U0116553

A family photo taken in the early 1960s: Kong Dong (middle left); Kong Dan's sister-in-law, Sun Yuzhen (middle right); Kong Dan's elder brother, Chen Mo (back left); Kong Dan (back right).

Mao Zedong
(May 1924–Jan 1925)

Chen Chuoxiu
(Jan 1925–May 1927)

Zhang Guotao (May 1927–May 1927, being expelled from the Party in April 1938)

Kong Yuan
(May 1931–Jan 1933)

Ren Bishi
(Jan 1933–May 1933)

This is a list of ministers of the Central Organization Department. Kong Yuan took the post in the 1930s. The original photos are from an exhibition on the history of the Central Organization Department.

Chen Yun
(Dec 1937–Mar 1944)

Peng Zhen (Mar 1944–Sep 1945, May 1948–Apr 1953)

Li Weihan (June 1927–Nov 1927, May 1933–Oct 1934, Oct 1935–Sep 1936)

Zhou Enlai (July 1928–Jan 1931)

Kang Sheng (Jan 1931–June 1931, being expelled from the Party in Oct 1980)

Zhang Wentian (Aug 1935–Oct 1935)

Qin Bangxian (Sept 1936–Dec 1937)

Rao Shushi (early 1946, Apr 1953–Feb 1954, being expelled from the Party in Mar 1956)

Zhang Dingchen (deputy minister, Feb 1954–Apr 1954)

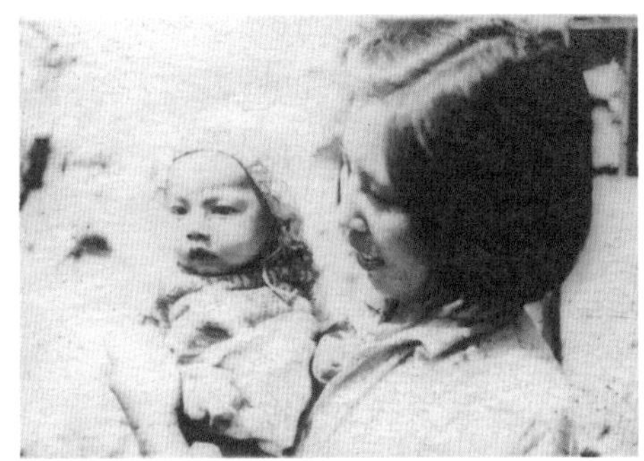

Top left: My mother Xu Ming as a middle school student in 1936

Top right: Xu Ming with her first daughter who died young in Yan'an in 1941

Bottom: Xu Ming in front of a cave in Yan'an

Top: Kong Dan's parents with Deng Xiaoping and Zhuo Lin on the day of their joint wedding in Yan'an in 1939 (from left: Xu Ming, Kong Yuan, Zhuo Lin and Deng Xiaoping)

Bottom: Kong Yuan with Dong Biwu at Hongyanzui Village near Chongqing, 1943

Top: Xu Ming with Kong Dan and Kong Dong in Fushun, 1948

Bottom: Kong Yuan holding Kong Dan in Yanji, 1948

Top: Xu Ming and Kong Dong in Fushun, 1949

Bottom: Kong Yuan and Kong Dan in Fushun, 1949

Kong Yuan and Kong Dan in Yanji, 1948

Top: Xu Ming, Xu Ming's mother and Kong Dan in Fushun, 1949

Bottom: Xu Ming and Kong Dan in Fushun, 1949

Xu Ming holding Kong Dong and Kong Dan in Fushun, 1949

Kong Yuan with Kong Dong and Kong Dan in Beijing, early 1950

Kong Yuan, Xu Ming, Kong Dong and Kong Dan, 1951

Top: Kong Yuan and Cai Chang (bottom right), 1950s

Bottom: Kong Yuan (right), Shuai Mengqi (center) and Qian Ying (left), 1950s

Xu Ming giving a speech in Beijing while working as the Director of Personnel at the customs, 1950

Kong Yuan (right) – then Deputy Minister of Foreign Trade – with Zhu De (center) at Tianzhen Railway Station in Datong, Shanxi, 1955

Top: Premier Zhou Enlai (center) at Lushan People's Theater in Jiangxi, with Xu Ming (left), 1959 – photo from Jiangxi Lushan Museum

Bottom: Xu Ming working in the office of Premier Zhou Enlai in Xihua Hall of Zhongnanhai, Beijing, 1956

Top left and Bottom left: Xu Ming and Kong Yuan at Beidaihe, 1960s

Top right: Xu Ming and Kong Yuan at Zhongnanhai, Beijing, 1960s

Bottom right: Xu Ming and Tong Xiao Peng, a colleague from Premier Zhou Enlai's office, at Zhongnanhai, Beijing, 1960s

Top: Xu Ming at Xihua Hall in Zhongnanhai, Beijing, 1960s

Bottom: Group photo of Premier Zhou Enlai, Deng Yingchao and staff of Zhou Enlai's office in Sanya, Hainan (Xu Ming is the fifth from left in the back row)

Top: Kong Yuan with his old comrades in army in Sanya, Hainan, winter of 1960: (from left) Kong Yuan, Liu Lantao, Li Bozhao, Yang Shangkun, Hu Qiaomu and Xu Bing

Bottom: Kong Yuan (third from right) after returning from a trip to Afghanistan with Vice Premier Chen Yi in the summer of 1960, together with Geng Biao and his wife Zhao Lanxiang (first and second from left), Chen Yi's wife Zhang Qian (second from right) and Xu Ming (third from left), who were there to greet them at the airport

Kong Yuan (right) with Premier Zhou Enlai (third from left in the front row) and Deputy Premier Chen Yi (second from right) at the front of the Great Sphynx in Cairo, Egypt during the 14-country tour of Asia and Africa, December 1963

Kong Yuan (left) and Premier Zhou Enlai returned from the 14-country tour of Asia and Africa, being greeted at the airport by Mao Zedong, Liu Shaoqi and other government leaders, 1963

Top: Kong Yuan in Tirana, Albania, December 1963

Bottom: Kong Yuan in a motor cavalcade in Ghana while accompanying Premier Zhou Enlai on the 14-county tour of Asia and Africa, 1964

Top: Memorial service held at *Babaoshan* Revolutionary Cemetery in Beijing to mark the rehabilitation of Xu Ming following the downfall of the Gang of Four, 1979 – (from left in the front row) Li Jingquan, Fang Yi, Yu Qiuli, Li Xiannian, Wang Zhen, Deng Yingchao, Geng Biao; and (second row) Wang Shoudao (second from left) and Kang Shi'en (third from left)

Bottom:
Ceremony to lay Xu Ming's ashes to rest at Babaoshan Revolutionary Cemetery in Beijing, attended by a number of elderly officials,including (from left) Wu Xiuquan, Yuan Renyuan, Wang Zhen, Wu Defeng, Wu Qingtong, Luo Qingchang and Lü Zhengcao, 1975

Kong Yuan (left), Yang Shangkun (second from left), Qu Wu (second from right) and Xi Zhongxun (right) in Guangzhou, Spring Festival of 1979

Kong Dan in his youth

Kong Dan and Kong Dong serving in the Beijing Public Security Corps in the summer of 1965, which left them unforgettable moments in their lives,, (from left) Luo Ting (Luo Qingchang's son), Ma Jia (Ma Lie's son), Kong Dan (Kong Yuan's son), Nie Ping (Nie Hongjun's son), Zeng Lu (Zeng Yifan's son), Wu Dan (Wu Lie's son), Xiao Song (Zhang Yuan's son), Zeng Yu (Zeng Yifan's son), Feng Hangjun (Feng Xian's son), company instructor, Zhang Yunjia (Zhang Jichun's son), Zhang Xiaopan (Zhang Qilong's son), Zhu Chunyuan (Zhu De's grandson), Kong Dong (Kong Yuan's son), Dong Lianghe (Dong Biwu's son), Liu Yuan (Liu Shaoqi's son) and Luo Yuan (Luo Qingchang's son)

Note: In 1965, Kong Yuan was Minister and Luo Qingchang was the Vice Minister of the Central Investigation Department; Ma Lie was Zhou Enlai's secretary; Nie Hongjun was Secretary of Ministry of Food Supplies; Zeng Yifan was Deputy Secretary of the State Council; Wu Lie was deputy commander and chief of staff of the Chinese People's Public Security Force; Zhang Yuan was Deng Yingchao's secretary; Feng Xian was Deputy Minister of the Central Investigation Department ; Zhang Jichun was Deputy Minister of the Central Propaganda Department and Director of the Second Office of the State Council; Zhang Qilong was Deputy Minister of the Central Organization Department; Zhu De was Chairman of the Standing Committee of the National People's Congress; Dong Biwu was Deputy Chairman of the People's Republic of China and Liu Shaoqi was Chairman of the People's Republic of China.

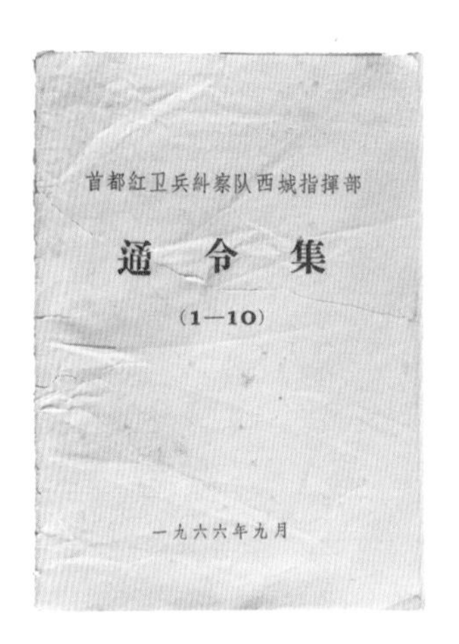

首都紅卫兵糾察队西城指揮部

通 令 集

(1—10)

一九六六年九月

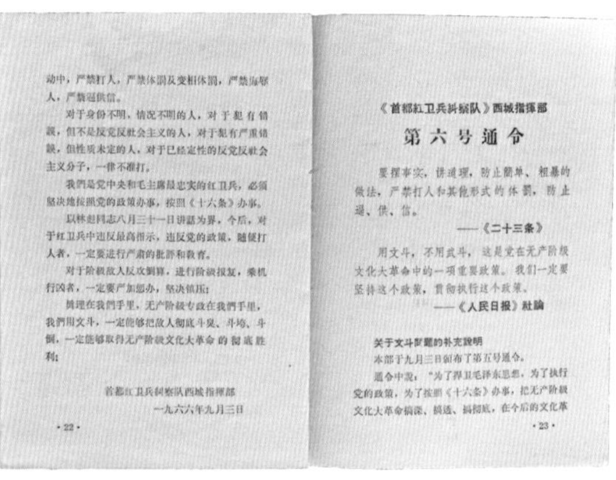

动中，严禁打人，严禁体罰及变相体罰，严禁侮辱人，严禁逼供信。

对于身份不明，情况不明的人，对于犯有错誤，但不是反党反社会主义的人，对于犯有严重错誤，但性质未定的人，对于已经定性的反党反社会主义分子，一律不准打。

我們是党中央和毛主席最忠实的紅卫兵，必須坚决地按照党的政策办事，按照《十六条》办事。

以林彪同志八月三十一日讲話为界，今后，对于紅卫兵中违反最高指示，违反党的政策，随便打人者，一定要进行严肃的批評和教育。

对于阶級敌人反攻倒算，进行阶級报复，乘机行凶者，一定要严加懲办，坚决镇压！

真理在我們手里，无产阶級专政在我們手里，我們用文斗，一定能够把敌人彻底斗臭、斗垮、斗倒，一定能够取得无产阶級文化大革命的彻底胜利！

首都紅卫兵糾察队西城指揮部

一九六六年九月三日

·22·

《首都紅卫兵糾察队》西城指揮部

第六号通令

要摆事实，讲道理，防止簡单、粗暴的做法，严禁打人和其他形式的体罰，防止逼、供、信。

——《二十三条》

用文斗，不用武斗，这是党在无产阶級文化大革命中的一项重要政策。我們一定要坚持这个政策，貫彻执行这个政策。

——《人民日报》社論

关于文斗問題的补充說明

本部于九月三日頒布了第五号通令。

通令中說："为了捍卫毛泽东思想，为了执行党的政策，为了按照《十六条》办事，把无产阶級文化大革命搞深、搞透、搞彻底，在今后的文化革

·23·

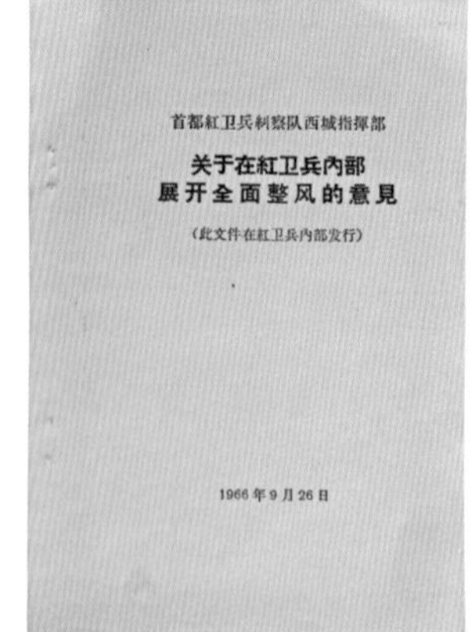

首都紅卫兵糾察队西城指揮部

关于在紅卫兵內部
展开全面整风的意見

(此文件在紅卫兵內部发行)

1966年9月26日

The Xicheng District Picket Corps of the Capital Red Guards published ten general orders and a paper on rectifying the Red Guards between the August and September of 1966. The photos are of the pamphlets collected by Kong Dan

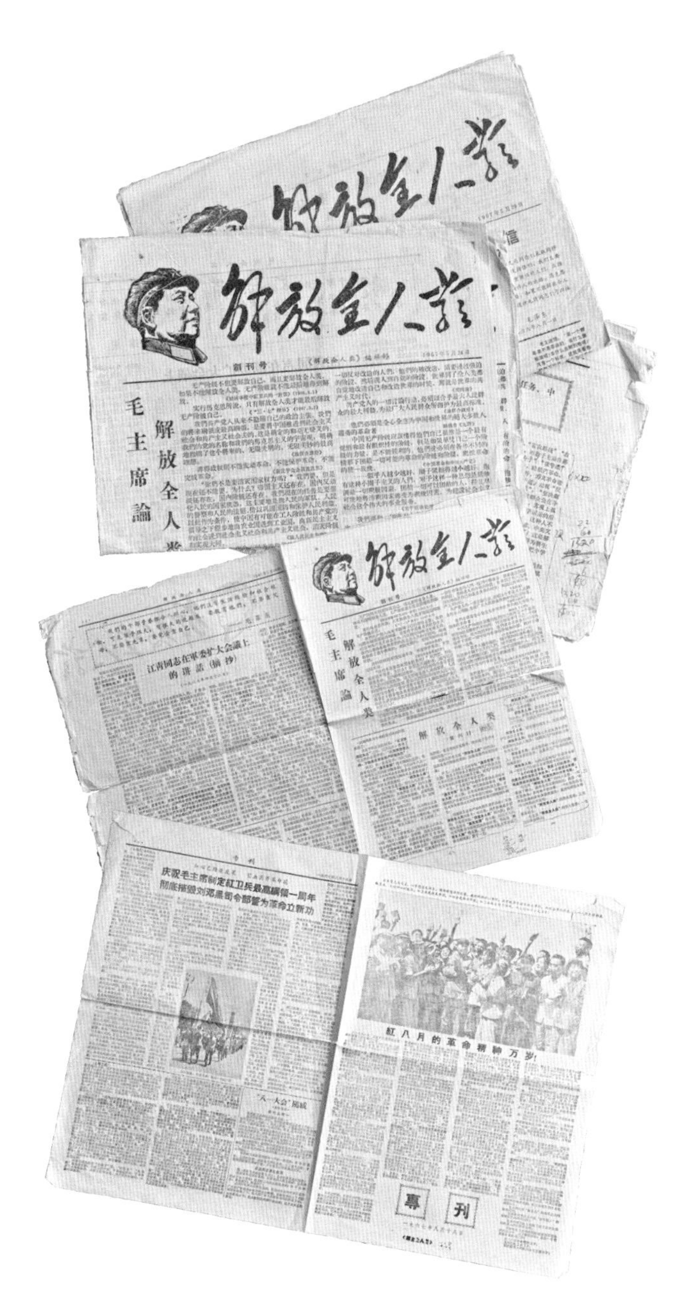

解放全人类

創刊号 《解放全人类》编辑部

毛主席論解放全人类

江青同志在軍委扩大会議上的讲話（摘抄）

解放全人类

庆祝毛主席制定紅卫兵最高綱領一周年
彻底摧毁刘邓黑司令部誓为革命立新功

紅八月的革命精神万岁！

專刊

Kong Dan was involved in publication of tabloid entitled Liberation of All Mankind, which ran for just three editions

Top left: Kong Dan was sent to work at the Gaojiachuan production team at the Angou Commune in Yanchang County, Shaanxi Province in February 1969 until the end of 1972 – here he strikes a sword-fighting pose with a fellow production team member Liu Jiandang (left)

Top right: The villagers praised Kong Dan as "a good lad," Yangchang county, Shaanxi

Bottom: Taking a break from hoeing, in Yangchang County, Shaanxi

Top: Kong Dan's good friend Zhang Haoyun (right) paid a visit to him in northern Shaanxi — (others from left) Chen Hui, Cai Danjiang, Liu Jiandang and Kong Dan, Yanchang County, Shaanxi

Bottom: Kong Dong paid a visit to Kong Dan in Shaanxi, Yanchang County, Shaanxi

Top: Winnowing (Kong Dan is third from left), Yanchang County, Shaanxi

Bottom: Plowing with the villagers (Kong Dan is second from right in the back row), Yanchang County, Shaanxi

Top: Lighting a cigarette (Kong Dan is first from right), Yanchang County, Shaanxi

Bottom: Kong Dong and Kong Dan read a letter in Beijing

Top: Taking a rest next to the Gaojiachuan River, Yanchang County, Shaanxi

Bottom left: Striking a pose while threshing wheat, Yanchang County, Shaanxi

Bottom right: One big happy family – Kong Dan with villagers and their children

Top: Sitting on the ground for lunch (Kong Dan is second from left), Yanhcang County, Shaanxi

Bottom: The cave Kong Dan lived in (photo taken by a friend of Kong Dan in 2010), Yanchang County, Shaanxi

Top: Kong Dan, Kong Yuan, Kong Dong and their sister-in-law Sun Yuzhen in Beijing, mid-1970s

Bottom: Kong Dan with Kong Yuan in Beijing shortly after Kong Yuan was granted his freedom, 1972

Top: With classmates at No. 4 High School in Beijing, early 1970s – (from left) Cai Danjiang, Wu Jian, Liu Jiandang, Kong Dan and Li Sanyou

Bottom: With friends in Beijing, mid 1970s – (from left) Cao Wuhan, Kong Dan, Song Yangzhi, Xiao Song and Cao Jidong

Top: With friends in Beijing, mid 1970s – Zhang Luning (second from left), Kong Dan (third from left), Wang Xing (fourth from left), Kong Dong (third from right), Su Yun (second from right) and Zhang Yanzhong (right)

Bottom left: Kong Dan being a heavy smoker, 1970s

Bottom right: Kong Dan and Kong Dong while travelling, 1970s

Top: (From left) Lu Shuqi, Kong Dan, Qin Xiao, Kong Dong and Feng Jianghua at Lushan, January 1972

Bottom: (From left on the bridge) Lu Shuqi, Li Sanyou, Kong Dan, Kong Dong and (at the front) Feng Jianghua at Jinggangshan Mountain, Jiangxi, January 1972

Top: (from left) Feng Jianghua, Li Sanyou, Lu Shuqi, Kong Dan, Qin Xiao and Kong Dong at Jianggang Mountain, Jiangxi, January 1972

Bottom: Kong Dan and Kong Dong while travelling, January 1972

Top: (from left) Kong Dong, Kong Dan, Li Sanyou and Lu Shuqi at Huangshan, Anhui, January 1972

Bottom: (from left) Feng Jianghua, Kong Dan, Lu Shuqi, Kong Dong and Li Sanyou at Jinggangshan Mountain, Jiangxi, January 1972

Top: Kong Dan, Kong Dong and Li Sanyou (left) outside the famous Fairy Cave at Lushan, January 1972

Bottom: (from left) Kong Dong, Feng Jianghua, Li Sanyou and Kong Dan at Huangshan, Anhui, January 1972

Top: Kong Dan paying a visit to Kong Dong, Jin Ancestral Temple, Taiyuan, Shanxi, early 1971

Bottom: Kong Dan and Kong Dong next to the Yangtze River Bridge in Nanjing, January 1972

Top: Kong Yuan while working as political commissar of the Second Department of the PLA General Staff Headquarters in Beijing, early 1980s

Bottom: Kong Dan (left) with Kong Dong (right) and his father, Kong Yuan, at home in Beijing, 1980s

Kong Dan, Li Xiaobei, Kong Ruomeng with Kong Yuan at Beidaihe, 1989

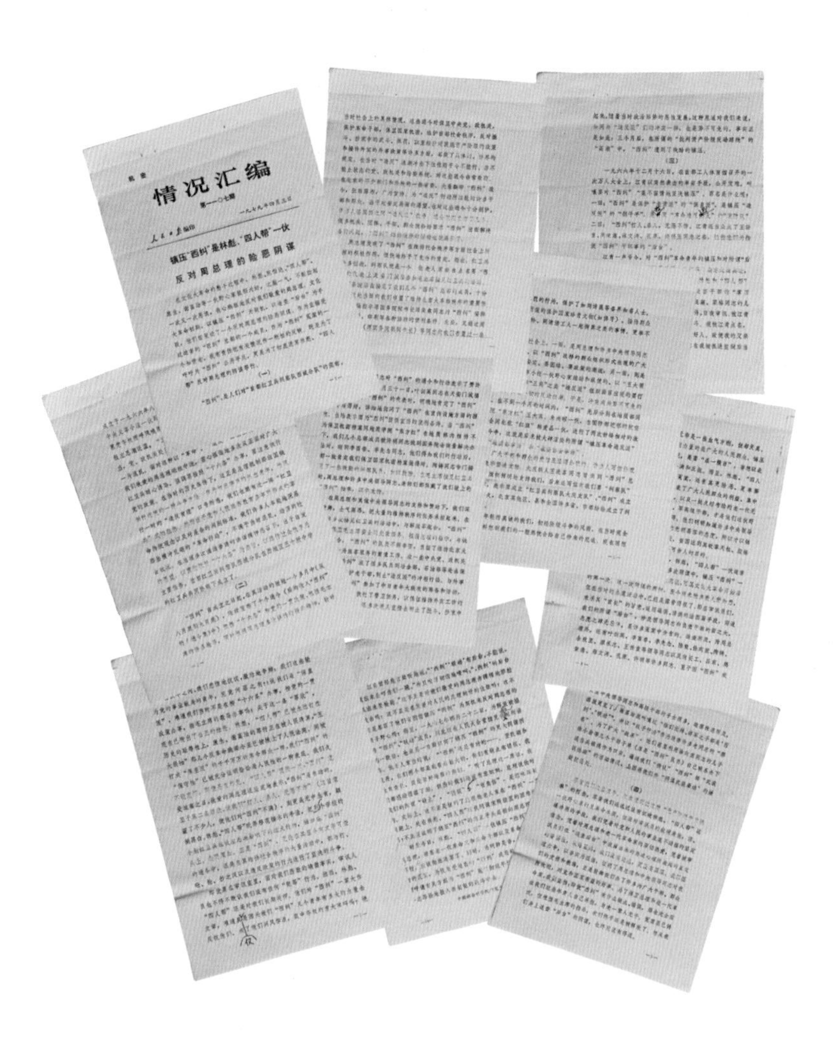
机密

情况汇编

第一〇七期

人民日报编印　　一九七九年四月五日

镇压"西纠"是林彪、"四人帮"一伙反对周总理的险恶阴谋

Report on problems with the Xicheng District Picket Corps written by Kong Dan, published in the "Collection of Situations" Section of People's Daily newspaper, April 1979

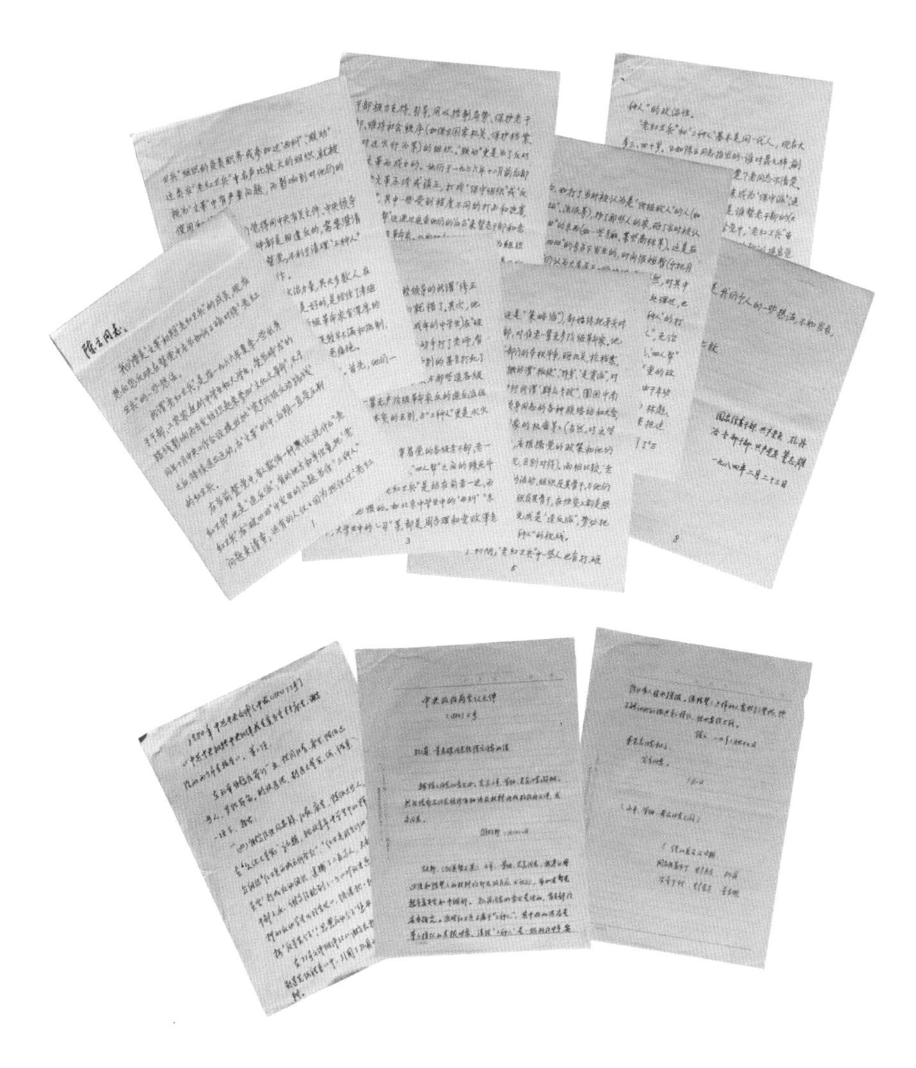

A Letter written by Kong Dan to Chen Yun containing suggestion on how to treat those who had been Red Guards, and related letters and instructions of Chen Yun and other leaders

Top: On a boat shortly after working at Everbright, 1984 – Kong Dan (left), Wang Guangying (third from left), Lee Ka-shing (fourth from left), Li Zhao (center), Li Xinshi (third from right) and Wang Sumin (right) in Hong Kong

Bottom: A visit to Tokyo, Japan, March 1990 – (front row) Sun Xiaoyan (second from left), Wang Qishan (second from right) and Zhu Yuening (right); (back row) Ma Kai (second from left), Kong Dan (center), Qin Xiao (second from right) and Tang Ruoxin (right)

Greeting Shanghai Party Secretary Yu Zhengsheng, November 2007 (Kong Dan is second from the left and Yu Zhengsheng is in the center, with Wang Jiong next to him)

Top: Zeng Qinghong meeting the Jiangxi delegation during the First Plenary Session of the Eleventh National People's Congress, March 2008 – Kong Dan (front left), Zeng Qinghong (front right)

Bottom: Kong Dan with Xi Jinping, Vice Chairman of China, during a visit to CITIC Luoyang Heavy Machinery Company, March 31, 2009 – Kong Dan (second from left in the front row), Xi Jinping (third from left in the front row) and Ren Qinxin of CITIC Luoyang Heavy Machinery Company (second from right)

Kong Dan with Fidel Castro during a visit to Havana, Cuba, November 2004

Top: Kong Dan with Indonesian President Susilo Bambang Yudhoyono in Beijing, July 2005

Bottom: Kong Dan with Venezuelan President Hugo Chavez in Beijing, August 2006

Kong Dan with Australian Prime Minister Kevin Rudd in Beijing, April 2008

Top: Kong Dan with Angolan President Jose Eduardo dos Santos in Luanda, Angola, August 2008

Bottom: Kong Dan with Belarusian President Alexander Lukashenko in Beijing, August 2008

Kong Dan with Argentine President Cristina Fernández de Kirchner during a visit to Buenos Aires, Argentina, March 2010

Top: Kong Dan with Kazakhstani President Nursultan Nazarbayev in Beijing, April 2009

Bottom left: Kong Dan with Kazakhstani President Nursultan Nazarbayev and Prime Minister Karim Massimov at a golf club in Kazakhstan, July 2009

Bottom right: Kong Dan with British Prime Minister Tony Blair in Beijing, August 2009

Kong Dan giving a speech in Hong Kong on the day CITIC Bank successfully listed on both the Shanghai and Hong Kong stock markets, April 27, 2007

Top: Kong Dan (left) visiting the Olympic "Bird's Nest" Stadium in Beijing during construction, June 2007

Bottom: Kong Dan (third from left) visiting the Candiota thermal power plant in Brazil, March 2010

Top: Kong Dan with Belarussian President Alexander Lukashenko during a visit to Belarus, August 2008

Bottom: Kong Dan (center) inspecting a social housing project in Angola, March 2010

Top: Kong Dan (second from right) inspecting a CITIC project at Yanhu, Qinghai, July 2007

Bottom: Kong Dan attending a poverty alleviation event in Yunnan, November 2009

Top: Surveying for Project in Xihai in Lushan, Jiujiang, Jiangxi, November 2010 – Ling Chengxing (second from left), Kong Dan (third from left), Zhu Hong (fourth from left)

Bottom: Launch of a joint credit card between CITIC and Air China by the two brothers, Kong Dong (third from left) and Kong Dan (third from right), July 2006

Kong Dong attending the Fifth Plenary Session of the Eleventh National People's Congress, March 2012

Top: Kong Dan at No. 4 High School with Kong Dong (left) and Li Sanyou (right) during the NPC and CPPCC sessions, 2010

Bottom: Kong Dan with his teacher Wu Jinglian and head of CITIC Publishing Group, Wang Bin, in front of a display at the National Book Fair in Beijing, December 2002

Top: Kong Dan visiting Nan Huaijin in Hong Kong, June 2000 – (from left) Zhu Ronghui, Qin Xiao, Yi Xiqun, Nan Huaijin, Kong Dan and Feng Danyun

Bottom: Kong Dan visiting Nan Huaijin at his Taihu Great Learning Center in Suzhou, Jiangsu, November 2009 – (from left) Kong Dan, Nan Huaijin, Li Xiaobei and Hong Jianling

Top: Reunion of classmates from Class 5, Grade 3 in No. 4 High School celebrating the birthday of their teacher Gu Dexi in Beijing, 2010

Bottom: Kong Dan (left) and Zhou Xiaozheng (second from left) congratulated Gu Dexi (center) on his birthday in Beijing, 2010

Kong Dan (second from right in the front row) at a reunion of schoolmates from No. 4 High School in Beijing, summer of 1997

From Red Guard to Business Mogul

An Oral Biography of Kong Dan

Dictated by Kong Dan

Complied by Mi Hedu

Translated by Central Compilation and Translation Bureau

Proofread by Wang Bo

Table of Contents

Preface

In China, the generation that has grown up with the People's Republic of China since its founding in 1949 is referred as the peers of the Republic.

A generation is not always categorized in terms of the physiological or coeval factors. The characteristics of the generation, including their behavioral habit, thinking patterns, emotional attitude, life outlook, measure value, moral standard, etc. would rather be considered. In 2011 I published a book through the Central Literature Publishing House entitled *Peers of the Republic*, in which I attempted to summarize a generation as people with shared social experiences, ideological experiences, behavioral patterns and historical characteristics, which have all been shaped within a particular social context. Specifically, the defining symbols for this generation refer to their common experiences from the Red Guard movement, the Up to the Mountains and Down to the Countryside Movement and Reform and Opening Up, together with their ideological experiences during the particular times, as well as their common behavioral patterns and historical characteristics shaped by the times. In other words, the special experiences are the key factors in the shaping of a generation.

For this generation, their wasted years were continuously accompanied by the fate of the People's Republic of China. After the previous sixty years, these morning suns are now at their dusk. With the Republic booming and entering a period of boundless opportunity, some of its peers stand at a new historical starting point after referring to the "law of double negation", while many others failed to rid themselves completely of the nightmares in their youths. In short, this is a very special generation. They have so many experiences worth recording and so many emotions waiting to be poured out. My oral histories series, *Memories and Reflections*, are aimed to provide a record of their experiences. Kong Dan's oral history, *From Red Guard to Business Mogul* (*Nande Bense Ren Tianran*), is one volume from this series.

This series of oral histories — *Memories and Reflections* has spanned the past sixty years, from the founding of the People's Republic of China to the present day, and it mainly focuses on the people who were still studying high school in Beijing at the start of the Cultural Revolution and were later heavily involved in the Red Guard Movement, the Up to the Mountains and Down to the Countryside Movement, and the country's Reform and Opening Up (a group referred as the '*lao san jie*' in Chinese). It is hoped that these personal oral histories will be a record of this generation, telling us who they were, how did they grow, how did they survive the turbulent times, what lessons they have learned in their youths, as well as their reflections on life and history. Perhaps these perspectives and thoughts would roughly sketch an outline of this generation and prevent us from forgetting about the past. Despite China's development and prosperity today, we should never forget a simple truth: a nation that never faces up to its history will never truly rise up.

It goes without saying that there are some defects for those contemporaries to write about their own histories. It is also difficult for the interviewees to eliminate their emotions from the recollected experiences. Meanwhile, the interviewees are all limited to the natural psychological tendency of forgetting about their negative past. In all, there would certainly be limitations for oral histories.

At present, there has been no academic consensus on oral histories. Our work here is merely one sort of exploration. In terms of form, in order to be coherent in style, all our books are written from the first-person point of view. This is not only easier for the interviewees to sort out their thoughts, but also makes it convenient for the readers. In terms of content, no amendments are made to the interviewees' basic ideas and understandings, and no revisions are made upon historical facts. The final versions are all revised and approved upon the interviewees' agreement, and they would ultimately be responsible for the content.

The Roman emperor Marcus Aurelius once said, "Everything we hear is an opinion, not a fact. Everything we see is a perspective, not the truth." This seems to offer an appropriate account on the qualitative nature of oral histories. An oral history is not a historical study, and is not equivalent to a trustworthy historical record. Even after some processing and sorting out, it is still a personal observation of the interviewee based on his or her personal understanding. With respect to the whole historical picture and the truth, it is inevitable that, like the parable of the blind men and the elephant, there is a failure to account for the truths, or simply because they are deeply involved in the events. Such is one characteristic of this type of history.

From Red Guard to Business Mogul (*Nande Bense Ren Tianran*) is our first attempt in the oral histories series of *Memories and Reflections*. Though it is merely one drop in the vast ocean of history, we have nevertheless tried our best.

History is like a complex and colorful jigsaw puzzle: only by gathering various perspectives can one reproduce the major historical scenes from the past. As this generation is now preparing to leave the arena of history, there is still a lack of comprehensive and accurate records as well as an objective and fair observations on their deeds and accomplishments. People of this generation not only have the responsibility to reflect on their own history in the first place, but they also have an obligation to offer their histories and reflections to the society.

Finally, I would like to thank Joint Publishing and Miss Tang Mingxing, the editor-in-charge of this project. I would also like to extend my thanks to those who helped me to compile and edit this book. Without the joint efforts by various people, we would never be able to present this book to the reader.

Mi Hedu

An Apprentice from Anyuan

My ancestral home is in the village of Zhangjiawan in the Anyuan District of Pingxiang City, Jiangxi Province, which was also the starting point of Autumn Harvest Uprising led by Mao Zedong in 1927. My grandfather, Chen Baochun, was a peasant, and his family did not own any land. When he was young, he had been to a private school. Later on, he first worked as an apprentice at a store selling delicacies from southern China and then at a pharmacy. He could therefore be considered as a so-called small businessman. While my father was a child, he was very clever, and had received his education at a private school. He was a good student, but was forced to drop out due to the financial situation of his family. He had also worked as an apprentice in various trades, such as a clerk for a pharmacist and an itinerant barber. He did all those jobs to make a living. It was in this kind of impoverished family that my father had grown up.

Two years ago, I went back to my home village. I was moved after the onsite visit. I wondered how my father embarked on the road of revolution and how he eventually became a government official. After I returned to Beijing, I consulted my father's biography. Then I knew it was his cousin that took him to a coal mine in Anyuan. That explained why he could join the revolution. At the coal mine, he witnessed the plight of the coal workers and sympathized them a lot. In those days, the workers' movement was already at its initial stage in China. Right at this place, my father got in touch with some early members of the Communist Party of China (hereafter CPC) and the Communist Youth League (hereafter CYL). Then, he was gradually involved in the revolution. I once asked my father for the reason of joining in the revolution. His reply was: there were progressive organizations run by students and the CYL back then in Anyuan. Those organizations inspired him, attracted him, and accepted him as a member of the CYL. They regarded him as a nice man with progressive thoughts, so they admitted him. Later on, they dispatched him to work in Pingxiang High School. It was the organization that helped him. In those days, one had to pass an English test so as to work in that school, but he knew little English. Therefore, during the examination, the CYL sent somebody else to help by giving him a slip of paper with answers on it. That was how he landed in Pingxiang High School.

My surname is Kong, but my family has nothing to do with the Kong family of Confucius. My father's original name was Chen Kaiyuan. After he went to Pingxiang High School, he changed his name to Chen Tiezheng, because the CYL had also given him a fake credential besides helping him to pass the English examination. These two traditional Chinese characters, *tie* (鐵) and *zheng* (錚), contained a lot of strokes, which made covering the original name on the credential a lot easier. That was how my father changed his name to Chen Tiezheng. He later changed his name to Chen Kunyuan while participating in underground activities. Since then, everyone called him Kunyuan. According to the accents of Hunan and Jiangxi Provinces, "Kunyuan" sounded similar to "Kongyuan". In this way, he was known as Kong Yuan.

I believed that, during the early days of the revolution, few people had chosen the path of action based on a strong consciousness, a sufficient study and a profound understanding of the Communist theory, and few had eventually stepped on the path of revolution based on his conviction. Many were simply attracted by some new ideas. When a social tide rushed in, those people got swept up in its path by the power of the tide. I described it as a sweeping tide, because many young people in those days, like my father, were swept up into the progressive organizations in schools, such as the Communist Party, the CYL, as well as the peripheral organizations. I did not think that my father had made a conscious choice in those days. He did not even have the time to think over it deeply, not to mention having an understanding of Communism.

Rather, he was swept up by the tide of revolution, which was quite different from the choices faced by the young people nowadays. I could still remember, when I joined the Communist Party at the age of 18, my father said that when he joined the Party, he was not as highly-educated as I was. Different from me and my peers, who had read many books and were theoretically acquainted with the Communist Party, he simply joined the student movement, and was later appointed as the chief judge in the trials of despotic landlords.

After the May Fourth Movement in China, there had been a surge of patriotic and political movements, in which young students played an active role. My father looked like a gentle man (many people said he looked like Saionji Kinkazu[1] due to his gold-rimmed glasses) with the air of an intellectual, but he was actually a "petty-bourgeois intellectual". His education background was similar to Chen Yun, who had not graduated from junior high school. Many Party members regarded Chen as a great intellectual and revolutionary theorist, but while filling in the forms on his educational attainments, he always wrote "elementary school". In those years, most Party members had received very little formal education, which eventually helped them to accept the new ideas circulating in those days and to be swept up by the revolutionary tide.

In the early 1920s, there was already a relatively high percentage of industrial workers in Anyuan. More than 10,000 workers were employed at the coal mines in Anyuan and the Zhuzhou-Pingxiang railway. There were also thousands of unemployed workers, which made Anyuan one of those places where most working class people were gathered in China. In 1921, not long after the CPC was founded, Mao Zedong, Li Lisan, Liu Shaoqi and many others had visited Anyuan, while Li Lisan had stayed on to organize workers and recruit members to the Party. Back then, at least half of all the CPC members came from Anyuan, so one can imagine how influential the Party was in this

1 Saionji Kinkazu was a prominent Japanese statesman during the 20th century and the founder of the Japan-China Friendship Association.

region. The local labor movements were organized vigorously and had a huge influence on society. In May 1922, the Anyuan Railway and Mine Workers' Club was established, which marked the beginning of the organized labor movement. Later on, conflicts between the owners of railway and coal mine as well as the workers had led to workers' strikes in Anyuan.[2] The strikes were led by Li Lisan, Liu Shaoqi, and others. It went down in the Party history as the defining moments often eulogized due to the quality of their organization and success in contrast to later strikes, such as the great strike launched by the Beijing-Hankou railway workers on February 7, 1923, which resulted in heavy casualties.

By September 1925, because of the armed forces, the Anyuan Workers' Club was disbanded, and some workers traveled southward to Guangdong to join in the Northern Expedition led by the Kuomintang Army. Pingxiang railway and mine workers accounted for two-thirds of Ye Ting's independent regiment in the Fourth Army. As a result, Ye Ting's independent regiment was a particularly effective fighting force during the Northern Expedition. Other workers returned to their villages when the club disbanded. In September 1927, Mao Zedong led the Autumn Harvest Uprising in the border region between Hunan and Jiangxi Provinces. Some railway and mine workers had constituted the main force in the uprising.

My father also participated in the Nanchang Uprising. After the failure of the uprising, he turned to the Communist University of the Toilers of the East in the Soviet Union to study, where he received systematic training on communist theories. After returning to China, he served as head of the Organization Department of the CPC Jiangsu Provincial Committee, and then worked for two years as the head of the Organization Department of the CPC Central Committee. Afterwards,

2 In September 1922, the Anyuan railway and mine authorities refused to pay the long-term wage arrears and tried to dissolve the workers' club. Mao Zedong and Liu Shaoqi quickly made their way to Anyuan to prepare for a strike. On the night of September 12, Li Lisan, acting as the general director, and Liu Shaoqi, acting as plenipotentiary of the club, led almost 20,000 workers in the strike. On September 18, thanks to the resolute struggle waged by the workers, railway and road authorities finally gave in and signed an agreement with 43 terms. This was a successful strike.

he went to Shanghai and worked as the representative from the northern region in the CPC Central Committee, where he remained in this important post for some time.

During the 1930s, when he served as the representative from the northern region in the CPC Central Committee, he was only at the age of 25 or 26, even Ke Qingshi was his subordinate.[3] I sometimes find it hard to imagine him having so much power within the Party at such a young age. Indeed, people used to say that my father was an old-timer, despite his young age.

However, during the days when my father was working for the Party Central Committee, the left-leaning thoughts have dominated the Party, and he was undoubtedly an important executor of the left-leaning thoughts. Before the Central Red Army reached northern Shaanxi, he had dispatched Guo Hongtao and Zhu Lizhi to the region. Upon their arrival, they purged various cadres of the Shaanxi-Gansu Red Army, including Gao Gang and Liu Zhidan. At that time, organization and discipline within the CPC was very strict, so the representatives dispatched by the Central Committee had the power to purge local Party organizations and base area of the Red Army tremendously. This was one of the most serious mistakes made by my father during his revolutionary career. The consequence of the leftist line as outlined in *Resolution on Certain Questions in the History of Our Party* [4] was 95 percent of the Red Area and almost 100 percent of the White Area were lost.

Later on, somebody joked to me, saying that my father was experienced in political campaigns. Indeed, my father did have made a number of mistakes in his career, and he did survive in several rectification campaigns. However, different opinions on certain issues did exist within the Party. When my father passed away, for example, Guo Hongtao came to offer his condolences, and he bluntly expressed

3 Ke Qingshi went on serving a number of senior posts, including Mayor of Shanghai and Vice Premier of the State Council.

4 It refers to the resolution passed by the Seventh National Congress of the Communist Party of China in 1945, which mainly criticized left and right opportunism prior to Mao Zedong attaining his leadership in the CPC Central Committee.

his disagreement with the *Resolution on Certain Questions in the History of Our Party*. He believed that the resolution gave an unfair account of the problems in northwestern China. But as I remembered, my father once said that he had no complaints about that period in history and he was totally convinced by the conclusions of the Party organization. While reflecting on those days, he said to me, "People like me had made several mistakes because of the influence of the Soviet Union and the Communist Party of the Soviet Union. It would be much better if we adopt Marxism to the local conditions." I later understood what he meant.

After making this mistake, the Party had once again sent him to study at the International Lenin School and the Moscow Sun Yat-sen University in Soviet Union. Zeng Qinghong later told me that, while studying at the International Lenin School, his father, Zeng Shan and my father had actually received the training in intelligence service. In 2011, I visited Moscow for the first time, and I especially paid a visit to the International Lenin School. There were portraits of Marx, Engels and Lenin carved on the old building, which had been used as an archive nowadays.

After the War of Resistance Against Japan broke out, my father returned to China with Mao Zemin and Chen Tanqiu. While traveling through the Xinjiang Uygur autonomous region, Mao and Chen were detained by Sheng Shicai to work there and were later killed by him. My father only stayed for a short time before being called back to Yan'an, and therefore spared the same fate. Upon arriving in Yan'an, the first person my father spoke to was Chairman Mao. He told Mao, "I have made several mistakes." Mao replied, "It did not matter. You had also been purged by Wang Ming, whose leadership was patriarchal. My father replied, "Yes, I had given Wang Ming some suggestions, and Wang Ming had treated me very seriously. His leadership was indeed patriarchal." Mao then said, "Since you are back, we will appoint you to be the deputy director of the Department of Social Affairs."

At that time, the director of the Ministry of Social Affairs was Kang Sheng, and the first deputy was Li Kenong. My father was the third most important person in the ministry. This could reveal that the CPC Central Committee still held him in high regard. Later on, he was transferred to the Southern Bureau, which was presided over by Premier Zhou Enlai, to take up the post of minister of the Organization Department. Song Ping and Rong Gaotang were secretaries, and Dong Biwu was the Minister of Propaganda at the Bureau in those days. During the War of Liberation, he followed the army to the northeastern region, and worked successively as the party secretary of Shenyang, Yanji, and Fushun.

When the Red Army took Beijing in 1949, Premier Zhou Enlai talked to my father, and dispatched him to work at the General Administration of Customs. However, my father had no idea of what customs was, so Zhou suggested him to learn. That was how my father came to be the first Minister of the General Administration of Customs. He later concurrently held the post of Deputy Minister of the Ministry of Foreign Trade. During his term, the first Customs Law of the People's Republic of China was formulated. In 1957, he was transferred to the Investigation Ministry of the CPC Central Committee, where he served as Deputy Minister. After Li Kenong died, he took over as the Minister. At that time, there were five ministries in the CPC Central Committee: the Organization Ministry, Propaganda Ministry, United Front Work Ministry, International Liaison Ministry, and Investigation Ministry. The Investigation Ministry was named by Chairman Mao, and was in fact an intelligence agency. It was mainly responsible for the external affairs instead of counterintelligence. My father worked there for nine years, which was a relatively long time within the history of the intelligence work in China.

A number of my father's old colleagues in the Ministry still missed him as well as the simple and efficient ways of working very much. They were jealous that he was in direct communication with the central leaders like Chairman Mao, Premier Zhou and Vice-Premier Chen Yi, and could solve all the problems directly. For instance, in every weekend, there were dancing parties, which Zhou and Chen would often go to, and Mao and Zhu De would sometimes attend.

Because they had formed close relationships during the Revolutionary War, so they would often attend parties or watch movies together, and whenever they met up, they could talk about their work. It was different from the ways of communicating with leaders nowadays, which had so many restrictions in terms of ranks and procedures. Chen Yi was then the Director of the Foreign Affairs Office of the State Council, while my father, Liao Chengzhi and Zhang Yan were all Deputy Directors. They need to appear often in public. In 1964, when Premier Zhou paid his visit to the fourteen countries, it was my father who traveled with him and did the external security works.

If the senior cadres of the CPC could be considered a group of leaders, people like my father were certainly part of that group. Unlike the bureaucrats in developed countries, they had not received any professional training, and many senior cadres had even never received higher education. The mission of their generation was to seize power and then to be in power. It was a miracle that after ten years of the civil war, eight years of the war against the Japanese, and another three years of the civil war, the CPC has seized political power only after 28 years of its foundation. What are the differences between them and the peasants whose revolts had brought about to the dynastic changes in the Chinese history? The difference lies in the brand new ideas as well as goals for national independence and liberation. Therefore, the dream that they were seeking to was different from those peasant uprisings. The word "democracy" was used frequently in the works of Mao Zedong, especially during the latter period of cooperation and struggle between the CPC and KMT, until the establishment of the People's Republic. This had reflected the spiritual pursuit of that generation. Occasionally I could observe those people from a closer distance, but I was never overawed by their presence. Perhaps it was because I was so close to them that I just regarded them as ordinary people. However, it was exactly this group of people that had seized political power and established this new society. That was how my father and the others had made their steps along the path.

My father was born in 1906. He joined the Youth League in

1924 and the Party in 1925 when he was only 19 years old. When my mother later joined the Party, she was only 17. This was also a reflection of the ideological vitality of young people that had turned them into the driving force of social change in the turbulent days in China. It was precisely because the CPC could attract young people from every classes and levels of the society that it constantly grew up until attaining its ultimate victory. I believed the reason my father joined in the revolution was related to his cultural knowledge and his thirst for new ideas. After all, many people from his village did not join the revolution. Many joined in but did not stick with it. And even more sacrificed their lives.

There was no way to know how many people from my hometown of Pingxiang in Jiangxi Province were swept up by the revolution and sacrificed their lives for the cause. More than 300,000 known martyrs were from Jiangxi Province, which probably counted the most comparing to any province in China. Among these people, half of them were killed during the purge of the Anti-Bolshevik League[5], which was particularly brutal. For example, there were two people known each other, and were from the same village. All it took was one person to claim the other as a counter-revolutionary, and then the other would be taken aside and killed. A number of people, including Liao Chengzhi, came very close to being killed during the purge.

The most prominent Communist Party member from Pingxiang was Zhang Guotao. If he had been a good man, then Pingxiang would have been known for producing a great leader. His younger brother Zhang Guoshu was at one time the Provincial Party Secretary of Jiangxi, but later he died in the revolution. Because of Zhang Guotao, Zhang Guoshu's reputation could not be rectified for a long time. In the

5 The Anti-Bolshevik League was a right-wing KMT organization established in Jiangxi during the Northern Expedition. The purge of the Anti-Bolshevik League was a movement to eliminate counter-revolutionaries within the Party. *History of the Communist Party of China* published by the Party History Research Center of the CPC Central Committee stated that the purge of the Anti-Bolshevik League and the struggle against social democrats were the product of speculation and confessions obtained under duress that blurred the line between friend and foe and led to many misjudged cases.

1980s, my father sought to Yang Shangkun and Feng Wenbin to suggest Zhang Guoshu be rehabilitated. This was eventually done, and he was designated a revolutionary martyr. Besides the Zhang brothers, the most important Party officials from Pingxiang were Kai Feng and my father. My father later became a senior Party cadre. He served as a Minister and was appointed an alternate member of the CPC Central Committee at the sixth and eighth National Congresses. He was also a member of the CPC Central Committee at the eleventh National Congress. He provided an inscription of the school name to his alma mater in Pingxiang, where there was also statue of him on the campus. He was considered an important local revolutionary figure in his hometown. His experiences and honors were important to him personally. However, more importantly, it was because he was a survivor.

A Talented Woman

My mother's hometown was Cangzhou in Hebei Province. Cangzhou is next to the sea and is considered a relatively open-up area in Hebei. My mother was born into a bureaucratic family, which was very different to my father's. My grandfather's name was Zhu Peilan, and he styled himself as Ai Ting. He was a local magistrate in the late Qing dynasty and a tax collector during the Nationalist period. He was also a talented calligrapher, and has his own style in calligraphy.

My mother's original name was Zhu Yujun, but she changed her name during her revolutionary career to Xu Ming. Both she and my grandfather were included in the *Records of Cangzhou* of Hebei Province. She was very smart and diligent from an early age. My mother and father were both very fond of me when I was a kid. An important reason was that I was like my mother, not merely in terms of appearance, but also because of intelligence and diligence. My daughter often asked me why she was not as smart as I was. I would always answer that she did not work as hard as I did. In fact, merely relying on one's natural talent is not enough. It must be coupled with hard work. My mother was a perfect example. She studied calligraphy and her handwriting was beautiful. She was an inheritance of an old-fashioned bureaucratic and intellectual family. When I was a child, she taught me how to write, and what she first taught was the official script used in the Han Dynasty and then the calligraphic style of tablet inscriptions from the Wei Dynasties. Then she taught me to facsimile the styles of famous calligraphers like Ouyang Xun and Liu Gongquan. But having fallen out of practice over the years, my calligraphy is now mediocre at best, which could never be compared to that of my mother and grandfather.

My father was a clever young man within his village, and my

mother was considered an outstanding student and a talented girl. She even got the highest marks in the unified examination of high schools in Hebei Province. While she was studying at the Second Provincial High School in Hebei, the Communist Party was recruiting members within the school. The Party was specifically looking for students who were good at study, with progressive thoughts and a good moral character. Being capable and eloquent, my mother quickly became a Party member. I knew many elder female Party members, and apart from a few, such as Deng Yingchao, Cai Chang and Shuai Mengqi, the others all joined the Party during the War of Resistance Against Japan. My mother joined the Party much earlier, during the agrarian revolution, only at the age of 17, in 1936. She was involved in the December 9th Movement and was one of the organizers. Later she did not go to university, but went directly to Yan'an.

My father was married to a woman called Zhang Yuexia before he met my mother, and I had a half-brother. They separated when my father went to the Soviet Union, and Zhang Yuexia married Bo Gu (also known as Qin Bangxian). At the initial stage of Anti-Japanese War, my mother was dispatched to work as a secretary at the Central Department of Social Affairs, and her seat was right opposite my father's in the office. That was how they got to know each other. Nowadays it is called an "office romance".

In the August of 1939, my mother and my father got married in Yan'an in a joint ceremony with Deng Xiaoping and his third wife, Zhuo Lin. I looked into the date of the wedding at the request of Deng Rong (Deng Xiaoping's daughter), who once lamented that she was feeling uneasy being unaware to know the date of their marriage. There was a photo that survived, in which the four of them were standing in front of Mao's cave dwelling. Deng Rong wrote about that day in her book, *Deng Xiaoping: My Father*. Chairman Mao and many other members of the central committee all came to attend the wedding, and afterwards they drank together. While drinking, Deng Xiaoping never refused the others, so he drank with everybody who proposed a toast. My father saw Deng doing this, and thought he should do the same. In the end, he was very drank and hid under the table. The next day my mother scolded him severely for getting drunk on his wedding night. My father wondered why Deng Xiaoping was not drunk after drinking so much wine. He did not know that someone was secretly giving Deng water instead of wine. When we talked about it years later, I berated my father for being so naïve and pointed out that Deng had got the better of being an official. He said: "In rank, I was also a vice-minister, but I did not expect that they were so cunning!"

After they got married, my mother stayed in Yan'an, while my father went to Chongqing. After victory in the War of Resistance Against Japan, they moved to Northeast China, as my father was appointed as the First Secretary of the Yanji Municipal Party Committee. In 1947, I was born in Yanji. In the following year, my younger brother, Kong Dong, was also born there. The area we lived in was called Longjing (龍井), which shares the same characters with Longjing tea, though the tea is not grown there. Later on, I had paid a visit to Longjing, as I wanted to have a look at the building where I was born. At that time, the government compound occupied the old headquarters of the Kwantung Army garrison. Because the Communist Party occupied the best buildings in the area, the building still stands today. According to the sayings of geomancy practitioners, those who were born in a government building would have a stronger life. No matter it was true or not, I did live with a strong life force.

My given name, Dan (丹), means "loyalty," and is not from the phrase "loyalty to the Party," as one might expect. It is actually the first character in the Chinese word for erysipelas (丹毒), which is an acute bacterial skin infection that causes reddening of the skin as well as other symptoms. When I was only 20 days old, I caught erysipelas, and my head swelled up like a basketball. My father, together with a member of his security guards, rode 20 kilometers on horseback to the nearest army field hospital to fetch vials of penicillin, which were put in a basin of cold water to prevent them from deteriorating. There was no doctor around, so my father had to find a trainee Japanese doctor to give me the injections. The young doctor did not know how to prescribe penicillin, and he failed to control the infection after several injections. As the infection was spread, he had to use a scalpel to make five incisions across my head, including cuts behind each ear, to relieve the pressure. I still bear the scars on my head until this day, but there was no doubt that he saved my life. That was how I came to be called Dan.

After the founding of the People's Republic of China in 1949, my mother also worked in the General Administration of Customs. My father was appointed as the Director, while my mother was the Director of Personnel. There were many married couples working in the same places or even the same organizations back then. It was very common during the years of war. If a husband worked in Yan'an, his wife would also be in Yan'an. If a husband worked in Northeast China, his wife would be there, too. Sometimes, however, couples had no choice but to live apart. When life became more stable after the founding of PRC in 1949, whether husbands and wives should work together had become an issue. Therefore, in 1953, my mother was transferred to Zhou Enlai's office, where she worked diligently both at day and night. She even forgot to eat or sleep. Her colleagues spoke very highly of her. Everyone thought she was sincere and honest, and regarded her as an outstanding female official. She worked methodically. She looked over important dossiers and would add some notes for Premier Zhou, which was greatly appreciated by him. My mother was responsible for these secretarial and ministrant works for Zhou until she committed suicide.

My parents had very different personalities. My father's status within the Party often changed back and forth. Not many people were like that. I thought it was his experience that had made him more resilient. I use the word "resilient", because he was flexible but tough. My mother, however, grew up in an old-style intellectual and scholarly family, so she would never lower herself to the power for personal gains. She treated people with a certain aloofness, but was always honest and frank. She had a very distinctive character. While working for Premier Zhou, she took on the liaison work in the fields of culture and education. For example, rehearsals of the large-scale song and dance epic *The East is Red* were personally overseen by Premier Zhou, and my mother had helped arrange the performances from start to finish. Then, Jiang Qing began her work on "model operas" to reform the Beijing opera. Jiang was not a novice of the literary and art; she understood the arts as well as Beijing opera. Some model operas were adapted quite well with classical singing. But Jiang was not satisfied. Being Chairman Mao's wife, the others all pandered to her, but my mother did not buy into it. She would do things in her own way and refuse to flatter Jiang, which angered her a lot. So even before the Cultural Revolution, my mother had already offended Jiang, which was indeed a hidden danger for her.

My mother's honesty and frankness also offended Chen Boda. My mother once accompanied Chen to carry out an investigation in Tianjin. When it was time to eat, Chen said that he did not want to, because the people were living in such dire poverty. The other cadres and staff were at a loss on facing such a hypocritical manner. So, my mother had to reply that they still had to eat as they still had to work. As a result, Chen Boda was not impressed by this at all.

My mother worked with Premier Zhou for 13 years, until she committed suicide. The reason she chose to die during the Cultural Revolution was largely related to her aloof and stubborn character. However, at the beginning of the Cultural Revolution, she urged the others not to resist the rebels. She could be authoritative and strict to me, but there was also another unknown side of her. In the 1980s, Wang Zhen once traveled to Hong Kong while I was working there. I went to see him and sat by his bedside to chat with him. During the conversation, we got into the topic of my mother. Wang said in his Hunan accent that my mother was a kind person. I replied, asking for his reason of saying so, also in Hunan accent to amuse him. He then talked about the start of the Cultural Revolution when Premier Zhou asked my mother to persuade him not to oppose the rebel faction so as not to suffer physically. He told her that he would never give in, but my mother implored him not to oppose them. She begged him with tears in her eyes. At that point, Wang relented and agreed not to oppose the rebels. He also said that he did not believe my mother had committed suicide and that she must have been murdered. I told him that, as far as I knew, she had committed suicide and that the sequence of events was very clear. He then replied that my mother had been a good comrade, the best comrade, and it was impossible for her to kill herself.

The Return of the Prodigal Son

The first school I attended was Yucai Elementary School, which was a boarding school mainly for the children of Party and government cadres. But I missed home terribly, so I put a blanket over my head and cried. I was not really sure why I got so upset. My classmate at the time, Ji Jun (son of the former foreign minister Ji Pengfei), later brought this up and said I was such a good for nothing! Half a year later, my parents had no choice but to take me out of the boarding school to become a non-resident student. I did not know why I was like that as a kid either. Because we lived next to the former General Administration of Customs building, near what is now Beijing Hospital, so they sent me to the Legation Quarter Elementary School.

After my father took up the post of Vice Minister of the Central Investigation Department, we moved to No. 4 of Miliangku Alley of Di'anmen Avenue. At that time, Li Kenong was still alive, and our two families shared a large courtyard. After this move, I went to Xibanqiao Elementary School from the Legation Quarter Elementary School. We later moved again to the first residence in Jingshan East Street, where Kang Sheng used to live, before moving back to the courtyard house at Miliangku Alley again until the Cultural Revolution erupted. The house at No. 4 of Miliangku Alley (later changed to No. 5) was very famous because it became Deng Xiaoping's residence after the Cultural Revolution. When Deng's wife, Aunt Zhuo Lin died, Kong Dong and I went to pay our respects. Because we had lived there, Deng Pufang (Deng Xiaoping's son) invited us into the courtyard to see the peonies. The peonies were planted more than 100 years ago and had witnessed many generations of people.

In 1958, during the Great Leap Forward, there was a great drive to produce iron and steel, and everyone, including school children, was called upon to donate scrap metal. I was still in elementary school, and could not find anything to donate, so I took a pot from home. My mother asked me, "How are we going to cook without a pot, and how can you do this?" I had nothing else to donate, but wanted to be active, so I went into a warehouse full of scrap metal from other people. I stole an old pot and donated it. During the Four Pests Campaign[6], we stood on the roof to scare the sparrows away from landing. I thought it was funny. Those were the elements of the Great Leap Forward we personally participated in. And such was the social atmosphere at the time.

At elementary school, I did not have the sense of superiority of being a son of a senior cadre, so I was happy to play with children who lived in the alleys near me. For a while, I even played around with some juvenile delinquents. We used to run down to the local shop and steal crabapples. Sometimes we would fight in the streets. I remember a kid surnamed Li, who was very badly behaved. I was quite stupid to get involved with such a bad crowd, and my grades suffered. You could say I was a bad apple at that point, and I used to swear and curse a lot. My little brother went to the same school, so I used to keep an eye out for people bullying him, then I went and sorted them out. I was quite aggressive. One time I was playing with a friend at school. I was holding a bamboo stick in my hand, which had a piece of scrap metal at its end. My friend grabbed the bit of metal, and I tried to snatch it back, but accidentally cut his hand open. He bled terribly, and it almost crippled him. His parents were extremely angry and came to my house. When my mother found out what had happened, she flew into a rage. Although she did not beat me, she made me stand in a corner and gave me a stern dressing down.

The incident happened when I was probably in the fifth grade of primary school. Afterwards I suddenly changed my ways and started to apply myself to study. It was like the return of a prodigal son. My

6 Campaign during the Great Leap Forward, which aimed at eliminating four pests, namely rats, flies, mosquitoes and sparrows.

elementary school never had any students admitted to Beijing No. 4 High School, but the next year I was allowed to sit the entrance examination. My class teacher at that time was Mr. Zhang. He was a very strict mathematics teacher. He was extremely happy when he found out that I had been accepted by Beijing No. 4 High School. He saw it as one of his greatest accomplishments in life. Things were done in a very orthodox fashion back then, and there was no way to get in by the back door. The only way was to pass the entrance examination. Later on, my younger brother failed the examination when he sat it. He was extremely upset, but he worked hard and passed the examination to the school for his senior high years, thereby fulfilling his dream.

When I sat the entrance examination for junior high school, I got 199.5 points (out of a possible 200). They deducted half a point for a character written incorrectly in my composition. When I started junior high school, I thought I was really something, and was quite complacent. But when I saw the scores of other students in my class, I found six or seven of them had scored 200. That really irritated me. I wondered how they could be so perfect. So when I started at No. 4 High School, I tried my best to improve myself. I wanted to be better than everybody else. First, I wanted to be the top of my class, then top of my grade, and finally top of the whole school. At that moment, I decided to study hard, and I never looked back.

In my third grade of junior middle school, I was selected as an "all-round good student"[7], and was given automatic entry to the senior high school of No. 4 High School, so I did not sit the examination. Back then, the senior high school entrance examination was extremely difficult. Because I was not sitting it, so I served for the other examinees by distributing them water and green bean soup. On one occasion, I saw some students had even passed out, perhaps because of the summer heat. In third grade, I received a silver good-conduct medal. I did not receive the gold medal because I misunderstood a question in my end-of-term chemistry examination, and had points deducted. The medals

---

7 An outstanding student who receives top marks for moral character, study and health.

were not awarded by the school but by the Beijing Municipal Bureau of Education in accordance with set standards. The requirements for each medal were extremely strict, and my mistake could not be overlooked. However, people said that, due to its status, No. 4 High School would rather admit its own junior high school students with silver medals into its senior high school than those with gold medals and recommendations from other schools. But actually some were admitted, including Qin Xiao, Xu Xiaodong and Lu Shuqi from Yucai School. For me and the other recommended students, we had enjoyed our wonderful summer life. While the others were still waiting nervously for their grades, we played happily, because we had no pressure at all.

Besides its long history, No. 4 High School had a large number of excellent teachers, who were the foundation for students to have good grades. The school's ethos was also important. The school laid emphasis on hard working and regarded idleness as a shame. Study was a form of competition, and all students competed to be the best. What went on in our minds was: "you may be good, but I can be better; you may be strong, but I can be stronger; you may work hard, but I can work harder."

I was so good at my study that my teachers decided to promote my study methods. This was done in my class first, then across my grade, and finally across the whole school. I have a strong capacity for self-study, and the overall emphasis of my technique was on the preparation for lessons before class. That meant I would know beforehand what to pay attention to in class and then review it. But I had different methods for different subjects and for different steps. For example, I used to have a cyclical method for memorizing words. Back then, not every high school encouraged students to prepare for lessons before classes. But No. 4 High School had attached great importance to encourage us studying on our own. The reason my school had such a good academic record was because it adopted a learning cycle of preparation before class, teaching in class and revision after class.

Moreover, the teachers were good at inducing and enlightening rather than simply indoctrinating students. This was also a crucial factor.

That year Chairman Mao advocated education reform towards the inducing and enlightening style of teaching. Some teachers had already started using this teaching technique of letting children ask questions in class rather than traditional cramming techniques. For example, in a Chinese class, the teacher would teach a word and students might say that they had looked up the dictionary and it had different meanings, and the teacher would listen to them. That was quite common in our classroom. In mathematics classes, for another example, the teacher would let the students work it out and then share their conclusions. If the teacher explained a way of doing it, students would sometimes find different ways. The teacher might even say their method was better. We had already started learning advanced mathematics on our own, and we found questions on analytic geometry would easily be solved with the help of infinitesimal calculus, but when I asked my teacher if we could use calculus to answer questions in the college entrance examination, he said that we could not do that due to the requirements and standards.

Some of the teachers at No. 4 High School were truly excellent. At the beginning, they told us that they were not there to give us fish, but to teach us how to fish. In other words, they would not just impart knowledge, but also train us to acquire knowledge on our own. My favorite teacher was Gu Dexi, who was a special-ranked teacher in Beijing who taught Chinese. He was also good at playing basketball, and was both a mentor and a friend to his students. I do not know if other people miss their days in high school, but I missed them terribly. I have benefited from the things I learned at that time throughout my life.

Due to this type of education, students at No. 4 High School took their studies very seriously, with a particular emphasis on independent study. I was never a bachelor student at the university, but I had taught myself advanced mathematics, general chemistry and general physics while living in the countryside. Apart from scientific experiments, there was almost nothing that cannot be learned outside the classroom. If you had a teacher who was willing to answer your questions, you could study almost all courses by yourself. Therefore, I self-studied all those basic courses for college. Though I was not a college student, I was still able to pass an examination and became Mr. Wu Jinglian's research student in 1978. This was largely due to the self-study skills I developed at No. 4 High School. And all my classmates gradually carried on their postgraduate studies.

The political demands to us were very clear. You would join the Communist Youth League at the age of 15 and the Communist Party at 18. After I joined the CYL, I quickly became the secretary of my league branch. As a class leader, I was in charge of the ideological works in my class. That was the relationship I had with my classmates at that time. I had to speak to them and enrolled them in the CYL. In order to do so, I also needed to know their family backgrounds. I had to patiently help those to make a clean break from the influence of their "exploiting class" background. My classmates used to ask what was so special about me. Every afternoon after class, my classmates would be around me in the playground. We walked together while talking. By the time I stopped talking, there was usually no one else left on the playground, then I would hurry home.

Because I had spent too much time that should have been used on study on extracurricular duties including ideological work with classmates, I thus had a very tight study schedule. Therefore, I developed a habit of studying until 11pm, which was similar to the high school students in China nowadays. I did so, because it was impossible to get good grades without hard work. Conversely, if you got bad grades, you would lose your face in class, and would not be persuasive to enroll other students to CYL. It was only by studying hard and being the best that you gained prestige and influence, and would be potent of persuading the others. I was good at almost every subject, particularly two of them, one of which was Chinese. Starting from junior high school, almost every essay I wrote served as a model and was shown to the whole school. I later had published essays in the *Junior High School Students* magazine. While still at junior high school, I went to Guilin with my father. When returned, I wrote an essay about my travel in Guilin on a whole notebook, which was later used as another model essay. As I got older, I tried to make my writing more concise and meaningful. I read widely and was influenced by various styles, including the works of Lu Xun. The other subject I particularly excelled at was foreign language. I studied Russian for several years, and had passed the Russian examination in Grade Two at high school. Afterwards, when my classmates were having Russian classes, I would carry my schoolbag under my arm, and go to the library to study English on my own.

I was also surrounded by a lot of very good students. There was a classmate called Wang Tianbo, who had won a gold medal for good conducts, and was the child of an intellectual. Wang is now a professor in France. When I referred him as a good student, I regarded him as the best, not in a general sense of being in the top five or top three. Top-notch means they were at the very top and were incomparable. Wang Tianbo was the best at mathematics. Another classmate, Xu Yijing, was the best at physics. I was the best at Chinese and foreign language. But comparatively speaking, being the best at Chinese was advantageous for me, given that my essays were promoted as model essays and showcased around the school. At the start, I was the best at Chinese in my class. Later on, I was the best in my grade. Then, because I was a senior, I became the best in the school.

The school placed particular emphasis on developing students in an all-round manner: morally, intellectually and physically. To be an all-round good student, one had to excel in everything. For example, all-round good students could not just excel in one subject, but in all subjects. There were also moral and physical requirements of being an all-round good student. In those days, joining the CYL was a sign of moral achievement. As soon as I came of age, I joined the CYL. Then in the second year of high school, I became the deputy secretary of the school CYL committee. It was the top position for a student, and was usually given to a third-year student. Obtaining this post one year earlier than most predecessors was largely due to the foundations I had laid in junior middle school. The experience of working as a student leader had made me different from other top students. It was rumored that I was desperate to become an official in class. Actually that was not the truth.

It was just all because of the situation that I was involved in. The school was just looking for someone who was held in high regard, so as to lead and motivate the others. After I became the deputy secretary, I held great influence over the students. I later also became head of the student council at No. 4 High School.

In order to stay fit, I did not "ride" bicycle to school each morning. Instead, I inserted some flash cards on the handlebars of my bike and pushed my bike to school from my home in Miliang Alley near Di'anmen. In this way, I could memorize new vocabulary and also did some physical exercises. One should neglect neither study nor body buildup. In the evening, I went home by riding my bicycle to maximize my study time.

My impression is that there were not a lot of all-rounders like me at No. 4 High School. When I considered about all-round development now, it seems extremely difficult. When Bo Xilai used to see me in meetings, he would joke about my model essays and recite the last sentences of them. I know he was flattering me. In fact, my generation loved to do that.

The Environment We Grew Up In

From my own respect, I believed that I had received the best education in my family, comparing with the families of other senior cadres of the Communist Party. My parents set a very good example and instilled a good work ethic to the family. They also had clear political and ideological expectations of us. We were expected to approach the organization by joining Youth League and then the Party. There were no other choices. This later became so ingrained in me that it had become an instinct. My parents demanded that we should study hard and be well developed ideologically, intellectually and physically — to be an all-round good student students. That was how I was motivated.

My parents were very strict with us. For example, we did not get special treatment and led a simple life. Looking back, I found it almost rigorous. In 1953, for instance, my mother had been transferred to Premier Zhou's office to be the secretary and deputy director there. After that, we were normally not allowed to eat together. They got very strict rules. But we still enjoyed the rigorous life then. We never felt being restricted in any way. Meanwhile, we were not living a special life, and had no real privileges.

I'm not sure about the life of other families of senior officials during the great famine, but my younger brother and I had experienced extreme hunger. We ate blackened sweet potato flour supplied to us. We even ate seeds from the elm tree, wild herbs, and elm flowers. As I remembered, one day we went into the kitchen to find our housemaid secretly scoffing down some cornmeal porridge she boiled. We coveted the porridge, and were very angry, so we told on her. According to the vocabulary today, she would have been "fired" for doing such.

The only special treatment I got was that my father would

sometimes take me and my brother on trips with him, such as our trip to Guilin. In another trip, we went to Guangdong and Hainan by taking Deng Xiaoping's special train when he visited the south. Looking back, this was an amazing experience for a young man like me. I got to see things I never got to see or learn in school. It was a real treat. That was why I could write compositions about the Guilin trip. It was these trips and activities that provided me with inspiration to write about experiences other than student life. Once I went to see *The East is Red* with my mother, and I wrote about the performance as well.

After I became the prodigal son, my parents no longer had to worry about my study. I know that some senior cadres worried terribly about their children's education. They worried about them playing too much, not studying much, not making much progress, not being motivated enough, and so on. But that was not the case in my house. In that respect, we did have a free hand, and the impetus was on us. From time to time, my parents would remind us to mingle with our classmates so as not to develop a sense of superiority. I was quite well known at that time among the children of senior cadres. My parents took pride in hearing other people praise me.

Another element of the school's ethos was advocating frugality and shunning luxuries. No. 4 High School was not the place for the arrogant and domineering offspring of government officials. Those children all kept a low profile at school. To wear clothes with patches was quite normal. I also found that all my classmates, regardless of their background, were good students. It was not possible to distinguish children of cadres from the others simply based on their behavior. I was particularly aware of not acting superior, as taught by my parents. Therefore, after I had been at No. 4 High School for a number of years, a classmate approached me, and asked me if my father was a senior cadre. I said he was sort of that, but I was afraid of other people knowing and assuming I had made any achievements only because of my family. I preferred to rely on my own abilities to be the best student in school.

Not all the children of senior cadres were the same, however.

When I was in senior high school, a student whose father was a major general was transferred from Bayi Army School. We had been classmates for two years. When we were about to step into the third grade, he approached me one day and said: "Someone told me that your father is holding a higher position than my father." I was taken aback as I had no idea where this had come from. There were some children of cadres who had a strong sense of hierarchy and paid attention to that stuff. Nevertheless, we never publicized who we were or what our parents did.

Essentially, according to the tradition of No. 4 High School, family background did not matter. There was no place for that. The children of Liu Shaoqi, Lin Biao, Chen Yun, Chen Yi, He Long, and Xu Xiangqian, both children of Peng Zhen, and the three children of Bo Yibo were all studying at No. 4 High School at that time. I was in the same class with Chen Xiaolu in junior high, and the same class with Bo Xiyong in senior high, but nobody acted arrogantly or condescendingly because their father held a high position. Thinking back, I found No. 4 High School was never like that. There was no atmosphere of finding out whose dad was the most important. The children of central government leaders were all very conscientious. If someone tried to use his background to bully the others, nobody would support him.

I was a student leader throughout junior and senior high school, first within the class and then among the school. After I became a student leader, I developed a habit of helping the others. Not only did I study hard myself, I also found some time to help my classmates, whether politically, ideologically, academically, or even emotionally. There were some students in my class from rural areas, and I often helped them catch up with their study. We very much encouraged students to help each other and share what we had learned. That was exactly what I did. There was fierce competition to be the best in grades, but that did not mean being defensive and taking precautions against others. In Liu Huixuan's oral autobiography, he talks about students at No. 4 High School who struggled to compete without helping each other. Perhaps that was how students behaved in his class. Our class was very united, and my position as the branch secretary of CYL committee still holds sways until today. My classmates are all in their 60s now, but they still see me as the branch secretary. In our class, I had more contact with classmates from ordinary families than cadre families, and I am still like that now. This is a reflection of my ideas at that time. We established an equal relationship lasting till today.

In the 1960s, class struggle in society had intensified, which had a major effect on my generation. I have already mentioned my parents' experiences, which are very different from those of my generation. First of all, the way we joined the Party was very different. We were not simply asked to join in. If you analyze our behavior and characteristics, you may find that we did not become members in one day or two; long-term political and ideological education has been required. We may have the same belief with them, but there are also differences. We have our own ways of behaving and thinking.

I still believed that there were no concepts of a privileged class in the eyes of my parent's generation. They sincerely wanted to govern the country well and bring benefits to the people. However, in terms of thoughts, there did exist some limitations and shortcomings brought about by the era. After the founding of the People's Republic of China, they quickly found themselves in a turbulent period of ideological struggle. Except for a small number of movements, such as those against the "three evils" and the "five evils," most of the movements were part of the anti-rightist struggle in the Party and had pervaded along with the development of the nation. For example, the Anti-Rightist Movement had shed its impact on the Party. My uncle joined the Communist Party when he was 15, and was a senior revolutionist despite his young age. In his youth, he was captured by the Japanese, but he never flinched while facing their bayonets. However, because he liked to share his opinions and often commented on government affairs, he had been eventually labeled as a rightist in 1957. My mother could not of any help for him, so he was sent off to do manual labor. My mother really cared about him and felt great sympathy for him, but she could say nothing. She had no choice but to obediently accept the Party committee's decision. This incident had revealed her generation's attitude towards the Party.

In 1959, my father was in Lushan when criticizing Peng Dehuai. Li Rui had quoted several speakers at the Lushan Conference, including my father, who criticized Peng Dehuai as demanded by Chairman Mao. Before the Cultural Revolution, we could never discuss these affairs openly. Only after the Cultural Revolution could my father and I discuss political problems in depth. Thinking back, as the struggles within the Party intensified, Party members became increasingly reluctant to speak about the truth. As for the case of Peng Dehuai, everyone knew that it was a personal disagreement with Mao and had nothing to do with anti-Party clique or struggles between opposing lines.

In 1965, Luo Ruiqing was denounced by the Party. By that time I was already a Party member, and I remembered my parents talking about how could Luo Ruiqing be against Chairman Mao at home. They had been told that Luo Ruiqing was against the Party, in spite of Chairman Mao's trust. I was still politically naïve back then, so I did not understand what they were talking about.

Back then, I was completely unaware of the internal struggles and conflicts took place among the upper echelons of the Party. It was because my father was in charge of intelligence work and my mother worked for Premier Zhou, which required them to have a strong sense of organizational discipline. Therefore, they never discussed their work with me. As such, we were not like the other children of high-level cadres, who were privy to large amounts of Party gossip. Besides, from the perspective today, I thought Chairman Mao's ideas resulted in to economic romanticism in the early period and political romanticism in the later period. After 1949, the developments had for a long time deviated from the ideological line of "seeking truth from facts", which he had advocated and practiced. Developments were divorced from realities, which resulted in detours. During those days, the ideas of my parents' generation were also changing and developing. They were first executives of Mao's ideas, and later reduced to the victims.

Student Protests led by No. 4, 6 and 8 High Schools

During the Four Cleanups Movement in 1965, there had been protests led by students from the No. 4, 6 and 8 high schools.[8] I was not responsible for organizing the protests, but was embroiled rather passively in the certain situation. The student protests began while I was in Grade 1 at high school and ended while I was in Grade 2. The main leaders were students then in Grade 2, who were later in Grade 3. They did not consider us as members of the main movement, but we followed them anyway.

Indeed, we were not of the same type of students. Within the school, I was a fairly standard student. Student movements were never started by students like me, but were rather started by those who were more avant-garde in thinking and who acted more freely. At that time, the leading students in No. 4 High School were in a higher grade than me. Those students, such as Qiu Huizuo's son Qiu Chengguang, Liu Lanbo's son Liu Andong, Song Renqiong's son Song Kehuang, Li Jingquan's son Li Xinwei, and Song Zhiguang's son Song Yangzhi, were more independent-minded. Nowadays, these people are all my good friends. Back then, I did not have as firm a grasp of political issues as they did, and my views were not as independent as theirs. I

8 The protests by students of No. 4, 6 and 8 high schools took place in 1965 during the Four Cleanups Campaign, which was part of the Socialist Education Movement. The students organized classroom boycotts and wrote advisory letters to the CPC Central Committee. Their main demand was that the "Four Cleanups" working groups should be dispatched to the high school, and they wanted to temper themselves in the great storm of class struggle. They also sharply criticized the education system and strongly urged implementing the class line among students and establishing a class-based organization similar to a poor and lower-middle peasants' association. In a sense, the protests by students of No. 4, 6 and 8 high schools can be seen as a preview to the Red Guard movement. See relevant sections of *Xin Lu—Toushi Gongheguo Tonglingren* by Mi Hedu (Central Literature Publishing House, 2011).

was completely shaped both by my family and my school, and was used to the standard form of education. I totally respected my school, my teachers and the principal. But the school was not that sacred in the eyes of those students. When they heard Chairman Mao's rousing words and arguments, they wanted to do something. I believed they understood some of Mao's ideas on education reform. That was probably a very important reason.

In 1964, some of them wrote a letter to the Party Central Committee, and then started the student protests. They believed that the school leadership was rotten, and was following a revisionist education path. Personally, I thought the school's leaders simply had not put enough emphasis on class struggle, and had not focused enough on political ideology. Besides, they did not adopt more stimulating teaching methods. Overall speaking, I thought that the school leaders were flawed and even wrong in some respects, but I did not think the entire leadership was bad and needed to be replaced. During the student protests, the students from No. 4 High School who wrote the letter to the Central Committee felt that they were being oppressed at school. I, on the other hand, did not feel being oppressed, but felt highly valued and esteemed, and was held up as a model within the school. Therefore, it should be said that there were considerable differences between me and them.

However, I was influential within the school, rather than merely among the children of cadres. Students in Grade 1 and 2 at No. 4 High School all took me as an all-round good student, but students in the higher grade did not know who I was. After the student protests began, I contacted them, but they were not particularly impressed by me. I remembered them saying that I should have my own views on the education system instead of being such a conformist.

Around that time, another incident took place at school. There was a well-known student at our high school called Cao Xiaoping. He was particularly good at table tennis, and was a first-class athlete in China. I greatly admired his skills in playing table tennis. He wrote a poem, two lines of which I could still remember: "A faithful employee shall not abandon the monarch in peril; A brave man should save people on a toppled boat at risk." However, the poem aroused an incident, as people claimed the "monarch in peril" referred to Chiang Kai-shek, and the "toppled boat" referred to Taiwan, so they thought he was advocating Chiang Kai-shek to retake the mainland, and was therefore labeled a reactionary student. I did not know how such a big issue came out of it, but it was regarded as an instance of high school students waging class struggle.

An incident also took place within our class. There was a boy in our class called Zhou Xiaozheng, who is now a professor at Renmin University. In the second half of the semester in Grade 1, Zhou Xiaozheng speculatively raised a number of questions, which became known as the "twenty-one items," for which he was criticized. As it had happened a long time ago, I could not remember the circumstances very clearly. Not long ago, more than 20 of my classmates from Class 5 in Grade 3 had arranged a reunion, and I deliberately raised this topic, so that we would recall it. Everyone started to talk about this issue, and it occurred to me that when we went to Nankou to do manual labor, the section chief of a tank regiment garrisoned there named Kang had given us a report, which Zhou Xiaozheng doubted. As a result of this, the section chief reported him to our school principal, who in turn asked me, as branch secretary, to look into the matter.

When we met up again recently, I asked Zhou Xiaozheng his recollections on the event. Afterwards he sent me a text message that said, "The so-called 'twenty-one items' were a number of questions that I thought up in political education classes in high school. They included the following ideas: "Mao advocates utter devotion to others without any thought of oneself', while Marx said 'Only by liberating the whole of mankind can the proletariat liberate himself.' The world's population was 3 billion at that time, so does that mean that the Communist Party has one-three billionth of individualism? Is the slogan 'all for one and one for all' correct? Is an unsung hero greater than a famous hero? Is there a contradiction between learning from Dong Jiageng's quote 'A foot stuck in mud, a heart longing for the motherland' and Mencius' saying of 'Troubled, improve yourself; valued, improve the world'? Someone in the class asked me to write out these questions, so I wrote the questions on the back of a piece of paper from my father's notebook. There may have been 21 questions, but I could not remember all of them clearly." Another classmate, Lu Xiaowei, remembered another item, which stated, "Communists are visionary individualists." Talking about it now, it shows independent thinking, though it is slightly superficial. He simply wrote down a number of questions, but in the environment of class struggle that predominated in those days, daring to question was also as a kind of challenge.

I then arranged a discussion on his "twenty-one items" in class. We went through them, and criticized each in turn. He debated with us, and I reprimanded him for daring to speak to us in such a way. He was such a person. He had an active mind and was an individualistic that dared to say anything. Our classmates criticized him heavily by using very strong language. On the whole, though, it was carried out with decorum in the style of a debate. Nevertheless, we had more people, and we quoted Party newspapers to level our accusations in a suppressed manner, stating that it was the influence of revisionist thinking. People also looked into his family's roots. His ancestors had been small proprietors, which did not in fact belong to the exploiting classes. I was the branch secretary of the CYL, but since we were all classmates, there was no need to treat it too seriously. But we did treat it seriously. Back then, it was normal to take political matters like that. All of us remembered, while we were holding a meeting to criticize Zhou Xiaozheng, several students from the higher grade rushed in, and demanded that it be elevated to an ideological issue. As the presiding officer, I quickly brought the class meeting to an end. Looking back now, I thought I had done the right thing.

During the student riots, we did not divide students into right, center and left. Nor did we divide people into friends and enemies based on their family backgrounds. An important job of mine at that time was to provide children born into families of the exploiting classes with ideological education, so that they could get to the root of any erroneous ideas, and make a clean break from their family background. Sometimes it was hard to tell what I was meant to be doing. Our class monitor was called Huang Hanwen. He was from a family of landlord status, but we got on very well. It was hard to see how much influence his family background had exerted on him. But we still had to look into it. That was exactly class struggle! Another difference between my grade and the senior grade was that we made a conscious effort to maintain good relations between classmates on dealing with those issues. We were more moderate, and did not try to make an enemy of anyone. Although we criticized Zhou Xiaozheng's "twenty-one items" as well as some remarks made by teachers, we were merely pointing out the errors in their thinking or understanding. We did not consider them as reactionaries. I even talked to the head of the Four Cleanups work group, Li Chen, about Zhou Xiaozheng's incident. I explained that it was just an ideological issue, and there was no reason to keep criticizing him.

After the students of No. 4, 6 and 8 high schools began to make trouble, the question of how to carry out the Four Cleanups Movement was raised. The Beijing Municipal Party Committee dispatched a working group to No. 4 High School, and the group leaders were the head of Culture and Education Department of the Municipal Party Committee called Zhang Wensong, and the head of the Municipal Education Bureau, Li Chen. Members of the working group included Yang Bin and Sun Yan. Yang Bin later stayed on and became the headmaster of our school. After the working group arrived, Zhang Wensong, Li Chen, Yang Bin and Sun Yan talked to me on a number of occasions, particularly Li Chen and Yang Bin. The four of them had a distinctive way of speaking. Li Chen had gray hair and impressed me greatly. He came across as being very sincere and did things in a straightforward manner. He informed me cogently that we could raise any suggestions, but it was not wise to do so in that manner, and had to be done only with the support of the work group. This left a deep impression on me. My feelings toward Zhang Wensong were not quite the same. He was very principled and talked very loudly and seriously. Maybe it was just because of his position. Yang Bin and Sun Yan talked to us like aunties. I had also talked with Sun Yan on a number of occasions. She also talked in a slow and kind manner.

The work style of the Municipal Four Cleanups Working Group was the same as those employed by Liu Shaoqi and Deng Xiaoping, which was later criticized during the Cultural Revolution. As a matter of fact, the Four Cleanups Movement was already quite left-leaning, but it still adhered to the Party's work traditions. Many of the Party's previous campaigns, including the Yan'an Rectification Movement, had involved leftist errors. They had already accumulated some experiences. The working group recognized that a number of students in Grade 3 were quite extreme and thus criticized them for it. The working group felt that all aspects of my background, my behavior in school and my relationships with teachers, as well as my understanding of the student movement, were compatible with their objectives. The key factor, however, was that I was influential among my fellow students, and they needed a backbone of students to implement the policies made by the working group.

Because of this, a number of students in higher grade thought that I was a strategist seeking amnesty. They said that I had been coerced. Some people later even called me a capitulationist. In short, a number of students in the higher grade had a very negative impression on me. Many of them felt that the very existence of Chinese education was at stake, but I was still encouraging everyone to concentrate on their study. They believed that No. 4 High School was one of the sources of revisionism, and was under bourgeois rule, whereas I suggested that although certain aspects of the school did not conform to Chairman Mao's educational principles, it was revolutionary on the whole. Their basic attitude toward the working group was one of antagonism, and they thought that we did not have the necessary fighting spirit. I simply thought that the working group had been sent by the Party and that we had to cooperate. However, I was slightly conflicted and also had the feeling I was being coerced.

When the working group felt that ideological work was going well, the Municipal Party Committee held a meeting of student cadres and those who led the protests. During his speech, Zhang Wensong first praised our revolutionary enthusiasm and our opinions on class struggle. But he also criticized us, saying that we should carry out our activities in an organized manner and under the correct leadership. I remembered Wan Li's speech quite well and was shocked by it. Back then, Wan Li was still the deputy mayor of Beijing, and I had no idea of how powerful or how severe he was. I remembered his Shandong accent clearly. He told us that Peng Zhen had authorized him to speak to us on behalf of the Secretariat of the CPC Central Committee. He asked us why we were making trouble. He said Peng Zhen had held a meeting with the Secretariat of the Central Committee, and nobody supported us. He accused us of just being fooling around, and warned us not to cause trouble, saying only on the day before he had sentenced two people to death for this reason, and he would deal with us in the same way. He pointed out that the Central Committee had contacted all of our parents, and we should go home and tell our parents we would study hard and cause no more trouble. He finished by saying we would be arrested if there were more trouble. On hearing that, I was bewildered. I thought he was going to say that the Central Committee was behind us. Instead, he viciously rebuked us. The thing I remember most is that he had two people sentenced to death just the day before. I wondered how he could be so uncompromising. He really scared us in his way.

Although my parents were quite lenient with us, I felt I had to tell them about this. After the meeting with Wan Li, I did not dare to keep it as a secret, so I related this to them as soon as I got home. They told me that we should listen to what Wan Li had said and do things according to the regulations. They were aware that a meeting had been held by the Secretariat of the Central Committee to discuss the matter of protests by students from the No. 4, 6 and 8 high schools, and they explained that what Wan Li had said was indeed the views of the Secretariat rather than his personal opinions. They also told me that Peng Zhen had given a speech at a meeting of the Secretariat, in which he had requested high-level cadres to keep an eye on their children and not let them cause troubles. As such, my parents' views on the matter were quite clear: though problems existed with the education system, we were not to engage in movements independently by holding anarchical student strikes. They believed that we could never carry on movements that were not supported by the government or Party organizations. The leadership of Party was essential. This was the traditional view of the vast majority of Party cadres at the time.

Looking back, many things can be seen as historically inevitable. From the Lushan Conference, to the split with the Soviet Union, Chairman Mao was thinking over these issues by promoting different forms of movements. I believed that he was behind those student disturbances. It was Mao that said, "No longer will the bourgeoisie rule our schools." It was our children of cadres who followed his lead and adapted to the major trends. The protests by students of the No. 4, 6 and 8 high schools were an example of children of senior cadres trying to implement the Party's ideas on class struggle in the field of education, especially in high schools.

I felt that a number of things we did prior to and during the initial stages of the Cultural Revolution were not done independently or consciously with careful consideration, but were simply following the trend. I was sure that the leaders of the student protests and those responsible for writing letters were simply echoing Chairman Mao's remarks, instructions and intentions. Nevertheless, they had gone too far. At least, their actions were not consistent with the main views of the Party Central Committee. Looking back now, perhaps Chairman Mao did not know about it at its beginning, so it was decisively suppressed by the Secretariat. Or perhaps he felt that the time was not ripe yet; maybe it was also possible that he agreed with it. It was, however, similar to his support of the Red Guards at the start of the Cultural Revolution.

Nevertheless, the lesson I drew from the student protests was that movements should be carried out in accordance with the requirements of the Central Committee and with the Party's support. The impression I gained from this episode had a direct impact on my position towards the Red Guards at the beginning of the Cultural Revolution.

A Young Party Member

It was during the student protests that I was chosen as a candidate for Party member. The Party branch at No. 4 High School informed me that I could apply to join the Party as an activist, and if conditions permitted, I would be considered to be a member. I remembered the Party branch also asked me to write some materials. Those methods of recruiting Party members in middle schools had previously stopped during the Anti-Rightist Movement, but it had been resumed because of the change of political situation.

I believed the student protests had drawn the attention of those higher up on student political movements. Before that, it was almost unthinkable that a bunch of high school students could launch a political movement. As a result, the Beijing Municipal Party Committee embarked on two areas of work. The first required every school to carry out top-down and positive "revolutionized education", the aim of which was to gain the initiative to reduce opportunities for students to cause trouble. The second was to recruit the most respected students as Party members so as to use them to control the other students.

I thought that we were a fairly rational group of people among our generation. I said so because we were rather traditional in that we relied on the organizational system and understood the policies. Even during the student protests, we were not particularly radical. We felt that we had to rely on Party organizations and stress policies throughout the movement. I always felt that I was exactly the sort of student leader the Party organization was seeking to cultivate. After the student protest incident, I found my thinking became more orthodox, more in line with the Central Committee's requirement of developing successors. It was because that in 1965, after the Four Cleanups Movement, Party members were once again recruited from among high school students in Beijing. I was one of the first to join the Party, which was in fact a result of the Four Cleanups Campaign.

On July 1, 1965, She Jing from the High School for Girls Affiliated to Beijing Normal University and I swore an oath at a meeting of the Xicheng District Party School to become probationary members of the Communist Party of China. We were among the first group of high school students in Beijing to be admitted to the Party. She went on to become China's Deputy Minister of Health. After I joined the Party, the Beijing Municipal Party Committee began recruiting more Party members from all the high schools in the city. In addition to Ren Xiaobin and Song Kehuang, Ma Kai, Qin Xiao, Li Sanyou, Zhao Liming and Liu Dong were all recruited from No. 4 High School. They were the only student members before the Cultural Revolution. Ma was in a higher grade than me, and he later became a political education teacher at our school. In fact, it was we who led the Cultural Revolution activities within the school and at the early stages of the campaign.

I still remembered, in the speech I gave while joining the Party, there contained the words like "to be an obedient tool of the Party". I wondered at the time whether I should still merely be an obedient tool after the Four Cleanups Movement. As a result, I changed it to "be an enthusiastic and obedient tool of the Party". I deliberately added the qualifier "enthusiastic", because it indicated that individuals should also show a certain amount of initiative. The key issue, however, was still to be obedient. This was something Liu Shaoqi had talked about. Being an obedient tool of the Party meant that you could not do whatever you want to. No matter how capable you were, the important thing was to obey the Party's decisions and accept its discipline. I believed what guided our thoughts and actions were the traditions cultivated by the Party over many years and its criterion of right and wrong. I was praised for this by the leaders. They thought that my version was much better and thoughtful.

The Party Central Committee had already raised the issue of training successors, and this was promoted more systematically after the Sino-Soviet split. From the perspective of propaganda, I believed that the training of successors, as mentioned by Mao in his criticisms of Khrushchev's leadership, was targeted at the Communist Party of the Soviet Union. The CPC Central Committee held, as the Communist Party of the Soviet Union evolved, they had already abandoned Stalin's line and betrayed the revolution. So, training the next generation in all walks of life and fields of work had become an important task in China. But the main emphasis in the succession issue was the selection and training of cadres.

I thought Chairman Mao was already aware that some of his ideas were not recognized within the Party, so he began promoting the theory of class struggle and training successors who would agree with, be loyal to and enforce his ideas. The training of successors was therefore a strategic suggestion. It was not about training people for the Communist Party in a broad sense; it was more targeted than that. The Central Party School had begun recruiting junior cadres from among graduated high school students, which revealed that the Party's organization and education departments had already begun to train professional cadres. We were then known as "political work cadres". Moreover, several cadres, including Shanxi Provincial Party Committee Secretary Zhou Mingshan, who was famous back then, were chosen from among professional cadres across the country and hailed as model successors for propaganda purposes. Had not for the Cultural Revolution, he would probably have quickly become a senior Party cadre.

I should mention one other point on the issue of training successors. Back then, the Party had not yet criticized famous literary works on patriotism, nationalism and social responsibility, including some quotes that most Chinese people are familiar with, such as, "Be the first to feel concern for the country and the last to enjoy oneself,"[9] and "A great shelter for all the world's scholars, together in joy".[10]

---

9 This is a line from *Yueyanglou Ji* (*Notes to the the Yueyang Tower*) (岳陽樓記) written by Fan Zhongyan (989-1052), a politician and literary figure during the Song dynasty.

10 This is a line from the poem "My Thatched Cottage was Torn Apart by Autumn Winds" (茅屋為秋風所破歌) by Du Fu (712-770), a famous poet of the Tang dynasty.

There was no shortage of social responsibility among the old scholars in China. Back in this time, the intellectuals were being asked to take on the social responsibility of helping to train successors for the sake of the nation.

In both broad and narrow senses, training successors became a more urgent task. Some people have questioned whether this was a direct response to the behavior of the children of senior cadres. But I did not think so. It was certainly in response to something, but I did not regard it as the behavior of senior cadres' children. Everybody, no matter from what family background, could have good and bad qualities. The Party was keen on training a generation of qualified cadres, which greatly stimulated the sense of social and class responsibility of my generation. We wanted to mold ourselves as successors of revolution. Amid this atmosphere, senior cadres naturally hoped that their own children would take over their work. But it was not because they wanted them to be government officials. A number of children of senior cadres also hoped to fill their parents' shoes and become professional revolutionaries, for instance, by attending the Party school as junior cadres. They demanded that they should be given priority when it came to the training, which led some people to question whether the system was fair or not. However, from another perspective, I did not think that the children of senior cadres were held back in any way within the school.

One of the five standards for successors was to "unite everybody that can be united, including those who have opposed you in the past and those who have been proved wrong". This practically became my creed. I tenaciously, strenuously and patiently sought to connect with the people around me. For example, there was the son of a general in our class. We criticized him for thinking that he would naturally be a model Communist just because he was the child of a revolutionary. However, he claimed that he was the sort of person that should be trained as a successor rather than the children of intellectuals and landlords. I told him that he would not meet the conditions to become a successor if he did not work hard on cultivating himself.

Although I had been a student leader for many years, I did not think I was planning to become an official. My only dream was to go to college. As far as I was concerned, graduating from high school and going to either the PLA Military Engineering Institute in Harbin or Tsinghua University were my only options. I considered the PLA Military Engineering Institute as important for building up China's national defenses. I felt that I wanted to work to help with constructing the country. Many students went to the PLA Military Engineering Institute to study technology about missile and nuclear weapon. I knew several male and female students older than me who studied there and then went to work at the Jiuquan Satellite Launch Center in the desert of northwest China. It was a very tough place to work back then, and one had to be stationed there a long time. But I was willing to, as long as I was requested by the Party to do so. Prior to the Cultural Revolution, the emphasis for students at No. 4 High School was keen on their grades, with a purpose of going to good universities, preferably Tsinghua, and help construct the motherland. Most people had dedicated to study science and engineering at Tsinghua. It was their first priority than Peking University at the time, as Tsinghua claimed to be the cradle of "red engineers". It originally claimed to be the cradle of engineers, but later added the word "red" just before the Cultural Revolution. If the Cultural Revolution had not taken place, I would then be leading such a life. It was slightly conceited of me to assume that I would get in to Tsinghua University, as only about 40 students from No. 4 High School were admitted each year, while another 40 of them would be admitted to Peking University. Many model students from No. 4 High School went to Tsinghua, including Chen Yuan[11] and Qiao Zhonghuai[12] or to the PLA Military Engineering Institute like Yu Zhengsheng.[13]

An incident worth mentioning occurred during our summer holidays in 1965. Kong Dong and I, together with other senior cadres'

11 Chen Yuan was Chairman of the China Development Bank until he retired in April 2013.

12 Qiao Zhonghuai was Deputy Foreign Minister from 2001 to 2002.

13 Yu Zhengsheng is currently the fourth ranked member of the CPC Politburo Standing Committee and Chairman of the CPPCC National Committee.

children, including Liu Yuan and Dong Lianghe, went to serve in the Beijing Public Security Corps. The fact that we served as soldiers reflected our attitude at the time. I later wrote an essay called "Diary of a Soldier", which was published in the *Middle School Students* magazine.

The Gathering Storm

Before the Cultural Revolution, people's state of mind had changed dramatically. It began with the Sino-Soviet controversy, and was a kind of crisis to us. It was a very open affair, with the Party Central Committee publishing nine editorials accusing the Soviet Union of revisionism. Everyone was aware that the Chinese and Soviet leaders had fallen out. And this had a significant impact on us. According to my memory, from the moment I went to high school, I felt the threat of war hanging over us. We were strongly aware that the split with the Soviet Union could end in warfare. This diplomatic environment coupled with the political environment within China made us feel that things had a momentum of their own, and we were headed on a collision course. It was against this backdrop that certain traditional elements of our lives were gradually discarded. Everything was focused on class struggle. This came to envelop and completely dominate our thinking. Something that was later referred to as "revolution of the soul". In other words, people's thoughts were ruled by such ideas.

Mao's movements from ideological campaigns to political campaigns had permeated in all walks of life, both inside and outside China, both among life inside and outside the Party, and both in China's domestic and international affairs. He was convinced that the Party was rotten at the primary level in many parts of the country, while many senior cadres were against him. His response was to fight against his perceived enemies for his own enjoyment. As I said above on the student strike, I believed Mao was responsible for inciting the earlier student protests. It seemed, in the eyes of the young students, Mao's talks with Mao Yuanxin and Wang Hairong were undoubtedly inflammatory.

On the eve of the Cultural Revolution, I already sensed the gathering storm. We had discussed it at home. My parents were well-disciplined and did not like to spread rumors, but they would ask me to focus on major issues. For example, when the Sino-Soviet split occurred, my father told me to read Mao's criticisms of the Soviet Union carefully. My father was closely connected to Kang Sheng, as they had both worked in intelligence prior to 1949, and they were in good terms after the founding of PRC. The first time my brother and I went to Beidaihe, my mother and father were unable to come due to work commitments, so we went there with Kang's family. We used to call his wife (Cao Yi'ou) Mama Cao. During the Sino-Soviet split and the Cultural Revolution, it was Kang Sheng who used to tell us what was going on. The signs became increasingly clear on the literary front. A number of articles appeared, which criticized literary works and movies from the perspective of class struggle, while works such as *Locust Tree Village* (*Huai Shu Zhuang*), *Seizing the Seal of Power* (*Duo Yin*) and *We Must Never Forget* (*Qian Wan Bu Yao Wang Ji*) were released. That was the political environment on the eve of the Cultural Revolution.

I remembered that in 1965, Cao Yi'ou's nephew, Su Han, wrote an essay criticizing *Early Spring in February* (*Zao Chun Er Yue*). He was in fact incited to do so. Besides, Kang also fanned the flames by saying that students should care about literature and art, look out for people who oppose the Party, and write articles from this perspective. There were all precursors to what would follow. And my thoughts were definitely affected by these events. I was aware that the Central Committee was up to something, so I was not particularly surprised when the Cultural Revolution began. It seemed to be the next logical step, though I had no idea about its connotation.

The first major incident of the Cultural Revolution that I was involved in was when Grade 3 students from Beijing No. 4 High School and No. 1 High School for Girls wrote to the CPC Central Committee demanding to abolish the college entrance examination. It was another example of children of senior cadres leading the way. The students involved at our school were from Class 5 in Grade 3, which was exactly my class. And it was a classmate, Bo Xiyong, who had heard that the college entrance examination was going to be scrapped in 1966. We were all studying hard for the examination at the time. Despite having experienced the Four Cleanups Movement and the campaign to revolutionize education, and regardless of the fact that I was already a probationary member of the Party and considered an "advanced element", all my efforts went into preparing for the examination. In one day, I was at the home of my mathematics teacher, Mr. Zhou, for an extra mathematics lesson together with Bo Xiyong and several other classmates who were perhaps from cadre families. Zhou was taking us through some difficult questions that had come up in examinations in previous years. During the class, Bo Xiyong told us about the Central Committee scrapping the examination and asked if we should take the initiative step and do something about it. He was sure that the Central Committee would support the idea of abolishing the college entrance examination, and I agreed. However, I was unaware of how the No. 1 High School for Girls got involved.

It was believed in the society that the college entrance examination was abolished because of the suggestions from Class 5, Grade 3 students from No. 4 High School, and the Central Committee had no choice but to accept it. But that was not the fact. The Central Committee had already thought about abolishing the college entrance examination. However, we did catch wind of it first. The children of senior cadres were always the first to hear about such things. There was a context to the letter we wrote to the Central Committee, and it did not come from nowhere. Personally I regretted having made the decision. I had worked hard for so long in preparation for the examination, I want to experience the honor, and I was itching to show what I could do. I felt that the examination was a way of testing myself and showing my capability. But it was suddenly taken away, and I was left feeling frustrated. Of course, my classmates who were not so good at their study were delighted that they no longer had to sit the examination. But the cruel reality was that university enrolment had also stopped, and none of us would go to college.

A working group then arrived and, a Cultural Revolution Committee was set up in our school. I was appointed as head of the committee because of my position among the students. However, there was a scramble among the children of senior cadres to assume leadership of this new body, and we came into conflict with a number of them. They felt that I represented a strategic faction that was relatively conservative, and as a result, I should not be in charge of the school's revolutionary activities. One evening, we called on a meeting mainly of the children of senior cadres in one of the large classrooms to hold a debate. I could not remember the details of the meeting, but maybe it was about how we should carry out our activities. Anyways, they argued that my methods were ineffective and too conservative. They also complained that I was always a student leader and suggested that somebody else be given a turn. In response, we said that we would proceed in accordance with the "Sixteen Points".[14] Actually, I felt that I had no choice as I had been involuntarily placed in that position by the authority.

The head of the working group was very nervous because both sides had support. The group led by me was larger and included almost every student Party members in our school. We also had the support of the majority of students, and were therefore very influential. The other side had a number of people in background positions. Later on, this was labeled as a "power struggle" between children of senior cadres within the No.4 Middle School. That, at least, was how the outsiders viewed it. The incident did not last long, however. The whole thing just blew over immediately after the working group withdrew from the school.

The group's withdrawal from the school left a power vacuum. Because the Cultural Revolution Committee had been established under the auspices of the working group, it had thus lost its authority. Then, I proposed to set up branches of Communist Youth League

14 Originally entitled *Decisions* of the Central Committee of the Chinese Communist Party *Concerning the Great Proletarian Cultural Revolution.*

according to different grades and put them in charge. Each class had a CYL branch, and the secretaries from each class branch could form grade branch, with the grade branch for Grade 3 being in charge of all grade branches. Most branch secretaries of CYL in Grade 3 were already Party members. Li Sanyou was the secretary of Class 2, Qin Xiao was of Class 4, I was of Class 5, and we were the student Party members who played the most important roles. There was also a joint organization above all the grade branches, which I was in charge of. I was deputy secretary of the school's CYL Committee, and one of the teachers acted as secretary. In fact, the CYL branch of Grade 3 could control the revolutionary activities of the whole school. Moreover, we used the old counselor system, whereby high school students were responsible for counseling junior high school students. This was used because I had learned from the lessons of the Four Cleanups Movement that we needed to act in an orderly and organized manner. Meanwhile, as students and Party members who were more mature, we should call the shots. This was probably a unique structure in Beijing.

I had not seized my position by starting a rebellion like Peng Xiaomeng of the Affiliated High School of Peking University or Bu Dahua of the Affiliated High School of Tsinghua University. Nor had I instigated troubles like the student leaders of No. 4 High School during the Four Cleanups Movement. Instead, I had become a student leader naturally by appointment. Some people were only interested in being in charge, but that was not my way of thinking. I found myself in that position because of the circumstances. When the school established a Cultural Revolution Committee, I was appointed as director. When the grade branches were established, I was put in charge of it. While facing mass movements, one cannot simply run away and hide. One must act. So, that was the position I found myself in at the start of the Cultural Revolution. It was largely beyond my control, and that was my fate.

Denouncing the School Principal and Teachers

Following our experience of the student protests during the Socialist Education Movement, student Party members behaved like political cadres during the Cultural Revolution. Personally, since junior high school, my way of thinking had continuously become mature under the guidance of the Party. At home, I had also been raised not to defy the Party's principles or policies. Due to this way of thinking, I was left behind during the student protests, which in turn led people to say that I had compromised and given in. It was also because I had been "given amnesty", so that I could join the Party. And as a Party member, I paid greater attention to the organizational discipline and the policies of the Central Committee. It was these circumstances that led us to place particular emphasis on following the Party's leadership and paying attention to policies at the start of the Cultural Revolution. On the one hand, my brain was hardwired to follow Chairman Mao and criticize revisionist education; on the other hand, I persisted to follow the Party's discipline and policies. I believed revolution was revolution, but it should be carried out methodically. We often studied the "May 16th Notice"[15] and the "Sixteen Points", and were well-versed on policy issues. However, as for the students of other schools, no one cared about the "Sixteen Points". During the Cultural Revolution, some students even used violence while denouncing their teachers. Because I tried to prevent some of these excesses, people claimed that I was some sort of policy faction and a conservative.

I could not totally remember the incident involving students from the No. 4, 6 and 8 high schools criticizing Li Chen and Yang Bin at the

15 Originally titled simply *Notice of the Central Committee of the Communist Party of China.*

Forbidden City Concert Hall. Chen Lu said in his autobiography that it was his idea, so he negotiated with me over it.[16] That may have been the case. Because I was the student leader at No. 4 High School, if an event was being organized jointly by several schools, they would coordinate with us. I was definitely on the rostrum at that event, along with Dong Lianghe from No. 6 High School and others. Struggle meetings against teachers and leaders were very common during the Cultural Revolution. I cannot remember whether we hung signs around the teachers' necks or not. I did not think we did that. Nor did I remember we made them wear tall paper hats.[17] At that time, Zhou Jian was the deputy director of the Cultural Revolution Committee. He was of the same age with me, but had missed a year of school due to illness, so he was only in Grade 2. He was a very capable person, and could talk and work in an organized way. I asked him to organize the struggle meetings, which meant he was responsible for organizing transportation to the meetings, how to arrive at the venue, how to maintain order, and so on.

Liu Huixuan was the CYL branch secretary for Grade 1. He also attended the branch meetings for his grade brunch, but he was very aggressive, and we would regularly come to blows. He accused us of being conservative and disliked us. He attended that particular meeting. As he was a branch secretary, Zhou Jian had given him a seat on the rostrum to help maintain the order. To our surprise, however, he was the first person at the meeting to turn violent, though I did not remember whom his target was. We had no idea why he was so violent. The stage then erupted into chaos as we tried to maintain a semblance of order. But a number of students from lower grades had already swarmed onto the rostrum trying to hit someone at the time. As far as I remembered, after Li Chen had been hit on the head by a belt buckle, blood streamed along his gray hair. It was a horrible sight. After that, we stopped the meeting, and took the denounced teachers away.

16 See Chen Xiaolu's Autobiography, *Huiyi Yu Fansi—Hongweibing Shidai Fengyun Renwu* (Memories and Reflections of a Red Guard Leader), compiled by Mi Hedu, p.26.

17 Making people being criticized to wear signs detailing their "crimes" and large hats to invoke ridicule were common practices at the time.

I later criticized Liu Huixuan for his behavior. I told him that he had gone too far, and it had not been our intention to turn out as that. I explained that we were not allowed to act like that, because it violated Party policy. By that time, the "Sixteen Points" had already been issued. It was stipulated that one must not use corporal punishment or beat people. This was made very clear. However, there was no shortage of people who took matters in to their own hands. They were simply brutal, destructive, and with a lust for violence.

Later on, another incident took place. One day at school, Yang Bin was suddenly surrounded by a group of students. We were having in a meeting when someone arrived with a message that Yang had been detained at the running track on the playground. I quickly ended the meeting and headed down there. Yang was already being kicked and punched, and her shirt was disheveled. I said that we could not act in such a way and called for order. I said that according to the "Sixteen Points", we could criticize her, but should not hit her. The students wanted a parade for Yang Bin through the streets, but Zhao Shengli and I wrestled her free, while Qin Xiao and others protected us. During the process, I was hit several times, but not too hard, because they did not dare mess with us. With us there, the situation quickly calmed down. Some clumps of soil and watery ink were thrown to us, but no real harm was done. Originally, they were using belts and sticks. It could have been much worse. An old lady like Yang could not have lasted for long. This had a profound impact on her. She even told her son later that I had saved her life. She said that if it had not been me and Zhao Shengli, she would have been killed.[18]

18 Mi Hedu interviewed one of the parties involved, Zhao Shengli, about this. During the interview, Zhao recalled the following: One afternoon, someone arrived with a message saying that something went wrong. Some Grade 1 students had cornered school leaders and teachers they had issues with, and that they wanted to hold a struggle session and parade them through the streets. Kong Dan arrived with members of the Cultural Revolution Committee and appealed to people by quoting *Quotations from Chairman Mao* and the "Sixteen Points". As he ran over, he said to us to use the situation to do the right thing, Yang Bin and some other leaders and teachers had already been seized. Kong Dan said that people should not do it like that and should abide by the "Sixteen Points". He said there should be a verbal struggle instead of a violent one. He quickly brought the situation under control. However, some students still demanded the leaders and teachers be paraded through the

Another incident took place in the school's small courtyard, when another gang of students suddenly seized a teacher. As soon as I heard what had happened, I rushed over there. The majority of the students in the playground were junior high school students, but they were really violent. They called out the names of teachers and dragged them on to the stage to shave half of their hair. Once their hair had been shaved, they would be prisoned in the so-called "cowshed". The teachers in the shed were all shaking with fear. Quite a few had already been called on, and had their heads shaved. On seeing this, I immediately climbed onto the stage and read the "Sixteen Points" to them. I told them that their behavior was unacceptable, and criticized them heavily for treating teachers in such a way. I said they could point out the teachers' shortcomings or errors, but not in such a humiliating way. Afterwards, a teacher told me that his heart was almost in his throat, because he knew they were just about to turn on him. He praised me for standing up for them. In that year, some teachers who were prisoned in the shed never came out alive. After my speech that day, however, those teachers had not been detained.

It was no accident that we managed to protect the principal, the teachers and students during those events. It was something we tried hard to do. From early on, we had decided to protect our class teacher, Gu Dexi, who was our mentor as well as friend. We did not let the other students touch him. We even directly intervened to protect the school

---

streets. So Kong and Zhou Jian escorted Yang away, with each by her side. Qian Xiao and I walked at the front, clearing the way. We knocked aside some students who were trying to attack them with sticks, brooms, basin and dustpans (filled with earth). Kong, Zhou Jian, Qin Xiao and I were hit in the process and were covered in mud. Back at the teaching and research group's courtyard, Kong Dan and I helped Yang into an outhouse away from the students. Kong told me to take good care of Yang and not let anything happen to her. He then went back outside to help the other leaders and teachers and encourage everyone to handle the mass movement correctly. He said all of the people being struggled against and paraded should be treated correctly. Afterwards, I asked the school nurse to give Yang a check-up, but the nurse saw her was covered in mud and said she could not examine her like that. Yang could not walk, so I carried her to her dormitory on my back and asked two young female teachers, Wang Simin and Peng Bowen, to help her get cleaned up. The school nurse then checked her over and said she had no major injuries. I was still afraid something might happen to her so I continued to look after her. Later on, two female teachers took it in turns to guard her. By the next afternoon, Yang had recovered her senses.

principal on a number of occasions. It was acceptable to criticize or denounce them. You could say that someone had followed the wrong line. But you could not hit them. As a result of our actions, teachers at No. 4 High School were not beaten in public like the teachers at the High School for Girls Affiliated to Beijing Normal University or those at Beijing No. 6 and 8 high schools. Nobody dared to do that because of the authority we wielded. In 1982, after the Cultural Revolution had ended, I went to work as Zhang Jinfu's secretary. Before I started to work, the Central Organization Department had investigated my behavior during the Cultural Revolution. They went to No. 4 High School and spoke to some of the teachers who experienced those days. They all said that I followed the Party's policies closely.

I did not say those to glorify myself. A lot of this happened because of the position I was in. It was just how a particular group of people at No. 4 High School was like. Our actions were the result of a common understanding. Nor am I trying to brag about how faultless we were. I am simply pointing out how a group of people reacted during that particular situation. Meanwhile, we also revolted against the larger background of the leftist movement. We started criticizing revisionism during the Four Cleanups Movement, including Zhou Xiaozheng's "twenty-one items". During the Cultural Revolution, we also criticized and denounced the headmaster and leaders in charge of education. However, we only criticized them verbally, without using any violence.

As a result, some students from lower grades were unhappy with us and accused us of opposing the revolutionary struggle and suppressing them. They said that we were not following the normal mode of development in the Red Guard Movement. They believed we had suppressed them. They also made big-character posters giving advices to the school's Cultural Revolution committee.

Passively Establishing the Red Guards

At the beginning of the Cultural Revolution, I had an opinion on the Red Guards, and thought they were too radical. Wang Ming, one of the Red Guard leaders, was a classmate of mine in junior high school, but he later attended the Affiliated High School of Tsinghua University, where he helped set up the Red Guards. One day, I went to the Old Summer Palace to talk with him. He told me that they were establishing an organization. For me, it was too radical and inappropriate, so I was strongly against it. I asked him why establishing an organization. And I told him that the purpose of the Cultural Revolution was to criticize the bourgeoisie line, and he should do so in accordance with the Central Committee's instructions and policies. I rather talked down to him at the time. I told him that they could not do it, because we had been warned and had to follow the Party's leadership during the Four Cleanups Movement. In those days, the struggle was aimed at school Party branches, but was only about criticizing their revisionist tendencies and problems with the educational policy over the previous 17 years. This could have been carried out in an orderly way. I had some sympathy for them. Wang explained that they were oppressed by the working group, so they felt that they had no choice but to set up an organization and fight. I advised him to talk to the working group and not resort to violence, but he did not listen to me.

There were a lot of students like me at No. 4 High School. Those of us in charge of activities linked to the Cultural Revolution at the school shunned the Red Guards due to their lack of legitimacy with the Central Committee. Nor did we accept the excessive practices employed by some students in Haidian District at the time. It did not seem to be the normal sort of organization that the Central Committee used to promote its political campaigns. Therefore, I felt that the Red Guards was not for me. To a certain extent, I even thought that, as student Party members, we represented a better standard of student than those who revolted in Haidian. We considered ourselves to be more aware of the Party's policies, with a better understanding of the Party's intentions and plans, and could carry out the movement in a better-planned and orderly fashion. We obeyed the working groups dispatched by the Party and acted in accordance with Party policies. That was our ideological states. It meant that activities were carried out in an orderly manner at the school from the start of the Cultural Revolution.

Moreover, people from Beijing No. 4 High School who became Red Guards later on were not as rebellious as the Red Guards from Haidian District. This had to do with the types of students that went to the schools and their different ideologies. If it had not turned to be promoted that way, I would personally be opposed to set up the Red Guards. In a way, I considered them a group of "brave members" in the revolutionary movement. I said so today not to absolve myself. This has already become history. Since the beginning, from the outset of the Four Cleanup Movements and joining the Party, I was seen by a number of fellow students as being conservative. But I did not agree with them. I always took my own way by upholding the Party's leadership and carrying out campaigns in a systematic and organized manner. This included solving the issue of whether or not the primary-level leadership had become degenerated during the Four Cleanups, as well as criticizing revisionist education during the Cultural Revolution. At least, that was what I believed.

The reality was that the school's Party branch was paralyzed as soon as the working group arrived. The group relied on students and the CYL organization. Later on, a Cultural Revolution Committee was set up. I was appointed director of the committee, and Zhou Jian was made vice director. There was absolutely no need for us to set up an organization of Red Guards. The whole concept of it was not compatible with our views and our system of CYL branches in one grade.

There was an important political sign during this period, but we did not pay sufficient attention to it. I was committed to adhering to the policies of the Party Central Committee, but I only found out later that the Central Committee had already been divided. Or one could say that, although it was not originally divided, Chairman Mao found a way to drive it apart. On July 29, 1966, Liu Shaoqi and Deng Xiaoping were holding a meeting for Beijing Cultural Revolution activists at the Great Hall of the People. I still remembered what Deng said in his Sichuan accent, "Let's sit and talk." Then Chairman Mao suddenly walked out from behind the rostrum curtain with the Cultural Revolution Group[19] and walked around the rostrum. Having done so, Liu and Deng had no choice but to greet him. But Mao looked really fierce, he simply ignored them, and said nothing to them. They looked utterly helpless and completely lost their faces. Everybody who attended the meeting had seen it. It was a strong signal. Nevertheless, I was too slow to catch on. It did not dawn on me that the Central Committee was already divided, and I still thought in the way of trying to uphold the leadership, the Central Committee and the Party organization.

Our school was relatively late in setting up a unit for Red Guards. We had still not established such a unit by the time of the mass rally held on Tiananmen Square on August 18, 1966. On that day, we chose five to ten students from each class in higher grades to help maintain the order in the vicinity of the Golden Water Bridges at the Forbidden City. Our school still had not come out in support of the Red Guards, so we did not wear their armbands. I heard over the loudspeakers that the person in charge of No. 4 High School students was to go up to Tiananmen gate tower, so I went upstairs.[20] During the rally, Mao

19 The Cultural Revolution Group was formed in May 1966 and consisted mainly of radical supporters of Mao, including Chen Boda, Jiang Qing, Kang Sheng, Yao Wenyuan, Zhang Chunqiao, Wang Li and Xie Fuzhi. The group was originally directly subordinated to the Political Bureau's Standing Committee but later gained *de facto* power.

20 According to Peng Xiaomeng, the Red Guards rally at Tiananmen on August 18, 1966 was organized by Yong Wentao. Yong asked Peng to recommend schools to send 20 students each. Peng recommended Beijing No. 4 High School, the High School for Girls Affiliated to Beijing Normal University, Affiliated High School of Peking University, Affiliated High School of Tsinghua University, and others. In total there were 400 students. Peng also specifically recommended Beijing No. 31 High School because its Red Guards unit had strongly opposed the working group. In the end, however, it was written down wrongly as

praised the actions of the Red Guards. The situation was clear.

After we got back from the rally, we decided that we could not fall behind, so we set up a Red Guards unit. Liu Huixuan criticized us at the time for being slow in action. That was one reason for us to do so, but it was not the decisive reason. The main reason was Mao's public support for the Red Guards, so we could not act as we originally planned. After the rally, the combination of the overall situation and internal pressures, including Liu Huixuan's criticism and the children of some cadres' accusation of being conservative, meant that the school had no choice but to establish a Red Guards unit.

However, the unit did not have a complete organizational system. There were no headquarters or body responsible for running the unit. Instead, the grade group of CYL branches, Cultural Revolution Committee and Cultural Revolution directors from each class were still put in charge. As such, the Red Guards was not the main organization through which we participated in the Cultural Revolution.

In those days, we had to say that we were Red Guards and revolutionary, but we did not believe in the "bloodline theory" (that the children of revolutionaries were naturally the best people to follow in the footsteps of their fathers) and violence. Thus, we had become a different breed of Red Guards.

The violence that occurred during the Cultural Revolution was a sudden outburst of the dark side of human nature. The general order of the Xicheng District Picket Corps was supported by so many people, because older comrades hoped we could protect them. For the so-called "five black categories"[21], their homes would be searched and their property would be confiscated. Many people who belonged to the five black categories in the city had been rooted out, but some still remained. During the frenzied house searches of August 1966, sub-district offices and police stations even helped look into people's backgrounds. Many

---

No. 13 High School, so nobody from No. 31 High School was on Tiananmen gate tower that day. For other perspectives on the Red Guards see relevant sections of *Xin Lu—Toushi Gongheguo Tonglingren* by Mi Hedu (Central Literature Publishing House, 2011).

21 Landlords, rich peasants, anti-revolutionists, bad elements and rightists.

house searches were done by Red Guards from different schools and districts. Often they were carried out near schools, and whoever happened to be there could join in. House searches were accompanied by a great deal of violence. The whole thing was completely chaotic. This was widespread at that time, as if it were organized by those in power. It was a terrible time and a major event.

When the campaign to destroy the "Four Olds"[22] gathered pace, I did not want students at the school to treat children from exploiting classes unfairly, so I instructed my classmates and schoolmates in the same grade of mine to conduct organized and protective searches of homes of those from families with questionable backgrounds. One such student, Zhou Xuezhong, had been in the same class with me throughout junior and senior high school, and his family lived right opposite my home. I often went to his house, and we both sat at the small desk in the communal courtyard doing our homework. We carried out a "protective search" of his home. We went but did not really search his home or confiscate items. But left a notice stating that Red Guards from Beijing No. 4 High School had already searched the house, which they could show other Red Guards if they showed up to search the premises. I personally organized the protective search of Zhou Xuezhong's home. And Zhou Xiaozheng was there too. Zhou Xuezhong and I were close friends. Considering my status, my personal participation could show that I had attached great importance to the search.

At our recent reunion, a number of us recalled the protective searches. Lu Xiaowei later sent me a message to tell me, "The only time I went to the homes of Xu Yijing and Chang Yue was during the house searches. I had not been there before and did not go again afterwards. As such, it left a deep impression on me. Chang lived in the first alley of Xisi. His father was tall and with a large potbelly, while his mother looked small and frail. I went to his home and entered his father's study. Chang opened a drawer in the bookcase. Inside there were several tins of food. We ate a few of them and then had a quick look around. We did

22 The "Four Olds" refers to old customs, old culture, old habits and old ideas.

not take anything. We just left behind the notice you had given us and left. The whole thing lasted within less than half an hour." Lu Xiaowei and Zhou Xiaozheng were obviously not true Red Guards.

Other people also remembered who had been in charge of the searches of different homes. For example, Liu Dong was in charge of searching Huang Hanwen's home, Dong Zhixiong was in charge of Jin Yijian's home, and so on. They were all conducted in a peaceful and friendly manner, which was unusual given the climate of violence at the time. In fact, it still surprises me today. Lu Xiaowei emotionally stated that the way people acted at the time meant there was no hatred among the students, and nobody was left hurt, which was the reason we could all still meet up today.

Later on, we stipulated that the CYL branches of each grade should quickly arrange for house searches of students from the so-called "five black categories" to be carried out by Red Guards from their class in order to prevent students from nearby schools interfering in. Back then violence could break out at the drop of a hat. If we had not been there, Red Guards from other schools would come. There were quite a few students from "undesirable backgrounds" in our school, whose homes were searched by Red Guards from their class. I cannot say with absolute certainty that no violent incidents took place during these searches, but for classmates, there was greater compassion, so it was a lot more moderate. We came up with this policy because we wanted to protect our classmates by preventing Red Guards from other schools from searching their homes. If a police station or sub-district office passed the information of those families to the Red Guards, there would often be brutal methods. What we proposed was actually a protective measure. That was what we had been thinking about. It was not like what had been rumored in the society.

By the way, I did not totally agree with the bloodline theory, which sparked a great debate in society. I took it as reactionary. I had read about Tan Lifu's speeches and was greatly admired by his eloquence and the way he quoted from ancient works. But his arguments were not persuasive enough. The things he said could not explain anything because the Party's aims, policies, development and organizational structure were not able to accommodate his views. My mother's family background was bureaucratic, so how could one say "if the parent is reactionary, the son is a wretch"? I could not accept that. Therefore, I had a fairly negative view of the bloodline theory. Liu Huixuan and others disagreed with me, however. He made up songs based on the couplet of "the son of a hero must be a good man." He was very talented, and I admired him a lot. I was on good terms with him, but we had different political opinions at school. We considered him as a "brave member" and he considered us conservatives. It was said that he had written more than eleven revolutionary songs. I remembered a very popular one about the Red Guards written to the music of Beijing opera. His talent was demonstrated in the book entitled *When Xiao Xia Disappeared* that he wrote with his pseudo name Liping. I appreciated and respected him for mentioning my rational behavior in his autobiography and his reflections on the Cultural Revolution.

My feelings toward the bloodline theory were certainly influenced by my mother. Because of her disagreement, she had once been criticized by Chairman Mao. I will talk more about this later. In general, though, during the early stages of the Cultural Revolution, I adhered to the traditional view of being guided by the Party's policies, and tried my best to protect students with undesirable family backgrounds. Part of the reason we carried out protective searches was that we did not believe in the bloodline theory. This was also related to the friendships we had established within the school. The bloodline theory could never bring our friendships to an end.

General Orders of the Xicheng District Picket Corps

There was both inevitability and fortuity about the establishment of the Beijing Xicheng District Picket Corps. I say there was inevitability because it was closely related to our views toward the Red Guards, which were part of a larger ideological foundation. One can obviously identify why it was fortuitous by looking at the process of establishing the picket corps. Wang Xiangrong was in Grade 2 at No. 4 High School. He was not one of the school leaders, but he attended an event involving Red Guards from a number of schools, at which they decided to set up the Red Guards Picket Corps. He came back from the meeting and told us about it. I said I was too busy to get involved and told him to deal with it. He said that he could not handle it, and that I was the only capable people. Meanwhile, he said since our school had the capacity to do this, we should therefore take the initiative.

Chen Xiaolu recalled that it was he who called for the establishment of the Picket Corps.[23] And I heard about it from Wang Xiangrong. It did not really matter how it was established, but that we all agreed and were quickly involved. The Picket Corps had its own headquarters, but those of us in charge of it did not have clear titles, and there was no commander-in-chief to give the orders. We did, however, have numbers and ranks. For example, I was number one. None of us would deny that I was in charge, and Chen Xiaolu and Dong Lianghe were my deputies, but I never considered myself as the person in charge or the organizer from No. 4 High School. The organizational structure of the Xicheng District Picket Corps had a lot to do with our school's

23 See Chen Xiaolu's oral history: "Do unto others as youwould be done," *Huiyi Yu Fansi—Hongweibing Shidai Fengyun Renwu* (Memories and Reflections of a Red Guard Leader), compiled by MiHedu.

status among the other schools, as well as the personalities of Chen and Dong. As a student leader, I was quite experienced, so it was natural for me to take a leading role.

There were several groups within the headquarters of the picket corps. Some people recalled that there was a propaganda department, but that was incorrect. It was merely a publicity group. Wang Xiangrong was in charge of one of the groups, and Zhao Shengli was the head of the logistics group. Qin Xiao was in charge of the publicity group. Li Sanyou was an important member of the publicity group. He was an excellent writer who composed all the drafts of our sixth and seventh general orders. Before the Cultural Revolution, Li Sanyou's father was the deputy director of the Beijing Public Security Bureau. By then, he had already been labeled as a "gangster" of the Beijing Municipal Committee by the Red Guards. Despite this, we still considered Li Sanyou to be one of us, so we let him to play a role behind the scenes. Ma Kai also did a lot of work to help us. As far as I could remember, he was also involved in the discussions on drafting the general orders.

When the headquarters of the picket corps was set up in Yuxiang Primary School, two teams of marshals were formed. One was made up entirely of students from No. 4 High School. The other was made up of students from the High School for Girls Affiliated to Beijing Normal University. At that time, my brother, Kong Dong, was in Grade 2, and was one year younger than me. He was the head of the team from our school. Xu Haidong's son, Xu Wenlian, served as the supervisor. I could not remember who was in charge of the other team, but Deng Rong was one of its members. Each team was made up of about dozens of people. The duties of the marshal teams were to station in the headquarters and deal with emergencies by organizing combined action. We had only several organized actions. For example, the incident involving a dispute between the Ministry of Geology and the Geological Institute "East Is Red" Red Guards groups and the dispute with "Red Flag" Red Guards group at the Commission of Science Technology and Industry for National Defense. On one occasion, Premier Zhou asked our picket corps to go to Beijing Railway Station to maintain order.

We immediately deployed more than 300 people from various schools in Beijing's Xicheng District. Dong Lianghe and Chen Xiaolu had led them to the station. The teams of marshals were not directly involved, but the picket corps was responsible for organizing it. There were other occasions when we were called upon temporarily, such as to protect the Panchen Lama.

When our picket corps was established, the society was really in chaos. On the one hand, veteran cadres were being targeted, which was conflictual. Students and Red Guards were targeting school head teachers and school Party branch secretaries. But many of these people, especially at key high schools in Beijing, were veterans of the anti-Japanese war. The headmaster of No. 4 High School, for example, was Yang Bin. She had joined the revolution in 1938 and was the wife of Song Yangchun, who was the Minister of Construction. When the movement had developed to a certain extent, some of the children of senior cadres realized this and began to question whom they were struggling against. We had an inherent instinctive reaction to this. On the other hand, our traditional education had taught us not to accept things like the bloodline theory, the prevailing chaos and the violent behaviors. For my part, I was the CYL branch secretary of my class, and I had long been instilled with the ideas of uniting students and always adhering to the Party's policies. My mother and father had never said anything like that to me, such as "A dragon begets a dragon. A phoenix begets a phoenix. Those begotten by rats are good at digging holes." Their origins and careers stood in complete contrast to such notions. The path that people had taken is determined by future influences and their own choices.

The establishment of the picket corps took place against the larger backdrop of a reaction to the Cultural Revolution. We formed the basis and backbone of the Picket Corps because of our identity. We naturally had close links to veteran cadres, and we wanted to protect them. We also had a strong affiliation to the Party. We wanted to protect the confidentiality of the Party and state. Moreover, we could not tolerate the use of violence against the public, even those who were considered bad elements or problematic. Those were the basic reasons that we started the Xicheng District Picket Corps. Not everybody agreed with us, however, and our organization later became unviable. We were eventually turned on from all sides. It was no surprise that the Cultural Revolution Group did not support us; even activists did not support us. Many of the younger students at school also expressed their dissatisfaction. They called me strategist and accused us of being conservatives and not being true Red Guards. Those were the particular circumstances that led to us setting up the Picket Corps. It happened naturally, and it had the effect of suppressing and resisting erroneous views and practices for a time.

By that time, the Red Guards were active throughout the society. I remembered an incident during which some Red Guards went to Xinhua Bookstore and stopped them from selling the works of Chairman Mao. They said that selling Chairman Mao's works was akin to blasphemy against a great leader. Workers at the bookstore were panic-stricken by this because they could not afford to just give the books away for free. So, they contacted the Picket Corps to seek our help. We discussed it with them and it was decided that studying Mao's works was important and his books were national commodities, so it was not appropriate to prohibit selling them. The Xicheng District Picket Corps signed a document which said that Xinhua Bookstore could continue to sell Mao's works. A subsequent general order provided further provisions over the matter.

Another incident involved the Yili Food Factory. Workers from the factory came to us saying Red Guards had told them that their packaging, which featured a pair of doves, was revisionist and could no longer be used. Yili was the most important food factory in Beijing at the time. Had their production been interrupted, it would have had a significant impact on Beijing's markets. Those in charge of the factory were anxious given how close it was to the National Day holiday, which meant they did not have enough time to change the packaging. They explained that if they did not use the old packaging they would not be able to complete their work for the holiday. They asked us to help in the hope that we would find a way for them to use the old packaging without offending the Red Guards. I sent Zhao Shengli and a few others to investigate. They did not think it was a big issue, so Zhao signed a document stating that the Xicheng District Picket Corps agreed they could continue using the old packaging. That seemed to be the end of the issue.

The Xicheng District Picket Corps mainly exerted its influence through general orders, and it issued ten of them. The first few were issued piecemeal. Our fourth general order was quite useful as it specifically prohibited beating people. We opened this general order with a quote from *Quotations from Chairman Mao Zedong*: "Policy and tactics are the lifeline of the Party; leading comrades at all levels must give them full attention and must never on any account be negligent." In our fourth general order, there contained seven provisions, while our fifth general order concerned policies regarding to house searches.

I remembered that Li Sanyou told me that we should not issue orders in such a piecemeal fashion and that we should make a policy-oriented point in the next order aimed at the whole society and things we thought needed to be stopped or rectified. For example, how to deal with sending landlords, rich farmers, anti-revolutionaries and bad elements back to their hometowns, how to manage the arrival in the capital of Red Guards from around the country, how to deal with the beatings, lootings and raids, how to interpret policies, and so on. I had taken the previous general orders home and showed my mother. She also thought that they were not systematic enough and too fragmented, which felt like she was giving me guidance. This was the origin of the sixth and seventh general orders, which were the most important ones issued by the picket corps.

Li Sanyou was in charge of drafting those two general orders. Qin Xiao and I made some modifications to them afterwards. We worked very hard on the wording in particular. The orders constituted fairly complete policy advice aimed at the increasingly serious situation at the time. Looking at it now, it reads rather like a document of the Party's Central Committee. We certainly based it on the documents issued by

Central Committee. But this meant the tone was rather condescending. This perhaps stemmed from that we believed our understanding of the Party's traditions and policies as well as the "Sixteen Points" was absolutely correct. It may also have stemmed from the fact that we often talked to younger students as experienced student leaders. We were, nevertheless, very aware that the general orders should not contradict the Red Guards too much. We did not use negative language like, "you must not do something." Rather, we used "these are not the practices that we should adopt." For example, we said, "beating people and obtaining confessions by compulsion and then giving them credence are not methods we should adopt." With regard to corporal punishment, we said, "making people kneel, lie down, bend over, carry things, walk through the streets, or stand, hold their arms up, hang their heads and do heavy work for long periods are all considered forms of corporal punishment, and are not practices that we should adopt." With regard to insulting people, we said, "making people carry black boards, wear tall paper hats and sing songs, as well as shaving people's heads, are types of insults and are not practices that we should adopt."

Everybody who read those two general orders, regardless of whether they were from the municipal Party committee, the government or which social faction all thought that somebody in government was behind them. The people who investigated us later also had the same thought. By that time, two different groups already existed. One was the Cultural Revolution Group, which was building its support base and encouraging the Red Guards. The other group was led by Zhou Enlai, who was trying desperately to bring the situation under control and to maintain social order. It had been widely believed that an experienced cadre was behind us. The Cultural Revolution Group assumed Zhou was behind our general orders. They had viewed him as an obstacle to the Cultural Revolution from the start, because he was their most powerful opponent after Liu Shaoqi. In fact, I and my mates also believed that Zhou was behind us, or that we were being supported, counted on, or commanded by him through the State Council.

I took home all the general orders issued by Xicheng District

Picket Corps to my mother, but always only after they had been issued. She was positive about all of them. She thought the sixth and seventh general orders were clear, with a grasp of policies, and well-written. Having worked in Premier Zhou's office for a long time, she had a lot of contact with important documents, so she particularly looked at the style they were written. I then told her that they were written by Li Sanyou. I want to make it very clear that she never suggested us what should be included in the general orders. Nor did she ever tell me to pay attention to what certain issue or topic. And she never explicitly told me that she was going to show the orders to Premier Zhou Enlai. It was simply my impression that she was positive about them. But I never received any orders or cues from her or from Premier Zhou through her.

This could be confirmed from the inconsistencies that existed in the ten general orders. For example, much of the content was repetitive, and the policies were stated inconsistently and unsystematically. This was especially true of the eighth general order. After the sixth and seventh orders, we changed our tune and decided that people should do what they wanted. That was because the previous sixth and seventh orders had been criticized by a lot of Red Guards, which forced us to backtrack. The orders reflected our thinking and understanding during the particular moment. We spontaneously attempted to steer the direction of the Red Guard movement, but at no point did we do it at someone else's behest. That was much certain.

The Picket Corps' Activities

The Xicheng District Picket Corps was established on August 25, 1966. On August 31 of that year, it was given an important mission. Together with the Beijing Garrison and the police, it was asked to provide security for Mao's second reception of the Red Guards at Tiananmen Square. On that day, I was in command of a team of marshals and was responsible for protecting Chairman Mao along with the soldiers of the Beijing Garrison. I later received an order stating that several members of the Picket Corps were to go upstairs of Tiananmen gate tower, so I went upstairs. I was not up there for long when Mao's jeep and that of Premier Zhou and Xie Fuzhi arrived, and they were surrounded by Red Guards in front of the Golden Water Bridge. The Red Guards were from all over the country and nobody dared to touch them, not even the soldiers. The whole thing was out of control. Xie Fuzhi, who was in charge of security, was extremely nervous, so he quickly got out of the car to maintain the order, but to no avail. None of the Red Guards paid any attention to the leaders in charge of security, such as Xie Fuzhi and Fu Chongbi. Eventually, they had to call on the Picket Corps for help. Members of the Picket Corps took off their belts and waved them in the air and hit those that got in the way until a path was cleared for the cars to get over the Golden Water Bridge. That was what had truly happened. I was up on Tiananmen gate tower and had a clear view of the whole thing. In the eyes of the Picket Corps, Chairman Mao was the commander of the Red Guards, and we could not put him in any danger.

On the next day, which was September 1, Xie Fuzhi visited us at the Picket Corps' original headquarters at the Jiusan Society. I remembered him walking into the courtyard and excitedly declaring,

"The Xicheng District Picket Corps did an excellent job." He lifted up his trouser legs and said, "Look at my legs. They're black and blue. If it were not for the Picket Corps, I would have been trampled to death. You saved my life, and you protected Chairman Mao. If you had not been there, and something had happened to the Chairman, I do not know how I would have explained it." Nevertheless, when the Picket Corps was later subjected to persecution, Xie was merciless and showed no leniency.

On the day of the rally on August 31, after I had climbed up onto Tiananmen gate tower, I got out some Picket Corps armbands to give them to the leaders. Our armbands were much bigger than those worn by the Red Guards. I also gave one to Jiang Qing who would probably know me. I introduced myself by telling her I was Kong Yuan's and Xu Ming's son. She just grunted her acknowledgement. That was all I got from her. I later saw her wearing the armband. She had covered it with her large coat. I did not think too much about it at the time. I just thought that she might have an unfavorable opinion towards the Picket Corps. The fact was that there were already acute differences within the Party.

When Chairman Mao and the other leaders arrived, I gave an armband to Premier Zhou. I also wanted to give one to Chairman Mao, but Zhou stopped me. He told me that it would be inappropriate for Mao to wear our armband only, given that Mao was the leader of the Red Guards. But he said I could give them to the other leaders. I then walked up to Lin Biao and gave him an armband. He took it without saying anything. I also gave an armband to Ye Jianying and several of the PLA marshals. Ye asked me what work we were doing. I explained that we were trying to maintain the order, for example, there had been many Red Guards arrived the railway station from around the country, which caused some chaos, so we went there to keep the order in accordance with the instructions from Premier Zhou. Ye listened and praised us for our actions. He also asked if we needed any help from him. I said that we were lacking transport and we needed bedding, as we often had to work late. He said that he would take care of it.

We later produced identification certificates for our corps, which had a portrait of Chairman Mao on the first page. On the second page, there was a picture of Lin Biao wearing a Picket Corps armband. This type of document carried a lot of weight. Lin Biao's armband number was 00001, but originally we intended Chairman Mao to have this number. I wore armband with the number of 10001. My certificate carried the same number. Some people would say this made me the commander. I was not officially, and I was just one of the main people in charge.

That night I went home and told my mother that I had met Marshall Ye Jianying and spoken to him about the Picket Corps. I said that I had told him what we were doing and he had offered his support. My mother said that I should not have bothered the army and Ye. She said that it was the responsibility of the State Council and its Government Offices Administration. She asked what we needed, so I told her we needed better headquarters as our temporary headquarters at the Jiusan Society were not quite adequate as well as vehicles and bedding. She said she would arrange it and put the deputy director of the Government Offices Administration, Li Mengfu, in charge. I passed these responsibilities onto Zhao Shengli, who was in charge of logistics. Li later arranged for us to move to the former site of Yuxiang Primary School (then used as a storehouse by the Education Bureau). He also allocated vehicles, bedding and funds to us.

Somebody suggested that it was during my conversation with Ye Jianying on Tiananmen gate tower that he talked to me about Liu Shikun being beaten up by Red Guards. Liu was Ye's son-in-law, Ye Xiangzhen's husband. I could not remember Ye Jianying speaking to me about it directly. As I recalled, it was Ye Jianying's son, Ye Xuanning who contacted me through Xu Wenlian and said he had something to discuss with me. I went to see him at Marshall Ye Jianying's home on Beichang Street next to the Forbidden City. Liu Shikun was there and had a bandage on his hand. Ye Xuanning asked for my help, as Red Guards had hurt Liu Shikun's hand and he would not be able to play the piano if they carried on. As far as I was concerned, Liu

Shikun needed to be protected because he was an artist. I told him that I would do my best, and afterwards I asked Xu Wenliang to take a group to the conservatory to protect Li Shikun and prevent Red Guards from attacking him. It was possible that Ye Jianying mentioned it on Tiananmen gate tower because it concerned him. I cannot remember exactly. The thing that sticked on my mind was Ye Jianying's offer of support.

Prior to this, Premier Zhou had called a meeting and deployed the Xicheng District Picket Corps to maintain the order around Beijing Railway Station as Red Guards arrived from all over the country had made a mess. At the meeting, which was held at the State Council, there were the Deputy Minister of Railways Wu Jingtian and Secretary-General of the State Council Zhou Rongxin. He had also invited me, Chen Xiaolu and Dong Lianghe. At the meeting, my perception of Premier Zhou completely changed. Because he was a friend of my parents, he had always been kind and I had never seen him lose his temper. But on that day he reproved Wu for failing in his duties. Wu was of my father's generation. We watched as he was called up and made to stand there while Premier Zhou told him off. It was very awkward. I had never seen anything like that. Premier Zhou told him he had invited us to help. He then turned to us and said that the police and army had both failed, so he was relying on us to take control of Beijing Railway Station. He said this would take effect immediately, and we were to make the appropriate arrangements after the meeting.

We immediately organized hundreds of people led by Dong Lianghe and Chen Xiaolu to go to the station. This was no small task given our workload at the time. Dong, Chen and other members were there for a long time overseeing things. They had very little to eat and drink and had to sleep outside on the ground. I only went to see how things were going a couple of times, but I saw the sense of responsibility and dedication with which everyone was carrying out their duties, and I was very impressed. Dong and Chen had everything under control and managed to maintain order as tens of millions of Red Guards swarmed in and out of the city, which was unprecedented in history.

I remembered that as I left the meeting, I bumped into the two vice premiers, Li Fuchun and Li Xiannian. Li Fuchun had also been made a member of the Political Bureau Standing Committee during the reshuffle of the Eleventh Plenary Session of the Eighth Central Committee. They both said that they supported us and praised our general orders for seeking to protect senior cadres and protect state secrets. My mother happened to be standing next to them, so she said we should strive to live up to the praise of the vice premiers.

Tao Zhu, who was promoted to number four in the Party during the reshuffle, later spoke to us as well to offer his support. This was a disguised snub by senior cadres to Chairman Mao for launching the Cultural Revolution. Everyone in the Picket Corps at that time was committed to protecting senior cadres, but the whole political campaign was aimed at striking a blow at senior cadres eventually by disrupting state apparatus.

Of the senior cadres who had an interest in the Picket Corps, Premier Zhou had the most to worry about. Such was his fate. He not only sought to keep pace with Chairman Mao, but also to minimize the chaos to the greatest possible extent. He had to handle all the possibilities in order to do all those jobs. Looking at it now, Premier Zhou used us as a tool or a force at his disposal. Just as he said, the police and army were powerless to act. There was no organization at the time with the authority or ability to directly deal with these problems. Premier Zhou even had to ask Red Guards to take control of Beijing Railway Station. So, it was us who were called upon.

Around that time, Secretary-General of the State Council Zhou Rongxin also sought me and Zhao Shengli out and spoke to us about protecting the Panchen Lama. He said he had been entrusted by Premier Zhou to give us this task. The students of the Institute of Nationalities wanted to hold a struggle meeting against the Panchen Lama, so we were sent to protect him. Premier Zhou had stressed that the Panchen Lama was very important. He said that if it were not properly handled, it would be easy for the Panchen Lama to be killed, and you must keep him alive. He said no violence could be used, and the Panche Lama must not die. He also said the students would be aggressive, so we were to protect the Panchen Lama at all costs.

I personally led the Picket Corps that day. I organized the Red Guards to stand arm in arm in three circles to surround the Panchen Lama. By that time, the Xicheng District Picket Corps was already very well known, so nobody attacked us. I told the Red Guards that if anyone tried to attack the Panchen Lama, we would stop them. Nobody was allowed to get close to him. I told them that they were to repel anyone who would rush forward and that they could use their belts to fight, if anyone tried to resort to violence. Those were the only means at our disposal. I remembered that when we were encircling the Panchen Lama, I found that he looked strong and bearded. The students from the Institute of Nationalities were surrounding him, criticizing and denouncing. I looked at him and he was rolling his eyes. It seemed to me that he was contemptuous of the proceedings. If someone had really wanted to attack him, the consequences would have been terrible. He probably would not have survived. Luckily, the Red Guards protecting the Panchen Lama looked quite ferocious, so nobody dared to attack them. He was afforded an unusual level of protection.

Cheng Yanqiu was a Beijing Opera star. When he died in 1958, he left his widow, Guo Suzhen, some property and some antiques. At the beginning of the Cultural Revolution, the Red Guards raided Guo's home and tried to confiscate some of her belongings. In order to prevent this, she wrote a letter to Zhou Enlai stating that she wished to donate all of Cheng Yanqiu's scripts, costumes, artifacts and other belongings to the country. All she needed is some rooms to live in. Upon receiving the letter, Premier Zhou asked my mother to help protect Guo. My mother asked me to send some of the Picket Corps with her to Guo's home. Since my mother did not have the authority to call on the police or army, she asked the Picket Corps for help. Zhao Shengli later told me that when they arrived at Guo's house, Guo broke down in tears as soon as she saw my mother, because she knew that Zhou Enlai had sent someone to protect her.[24]

24 Zhao Shengli gave the following account: "After Comrade Xu Ming had been instructed by Premier Zhou, she held a meeting at the State Council and invited the Xicheng District Picket Corps, the first, second and third university Red Guards divisions, and representatives of the Academy of Drama, the bank and the Housing Management Bureau. Kong Dan sent me and Yao Ning to represent the Picket Corps. At the start of the meeting, Deputy Secretary Xu Ming read the letter from Cheng Yanqiu's widow to Premier Zhou and asked the representative from the Academy of Drama to introduce Cheng Yanqiu's achievements as an artist. She then asked the representatives from the bank and Housing Management Bureau to explain policies relevant to the case and suggested how we should process in accordance with the relevant policies. Finally, Comrade Xu Ming turned to me and Yao Ning and said that she had invited us along, so she could consider with us how to carry out Premier Zhou's instructions and deal with the situation together. We insisted that we would act in accordance with the Party's policies and agreed with the suggestions of the Academy of Drama, bank and Housing Management Bureau. After the meeting, all of us travelled to the home of Cheng Yanqiu's widow. When Comrade Xu Ming saw Guo Suzhen, she took her hand and explained that Premier Zhou had received her letter, and had asked her to pay a visit. Her eyes glistened with tears as she kept saying "Please extend my thanks to the Premier." They sat down and Comrade Xu Ming told her how they would deal with the situation. Guo was very happy with the arrangements. Afterwards, Comrade Xu Ming drafted a notice and posted it on the outer door to the effect that the house had already been checked by Red Guards and other revolutionary groups, and nobody was allowed to raid it again. The notice was inscribed with the names of the Xicheng District Picket Corps and the three university Red Guards command headquarters."

My Mother and the Picket Corps

I believed my mother had a dual identity when it came to her dealings with the Picket Corps.

On the one hand, she was close to the Premier and she knew what he was thinking and his intentions. She therefore had to do his bidding. Not that she was entirely passive, and she also used her initiative. She had been the deputy director of the Premier's office before Chairman Mao disbanded the office. Afterwards she became the Deputy Secretary of the State Council. My mother was considered an outstanding female Party member. She was already a vice-ministerial cadre by the time she was 40. Premier Zhou had a number of secretaries who dealt with different works. Around the same time, she and Fan Ruoyu both worked as one of the Premier's secretaries. Fan was responsible for theory and learning, while my mother had been in charge of agricultural and cultural work. There were also other secretaries who were responsible for works related to foreign affairs, the military and industry.

On the other hand, as my mother, she knows that my brother and I were good children as we did not fool around and showed promise in terms of our understanding of Party policies and in our studies. In that way, she had recognized our abilities. When she learned that we were opposing rebel factions of the Red Guards, she immediately phoned me and told me to stop. She strongly dissuaded us from going up against the Red Guard groups such as "East Is Red" from Geological Institute and "Red Flag" from Beijing Aviation Institute. The leaders of "East Is Red" from Geological Institute, Zhu Chengzhao and Wang Dabin, were in conflict with the Ministry of Geology and had seized and denounced Deputy Minister He Changgong. The Picket Corps had gone to stop it, but clashed with the group. The children of a number of leaders were part of the Picket Corps at the time, including Deng Xiaoping's daughter Deng Rong and Marshal Xu Xiangqian's son Xu Xiaoyan. The "East Is Red" from Geological Institute was very powerful. As I remembered, there were fights breaking out on a flight of stairs, and our two sides were deadlocked.

My mother could not find me over the phone, but she spoke to my brother. She told him to tell me to stop the conflict and withdraw. Later on, she spoke to me directly and told me to stop. I was not happy about it, but she obviously had access to more information than I did. It showed there was a dispute among the top leaders. I therefore told the Picket Corps to withdraw. A lot of people questioned my decision, but I simply told them to do as I said.

The same thing happened later with the dispute between the Commission of Science, Technology and Industry for National Defense and the "Red Flag" Red Guard group from Beijing Aviation Institute. On both occasions, my mother personally phoned me, saying that we should pull back. She told me that we should not go up against rebels supported by the Cultural Revolution Group. The only thing she did not say was that it was the order of the Premier. She could not say that, of course. I believed they had an understanding and communicated in a way that I did not know. My mother worked next to the Premier and she kept telling us not to stand up to the university rebels. I felt that it was Zhou Enlai's wish.

The main purpose of the Picket Corps was to maintain order. Jiang Qing later accused us of being loyalists. We were also referred to as the "fire brigade". We had helped maintain order at Beijing Railway Station and protected the Panchen Lama, Cheng Yanqiu's widow, Liu Shikun, He Changgong, Zhao Erlu and also Yu Qiuli from the Oil Ministry. People began seeking us out. "Iron man" Wang Jinxi[25] even contacted us, saying he wanted to set up a Daqing branch of the Picket Corps. We were later accused of protecting our parents as well as our

25 Wang Jinxi was famous for being a model worker of the Daqing oilfield in Heilongjiang Province.

vested interests. This was because the movement had already expanded to attack all cadres, which meant attacks on our friends and family members had started.

Soon afterwards, the Picket Corps' luck took a turn for the worse. The landmark events were the disputes with the two Red Guard groups. These two incidents marked a shift in our thinking. Whether as the result of instinct or a kind of consciousness, we already knew that the movement was not aimed at one or two Party branches but at all cadres, especially senior cadres. The movement also started in the army. At the beginning, the military was ordered not to get involved in the Cultural Revolution, but when it did become involved, it happened very quickly.

From August 25, 1966 when the Xicheng District Picket Corps was established to the end of September, in about 30 days, our corps was merely involved in the events mentioned above. However, its image and influence had been greatly exaggerated. At the end of September, we heard that Chen Boda had given a speech in which he said the children of senior cadres should not be in charge of mass organizations. I and several other leaders of the Picket Corps then left Beijing before the October 1st holiday to visit the Red Guards in other parts of the country. I did not concern myself with the Picket Corps again after that. Apart from returning once to Beijing in the interim, I spent my whole time traveling. After fulfilling its duty of maintaining order on the National Day, the Picket Corps basically ceased its operations. As soon as criticism of the bourgeois reactionary line began, the Picket Corps became a target. I should add that the Picket Corps was not a close-knit organization. Its headquarters had a very loose relationship with school Red Guard units. Each Red Guard unit had its own rules, and the Picket Corps headquarters cannot be held responsible for the violent behavior of some of the schools (such as the No. 6 High School in Beijing). Only the perpetrators can be held responsible.

While traveling across the country, I continuously cared about the political situation in Beijing, and particularly the situation my mother and father were in. My transformation during the Cultural Revolution was very natural, but I quickly found myself in opposition, as I deeply resented the movement. I had a feeling that something bad was going to happen. He Changgong of the Ministry of Geology and Zhao Erlu of the Commission of Science, Technology and Industry for National Defense were both good friends of my father, and they both became targets of the movement. Wang Zhen of the Land Reclamation Department was also treated harshly. Since that September, the Picket Corps was very active, but later my mother had told me not to go up against the rebels. By October, there was nothing we could do. I had a feeling that the movement would not just stop there. I sensed an impending threat and was quite fearful. So I kept an eye on the list of names of leaders appearing on the newspapers when Mao Zedong received the Red Guard rallies. Mao held a total of 11 rallies with the Red Guards, and each time a list of names of people who were with Mao on Tiananmen gate tower was published. My father attended all the rallies and his name was on the list every time. I felt uneasy, but I thought that maybe the worst had passed. As such, I did not expect the drastic changes that would take place, nor could I have foreseen how brutal it would be. In fact, at that moment everything was still unfolding.

Within days, the trouble had started. On December 16, 1966, a meeting attended by Premier Zhou and the Cultural Revolution Group was held at Beijing Workers' Stadium to criticize the bourgeois reactionary line. At the meeting, Jiang Qing read out five names who she claimed were the "sinister backstage bosses" of the Xicheng District Picket Corps: Wang Renzhong, Zhou Rongxin, Yong Wentao, Kong Yuan and Xu Ming. Jiang said that the arrest of these people would make quite a stir. It was said that Premier Zhou, who never smoked, lit a cigarette at that moment and turned pale. At the time, however, I was still away traveling across the country, so I did not witness the events myself. The disaster that was about to befall my parents and me had arrived. On December 21, I returned from Nanjing because it was starting to get cold and I had not brought any winter clothes with me. I arrived back at our house at night. When I walked in, it was dark, and I saw seals on many of the doors.

My brother Kong Dong got out of bed and told me that there

had been criticism meetings in the past several days, and Jiang Qing had called out our parents' names. Straight away the "East Is Red" rebel group from the Geological Institute had cooperated with the rebels in the Central Investigation Department to raid our home, after which they sealed the doors. I said that I had seen our father's name on the newspapers after each of Mao's Red Guard rallies, so I thought everything was fine. He said it had all happened in only a few days. One minute they had been free, suddenly Jiang Qing had called their names at a meeting, and my father was quarantined for investigation. My mother had also been prevented from returning home. My brother also said that somebody had set up a Capital Red Guards Joint Action Committee. I replied that I knew nothing about it.

We were still talking when somebody came to the door and said our father was in the hospital. We rushed over there, but the receptionist said there was no record of Kong Yuan at the hospital. I asked if there was Xu Ming. She looked up and found it. I told my brother that something bad had happened. Although I am only one year older than my brother, at that time I knew a lot more about our parents. My appearance and personality were also a lot more like our mother, so I knew more about her. My father had experienced a number of ups and downs, and he could withstand a great deal. My mother, on the other hand, was different. She had always been looked upon in the Party, and was rather highly qualified. Also unlike my father, she had an unyielding character. My intuition told me at that moment that she had committed suicide. On the way to the emergency room, somebody told us that she had tried to commit suicide by taking sleeping pills, and they were trying to save her.

Kong Dong admitted that my mother had phoned him yesterday and asked him to bring her sleeping pills from her bedside cabinet. He said he did not know what they looked like, so she told him to bring all the pills from the cabinet. Normally when we went to see her, we would go to her office, but that day she met Kong Dong outside. They met on the bridge between Beihai Lake and Zhongnanhai. The north gate of the State Council is just to the west of the bridge. They walked and chatted for a long time. Kong Dong was fired up and said he wanted to fight the rebel students and Cultural Revolution Group. My mother advised him to calm down and not to take on the Cultural Revolution Group. She also talked about the incidents at the Ministry of Geology and the Commission of Science, Technology and Industry for National Defense, and told Kong Dong how they should be handled. He would not listen though. He insisted it was their fault, and we had not done anything wrong. She asked him to speak to me when I got back, and tell me to stay clear of the rebels.

My biggest regret from that time was that I should not have gone traveling for so long at such a sensitive time. If I had been there I might have been able to save my mother. It was hard for her to communicate with other people. If I were there, I might have a chance to exchange my views with her.

Although my mother had not been taken in for questioning at that time, Jiang Qing had singled her out and even arrested her husband, who had nothing to do with the Picket Corps. What fate was waiting for her? I thought she knew the situation quite well. We later learned that on that day she had returned to her office. She set up a screen in front of the bed, which was used by people on duty at night, so that nobody could see her. Then, she poured all the sleeping pills she had into a glass, and swallowed them down with some water. After she had swallowed the pills, she switched off the light, and hid under the bed. When they came looking for her, they entered the room, switched on the light, but did not see her because of the screen. They thought she had disappeared. After looking for her for a long time, a colleague of her found her under the bed, and quickly sent her to the hospital.

This happened on the night of December 21, 1966. My mother had swallowed the sleeping pills just about the time I arrived home. She was discovered in the early hours of the morning, and was taken to the hospital. When we got to the emergency room, she was already unconscious. Medical care at that time was different from that today. Nothing could be done to her, except for intravenous drip. Twenty-four hours after her attempt of committing suicide, they gave her some hemodialysis. After that, she improved obviously. But the drug, which was highly toxic, had already entered her cells through her blood. They tried hemodialysis, but it had no effect. While I was in the hospital, my father, escorted by two rebels, came in. He only said a few words to us. He also said something to the rebels. He said, "Tell them that Kong Dan is back." I was quite surprised. I wondered whom he was talking with. And whom would they inform about my return.

I was up all night long, and the next day some classmates and friends paid us a visit. They were even willing to transfuse some blood for my mother. I thought she was getting better, so around 3 or 4 pm, I went home for a rest. Looking back now, her slight recovery was just the last radiance of her life. I was sitting down and about to take a shower, when somebody looing for me came to the door again. At the moment, six policemen entered, asked if I was Kong Dan and told me that I was detained. Then, I realized what my father had meant. They were intending to arrest me all along. I was arrested while my mother's life or death was still uncertain. I was put in jail during the afternoon, while she died that night. My father was subsequently transferred from isolation into prison as well.

My Parents and the Misfortunes of the Picket Corps

Following the first Red Guard rally led by Chairman Mao in Tiananmen Square, the Red Guard movement had taken on a momentum of its own. The Red Guards had already broken free of the confines of school playgrounds and made their way into society with house raids, the Four Olds campaign, attacks on leading organs, criticisms and denunciations. The whole thing was in chaos.

We set up the Xicheng District Picket Corps after the CPC Central Committee released the "Sixteen Points". I believed that, in a sense, the "Sixteen Points" were a compromise. On the one hand, they reflected the fact that Chairman Mao and the Cultural Revolution Group wanted to thoroughly continue the Cultural Revolution. On the other hand, they reflected the wishes of a group of leaders, led by Zhou Enlai, who wished to protect senior cadres and stabilize the social order. Throughout the history of the Communist Party of China, regardless of the circumstances, all political movements, whether nationwide or local, have been policy-based. Irrespective of whether the policy was left-wing or right-wing, there were always rules and regulations to be followed. For example, there were the "Twenty-Three Points" for the Four Cleanups movement, the "May 16th Notice" before the Cultural Revolution. Later after the "May 16th Notice" was put into practice, there were the "Sixteen Points". Just like policies in the past, the "Sixteen Points" was very clear about what was to be done: "We must conduct a verbal struggle, not a violent one." Looking back now, however, Chairman Mao wanted to mobilize the masses. He deliberately allowed the society, and particularly the Red Guards, to go beyond the boundaries of the policies. The society was out of control and chaos reigned. Although we were unaware of how deep the problems went, we established the Picket Corps due to the education we had received and our ideology and instincts. We felt that we had the responsibility and the ability to do what the "Sixteen Points" said for the sake of the Party and the stability of the entire society.

We noticed at the time as high school Red Guards went out into the society to destroy the Four Olds, and criticisms and denunciations were aimed at organizations like the Beijing Municipal Bureau of Education, the Ministry of Education and the CYL Central Committee. University students also started targeting Party and government organs as well as the leading cadres. The movement had therefore mutated from its humble beginnings of criticizing school Party branches and university Party committees from the confines of school and university campuses. It was no longer a struggle against the traditional class enemies — landlords, rich farmers, anti-revolutionaries, bad elements and rightists. This contradicted everything that we had been taught to think. We thought that capitalist roaders constituted only a small group, and the majority of war veterans were good people, though they might have shortcomings, which could be criticized. But we did not think they should be taken down. As such, we wanted to do our bit to protect the majority of senior cadres. But this intention was essentially seen as reactionary during the Cultural Revolution, and it was soon to be the root cause of the Picket Corps' downfall.

The establishment of the Picket Corps was a spontaneous act. For our part, we thought it was set up in accordance with the wishes of the CPC Central Committee. The spontaneous behavior of Peng Xiaomeng and Bu Dahua to set up the Red Guards allowed Chairman Mao to initiate a mass movement with one stroke. Our spontaneous behavior of setting up the Xicheng District Picket Corps was likewise seized upon by a group of senior leaders led by Zhou Enlai in an attempt to control the situation. Essentially, the incident involving the Xicheng District Picket Corps reflected the hopes of a few senior cadres to use a mass organization and a few Red Guards to steer the ideological course of the Cultural Revolution in their favor. When my mother found out that Ye Jianying had offered the Picket Corps some material assistance, she immediately took care of it for us, which reflected that she wanted to stem the chaos and control the situation by resorting to the State Council.

Premier Zhou personally convened meetings with us to assign work; one of his secretaries gave direct material support to her son; Premier Zhou arranged for the Secretary-General and Deputy-Secretary General of the State Council to assign work to us. All these facts show that Zhou was giving the Picket Corps background support. Therefore, one cannot say that it is groundless to claim that by arresting those behind the Picket Corps, the Central Cultural Group laid the blame at the door of the Premier. It was very much seen as an indictment against Zhou Enlai. Without his support, things may not have gone the same way. I did not believe my mother and Li Mengfu had the authority to sanction these things on their own, and I was sure they were reporting to Premier Zhou.

Before my mother died, she wrote note on her suicide. We were not allowed to read it at the time, and I had still never read it. According to those who read it though, she supposedly claimed responsibility for the problems involving the Picket Corps and said it had nothing to do with Premier Zhou. My mother committed suicide for two reasons: one was that she would not submit herself to humiliation; the other was that she wished to take responsibility for the events involving the Picket Corps and remove their association with anybody else, especially the Premier. In her note, she also said that, "My sons are already grown up and should temper themselves in the political movement." She was only at the age of 47 when she died. For us, we could not even find her posthumous papers nowadays. She resolutely chose death, and I was sure it was because she wanted to remove any association the incident might have with the Premier. I also held that it was because she had such an unyielding character, so she could not take the humiliation. In a eulogy I delivered at a memorial service for her after the Cultural Revolution, I included the following words: "She would rather have been a broken piece of jade than an unbroken piece of pottery." Although it was a metaphor, I believed its meaning was quite clear.

My mother had been under a great deal of pressure because of the Picket Corps, but she was suffering from other pressures as well. At the start of the Cultural Revolution, she had expressed her opposition to the saying "The son of a hero must be a good man, and the son of a reactionary must be a wretch," and had sought to have it changed. At the time she was working for the State Council's liaison department, in charge of liaising with the masses. Chen Boda sent her a letter proposing the saying be changed to "The son of a hero will succeed him, and the son of a reactionary will rebel him," and he asked her to announce the change to the liaison department. My mother assumed that this was the correct thing to do and put up a public announcement in the State Council's reception center. She did not foresee that this would stir up a hornet's nest.

There was a fierce reaction to this among Red Guards. The suggestion of changing the saying had been criticized by a number of people, but mainly Red Guards. They asked how Cheng Boda, the head of the Cultural Revolution Group could oppose the original saying and make such a change. Chen claimed that it was an attempt by Xu Ming of the State Council's liaison office to provoke a student attack against him. It did not end there, however, because Qi Benyu of the Cultural Revolution Group then wrote a letter to Chairman Mao, saying that my mother had called for the change to incite students to turn on Chen Boda. After he read the letter Mao accused her of "supporting the right and suppressing the left" and said that if she did not change her ways she would be transferred to a different position. These were really strong words for such a senior cadre, and it was probably the harshest criticism my mother had received since she joined in the revolution.

In addition, my mother and Jiang Qing had never got along. In Yan'an, they had been classmates at the Party School. There was no grudge between them. However, because my mother was so aloof that she did not show Jiang Qing the respect she thought she deserved as Mao's wife. My mother felt that people should be given positions of importance on ability, not based on whom they were married to. My mother was later put in charge of cultural work at the State Council, which included working on the model opera *Shajiabang* (originally named *Spark Amid the Reeds*). She quickly came into conflict with Jiang Qing again due to the differences in their characters. Jiang was a very dark and abnormal person and was extremely narrow-minded. She would always remember those who did not show respect to her. I believed she was of such disposition.

More important to my mother's downfall, though, was Mao's announcement that the Picket Corps was a force resisting the Cultural Revolution. The *modus operandi* of the Cultural Revolution Group was to seek conflict. It was convenient for them that my mother was involved with the Picket Corps, especially as somebody who was close to the Premier; because it gave them the excuse they wanted to criticize her. Paradoxically, my father, who was the director of the Investigation Department and had nothing to do with the Picket Corps, was also named by Jiang as being involved. I can only think that it was because he was married to my mother. He was immediately taken in for questioning and later given seven years in jail for supposedly giving tutelage. At the meeting in which they were denounced, Jiang said that those behind the Picket Corps would be arrested and shot dead. The pressure from people higher up had therefore intensified. Such was the background reasons that resulted to my mother's suicide. It was not simply events related to the Picket Corps. There were a number of things going on at a high level that we did not know.

My family and I paid a heavy price for the Picket Corps incident. My mother's suicide was certainly closely related to it. People back then were very harsh. Xie Fuzhi had supported the Picket Corps and said we had saved his life. But later on, according to his son, Xie Guoqing, Xie Fuzhi had even suggested executing some of us as a warning to the others.

Looking back now, if Ye Jianying had given the Picket Corps his direct support, my mother may not have taken over, and it may have relieved a bit of her pressure. If she had not become involved like that, my father would not have been dragged into it. In a sense, I was the root of the trouble. If it had not been for me, my mother would not have been involved to the same extent and would not have committed suicide. My father's downfall during the Cultural Revolution was inevitable. But it would not have happened so swiftly. After the meeting on December 16th, my father was arrested and investigated. On the 21st, my mother tried to commit suicide. On the 23rd, I was arrested and put in prison, and at that night, my mother passed away. Within just a few days, my family was torn apart.

Looking at those events from a historical perspective, I knew I never tried to be a student leader or head of the Red Guards. I was just concerned with the norms I had been taught, the so-called traditional views of the Party. If it had not been for this, I would not have been put to prison, my mother would not have been in the teeth of the storm, and such a tragedy would not have befallen my family. The Xicheng District Picket Corps became my nightmare, and it has affected a large span of my life. Moreover, the sudden ruin of my family had become the source of the misfortunes in my family.

In 1975, my mother's name as a Party member was rehabilitated at a ceremony when her ashes were placed in Babaoshan Revolutionary Cemetery. This was the first redress. After the downfall of the Gang of Four, a formal memorial service was held for my mother in 1978, attended by Li Xiannian, Wang Zhen, Yu Qiuli and many other senior cadres. This event marked the complete rehabilitation of her name and redress of her case. It also marked the end of her life.

Life in Prison

I had spent four months in prison. I was arrested on December 23, 1966, the same day my mother died, and was released in the following year on Lenin's birthday, April 22.

I was the only person of my generation to be arrested in connection with the Xicheng District Picket Corps. Dong Lianghe was also arrested, but mainly in connection with the so-called "concentration camp" affair at Beijing No.6 High School. When I was arrested, the spearhead was firmly pointed at Zhou Enlai. It was part of a conspiracy by the Gang of Four to persecute Premier Zhou and the veteran cadres. Many had been investigated, including Ye Jianying, Li Xiannian, Li Fuchun, Chen Yi, Xu Xiangqian, Tao Zhu, Yu Qiuli, Liao Chengzhi, Wang Renzhong, He Changgong, Lü Dong, Zhou Rongxin, Yong Wentao, Kong Yuan, Xu Ming and so on. The Cultural Revolution Group interrogated me in the hope of discovering who was behind the Picket Corps. My mother provided the Picket Corps with office space, transportation and bedding, which was enough for her to be seen as supporting us. That much could not be denied.

The main point of the investigation was to target at the so-called "sinister backstage bosses". But the plot did not work. As I clearly pointed out in prison, the Picket Corps was entirely our own idea, and that was the fact. They constantly asked me about this, but the interrogations were carried out in a fairly civilized manner. The investigator would ask things like, "Are you the head of the Picket Corps?", "What instructions did your mother give you?", "What instructions did Yong Wentao give you?", "What did Zhou Rongxin say to you?" All I could tell them was the truth, which did not lead to the conclusion that Premier Zhou Enlai gave me direct orders.

Naturally they were extremely interested in that. For example, they would ask, "Was there somebody in the background that instigated you to set up the Picket Corps?", "Who put you up to the general orders?", "Was somebody behind those incidents?" I answered those questions truthfully too. I can confirm that. But I did not say that my mother was affirmed with our methods. I would not say that. After a while, they realized that there was no point in questioning me any further. They may also have confirmed what I said in my "confession" through circumstantial evidence, so they stopped interrogating me.

In addition to being interrogated, I was also taken from the prison on one occasion for a denouncement session. This was organized by the rebel group at No. 4 High School and held across the road in the hall of Peking University Hospital. It was very cold that day, and I was wearing an army overcoat. They originally planned to denounce me and my father together onstage. When I was escorted onto the stage, my head was down, but I turned to look at the person next to me, and I was relieved to see it was not my father. It was Yong Wentao, Deputy Minister of the Ministry of Education. They said that when I was escorted to the bus, I turned around and smiled. Then they said that I was so extraordinary. I was similar to my mother in that respect, slightly aloof, and sometimes conceited and arrogant. My father, on the other hand, was well-tempered and had been in positions of great power, which seemed to make him more flexible. When I went to the prison, I was extremely indignant, but I persevered. I believed this was also down to my mother's aloofness and my father's resilience.

The most important thing in prison was to adapt to the environment. I was held at the Banbuqiao No. 1 Prison in Beijing. The building was called the Plum House because it had six tubular buildings stretching out from the center like plum petals. We were supervised by guards who were stationed in the central building at the heart of the flower. The other prisoners were put in large cells, while I was given special treatment to live in a small cell all by myself. Inside, the prison was extremely cold. The guards wore cotton clothes and had a circular coal stove to keep warm. However, in the four months from December to the beginning of spring in March, I had no heating facilities, and it was so cold that even the ink used to write confession documents froze. Meals consisted of 400 grams of grains a day, with two large pieces of steamed cornbread in the morning and three small pieces in the afternoon. There were only two meals in a day, and no vegetable except soup with bits of cabbage heads in it. It was no exaggeration to say that I was always starving and cold in prison. By the end of my time in prison, my stool looked like round pellets of sheep dung, because the little food I ate had been completely absorbed by my stomach and guts. By the time I was released, I already looked bloated.

Everybody talked about the dark side of the prison, but I just remember how poor the living conditions were in general. After I was released, I had to pay for the meals in prison, which cost me 6 yuan per month.[26] I was a stickler for rules, so I paid for it. I later demanded it back from the Beijing Public Security Bureau, because it was a trumped-up case. They did give it back to me, which proved that I was wrongly arrested. Since I was wrongly arrested, how could I pay the money? I was a really serious man.

While in prison, the main thing I thought about was how to deal with life there. I therefore invented a way of communicating with the female prisoners downstairs. The person in that cell was Zheng Zhongwei from the High School for Girls Affiliated to Beijing Normal University. I did not know why she was in prison, but we knew each other, so we started talking. I told her that I did not have enough to eat. She said that she had too much to eat and usually had some left. Then I had found my way. I asked the guard for a needle and thread to patch my clothes, then I took the thread from my bedding, twisted it into a cord and used it to sow a pocket from a handkerchief. I agreed on a time with Zheng. At the designated hour, I banged on the wall as a signal. I then lowered the pocket attached to some cord out of the barred window down to her window. She put a piece of cornbread in the pocket and I

26 US$ 2.44 in 1967.

pulled it back up. I was feeling so happy! In distress, I often dreamed about all kinds of food. At such times, one would no longer think about political pressures; survival was the first thing.

On our corridor, there were 19 inmates. I lived in the 19th cell. Cell number 20 was a toilet. One time when we were let out for fresh air, I found a nail. At one time there had been a hole in the wall of my cell for a chimney. It seemed there used to be a stove in here, but the hole had been blocked up. I used the nail I had found to scratch away at the filled hole and eventually managed to make a small hole. The guards were unaware that I was able to communicate with the other 18 inmates through this hole in the wall between my cell and the toilet. We used the paper we had been given for confession to write messages. We rolled the paper into rolls and passed them through the hole. After the incident involving the Capital Red Guards Joint Action Committee, many people were arrested. Using this method of exchanging messages, I was able to discover that Dong Lianghe, Su Yu's son Su Hansheng, and Li Jingquan's son Li Mingqing had all been arrested. I was also able to find out a lot of information about what was going on in the outside world, such as the struggle of Joint Action Committee against the Cultural Revolution Group.

I was not tortured while in prison. Nor did I suffer any direct harm physically. But I did witness policemen beating somebody. It was very intimidating. In the cell next to me, there was a tall worker surnamed Liu. His case was very unfortunate. He had inadvertently used a piece of newspaper with Chairman Mao's picture on it to cover up a window, and had subsequently been arrested as a counter-revolutionary. One day he was standing up in his cell, perhaps because he was sore from sitting so long, when a guard told him to sit down. He refused, so the guard called on four or five policemen. They dragged him out of his cell and handcuffed his hands behind his back. Then one police knocked his legs out from under him. He hit the wall hard and his face was immediately covered in blood. Several of the police started kicking and punching him. I was on toilet cleaning duty that day. I frequently went in and out, scrubbing the blood on the floor, and thus had a clearer view. Since then, I decided not to provoke the police there. A wise man does not fight when the odds are against him, and it would not be worth it for the pain they inflicted.

When inmates were released, I entrusted them to deliver messages for me. While in prison, I wrote one or two letters to my brother, Kong Dong. It said something like, "Please persuade mother to accept reality and weather the political movement." I assumed that my mother was still alive. In addition to letters, I also asked some people being released to deliver messages in person. Later on, when I had been released, I realized that Kong Dong never received any form of messages. I had wanted Kong Dong to bring me some salt, because I was so hungry. My message stated that he was to empty a toothpaste tube, pack salt at the bottom of it and then fill it up with toothpaste again. It would have been hard to detect. In the end though, the message was not delivered to him, so the salt in the tube of toothpaste never arrived.

I was so hungry that I diluted my bowls of soup with water to make four or five bowls out of one, which would make me feel full for a while. It was a method of staving off hunger, but it meant the soup was utterly tasteless, so I wanted some salt to at least give it some flavor. But I was not able to get any in the end.

I was released as part of a large group of people at around 10 o'clock on the night of April 22, 1967. That day our names were called out and we were taken out of our cells. I was afraid of what was going to happen to us. Some of the inmates' voices were even trembling. One of the female prisoners quietly asked if they were about to shoot us. I was older than them, so I assured her not to worry and that they would not shoot us. We were taken out into the yard. The light was bright, and we saw several cars stopped there. At first we kept order but quickly became frantic as we got onto the cars. More than a hundred people boarded those cars and then they pulled away. After a while, the cars eventually pulled up outside the south entrance of the Great Hall of the People. We got off the buses and were taken inside. I was not sure which hall we were taken to, but rows of chairs had already been set out. I had been walking next to Dong Lianghe, but by the time we were inside we had separated. I was not sure where they were seated.

We had just sat down when Premier Zhou, Chen Boda, Kang Sheng, Jiang Qing, Guan Feng, Qi Benyu and some other leaders walked in. They were all wearing military uniforms and sat in a row. A moment later, I heard Jiang Qing said, "Which one is Kong Dan? Stand up and let me see you." She had a look of sheer contempt. I stood up with a totally blank expression. She looked at me and told me to sit down. Premier Zhou then began talking.

In his speech, Zhou stated that Chairman Mao had said there was no need for any further investigations and we should be released to join in the revolution. He said that we had made mistakes, but we need to carry on the revolution. In the middle of his speech, Premier Zhou called out my name and that of Dong Lianghe. We quickly stood up. He then told us to sit and said, "I have known you both since you were very young, and I watched you grow up. I am also responsible for the mistakes you made." As somebody later recalled, he also said that the Picket Corps had rendered a great service. But I could not remember him saying that. I also thought that he could not have said that at the time, as it would have been tantamount to accepting his direct responsibility for the Picket Corps. Somebody else recalled that I cried. I certainly did not recall my crying, but when Premier Zhou said that, I certainly felt grieved. I was not sure whether Dong felt the same.

Kang Sheng was present that day. He and my father had known each other for a long time and had a very good personal relationship. He knew me quite well. When Premier Zhou and Jiang Qing asked me to stand up during the meeting, he smiled, but did not say anything. The meeting did not last long. When Premier Zhou had finished his talk, he declared the meeting over.

I felt as though it had all happened very suddenly. I later discovered that Peng Xiaomeng had written a letter to Chairman Mao in his blood, explaining that Niu Wanping and others from the joint action committee were all loyal to Mao's Revolutionary Guard and were not counter-revolutionaries; they just disagreed with Jiang Qing. He said that they should not be imprisoned any longer and strongly urged Mao to deal with the matter. The letter eventually made its way into Mao's hands, and he issued instructions stating that the investigation was to be stopped and the prisoners released to carry on their revolution. This is what led to the release of the joint action committee, which I had benefited.

After we had exited the Great Hall of the People, I asked the guard next to me what was to happen next. He said we could just leave on our own from there if we wanted. I said that some of my things, such as my toothpaste, laundry soap and a few bits and pieces, were still in my cell. I told him I would rather go back for them, and he said a bus would take me.

It was an interesting scene watching all those people heading out through the south gate of the Great Hall of the People and going their separate ways. I, on the other hand, got back on the bus and returned to the prison, so I could collect my things, which included some poems I had written. I seemed to remember them putting us back on the bus and dropping those of us who returned to collect our belongings near our houses. I was dropped on Di'anmen Avenue at around 3 am. When I went in, my brother was shocked to see me. I began to tell him what had happened that night at the meeting, but then I suddenly remembered how hungry I was. He gave me some peanuts and biscuits,which I scoffed down. Then I began to feel better.

I hurriedly asked Kong Dong, "Where's Mum? How is she?"

"Don't you know that?" Dong said.

"Know what?" I asked.

"Mum died on the night you went to prison," he said.

"But when I left the hospital, her breathing was stronger and some of the color had returned to her face!"

"People often recover for a moment before death. I thought she was going to make it too. It was her making a last minute effort, but she did not regain consciousness. She died that night."

"What about her funeral?" I asked.

Dong said, "The Government Offices Administration of the State Council sent somebody to handle it. They took her to the Babaoshan cemetery."

"Did they involve her family members?" I asked.

"No."

Then I understood, this meant the State Council considered her suicide a betrayal to the Party.

Tabloid Entitled *Liberation of All Mankind*

Shortly after I was released from the prison, the following saying circulated around the school: "Kong Dan is still ambitious. Qin Xiao is not at peace. San You writes in anger. They're staging a comeback". This was probably a truthful portrayal of our condition.

I was the sort of person who liked to perform real deeds during the Cultural Revolution. After spending time in the prison, my body was weak and swollen, so I used to drag a wicker chair out to our courtyard and sit under the sunshine. In around May or July, I had started to recover. I really should have rested much longer, but I could not stand the loneliness. In no time I was back on the road spreading the revolution, getting into lively discussions about problems arising in the course of the revolution and attempting to spread my views. So it was in the summer of 1967, Ma Kai, Qin Xiao, Li Sanyou and I established a tabloid entitled the *Liberation of All Mankind.*

Premier Zhou's speech on the night we were released had left such a deep impression on me. I took three messages from it: firstly, I should admit my errors; secondly, I should put the past behind me; and thirdly, I should continue the revolution. His speech certainly played a promoting role in our decision to set up the tabloid.

The tabloid's first issue was published on May 24, 1967. In total we published three issues. We took it very seriously and investigated issues in great earnest. This is particularly true of the editorial titled "History and Lessons" in the third issue published on August 18. It was two-and-a-half pages long, which analyzed and summarized the Red Guard movement since the start of the Cultural Revolution. Reading them today, one could see that our essays, with their reverence for Chairman Mao and the Cultural Revolution, reflected the mode of thinking prevalent at the time, but they also dealt with some of the issues facing us and the Red Guards in the early period. Our awareness of these issues, whether our views were right or wrong, showed our ideological track at the time.

In another respect, the newspaper reflected our theoretical explorations at the time. There were five people involved in its publication: me, Ma Kai, Qin Xiao, Li Sanyou — all four of us are Party members—as well as Kong Dong. Wang Xiangrong was not really involved in the newspaper, though we never communicated our opposition to Lin Biao to him in detail. The articles we wrote included one about continued revolution under the dictatorship of the proletariat written by Ma Kai, and an editorial I wrote titled "Only by liberating the whole of mankind can the proletariat liberate itself." We tended to have our own views on things like the bloodline theory, the five red categories and the five black categories. We were not looking to form small groups with Red Guards or the children of senior cadres. We had to unite as many people as possible.

I wrote the editorial for the first issue. In the essay I stated, "We believe it is necessary to completely rectify the way the Red Guards work, rectify their thoughts, and do away with harmful working methods. Through rectification, we can oppose personal heroism as well as freedom and sectarianism in organizations. The fundamental thought behind our writing was the liberation of all mankind." During that period, the Central Committee did not issue any instructions, but we just proposed rectifying anything that was incompatible with the situation. We also started reading the original works of Marx and Lenin at that time, about 30 volumes in all. This had a lot to do with our arguments regarding continuing the revolution under the dictatorship of the proletariat. It also encouraged us to better understand the purpose of the Cultural Revolution. Reading the works of Marx and Engels gave us a broader perspective than merely reading the works of Chairman Mao. From these classical Marxist works, we were able to view the wider world outside China, and see that there was also a give and take with these great teachers, and that they had roots and developments.

In total, we wrote three essays discussing continuing the revolution under the dictatorship of the proletariat. We were a very solemn group. We were not the sort of people who act on impulse. We tried to look beyond the fanfare and excitement of the Cultural Revolution in search of truth. However, our parents had suddenly become the targets of the Cultural Revolution and the masses. In other words, they had become the enemy, which we could not accept. This led to the theory on continuing the revolution under the dictatorship of the proletariat, which was more theoretical than the statements made by the rebels. The basic argument was that, even with the CPC in power, revisionists and capitalist roaders were still present within the ruling establishment at all levels. We did not understand this theory, and we felt that it did not fit with social realities. So we considered what kind of system could be used to continue the revolution, how it could be created and why it should be continued under a dictatorship of the proletariat. In this sense, we were quite orthodox. Besides, we also believed that we should not let our personal or family backgrounds get in the way to the negation and resistance of the Cultural Revolution. The tabloid had reflected our sincere search for truth.

There was an interlude here. Because my parents had been good friends with Wang Zhen, I often spent time with his son, Wang Jun since childhood. Wang Jun was six years older than me and was like an older brother. During the Cultural Revolution, he was already a naval officer and worked as a military representative at the Hubei Shipyard. The military held strong views during the Cultural Revolution and were the first to speak out against Lin Biao and the Central Committee. When he found out we were setting up the tabloid, he offered us financial support in exchange for us writing articles that opposed Lin Biao. We needed money to buy paper and to print the tabloid, so we agreed, and he gave us 200 yuan. A lot of the criticism of the Central Committee and Lin Biao during the Cultural Revolution was coordinated, but I had told Wang Jun that we should criticize Lin Biao and the Central Committee more subtly. As such, we published an article that stated we should be "alert to Khrushchev-style careerists in our Party". The article's logical reasoning was clear. The bourgeois headquarters of Liu Shaoqi and Deng Xiaoping had already been exposed, so it was quite apparent at whom the accusation was being made.

It was this sentence, however, that led to us being shut down. People asked what we meant by it and whether or not we were referring to Lin Biao. As such, in August 1967, just after the publication of the third issue, the PLA propaganda team from No. 4 High School and a group of rebels arrested us. That day I was sitting in Li Sanyou's courtyard playing chess when a large group of people led by Yang Fan suddenly rushed in. They had originally come for Li and had not expected to see me there. I thought Yang had been watching a lot of model operas, because as soon as he saw me, he made an exaggerated operatic action and shouted, "Nobody move! Kong Dan! You're coming with us." I looked up and said, "Fine. Let's go then." "Where's Li Sanyou," Yang shouted. Li, who was sitting right next to me, looked down at the chess set and then up at Yang Fan and said, "I'm here." We were both taken away.

Being arrested the second time was not nearly as bad as being arrested by the authorities. They took us to the school in a bus, and then locked us in separate rooms within the same courtyard. They arrested four of us that day — Qin Xiao, Li Sanyou, Wang Xiangrong and me — and announced that they were going to implement the dictatorship of the masses. Liu Huixuan was also arrested but on different charges.

I was able to put some of the tricks I had learned at Banbuqiao Prison to good use. It was important that we had the same story during the investigation at No. 4 High School, so I wrote a note telling everyone that we would exchange information by leaving messages in a corner of the toilets. We were escorted by students to the canteen for food each day, and on one occasion as I was walking at the front of the group, I turned and gave Li Sanyou a wink before I knelt down and pretended to tie my shoe laces. As I knelt on the ground, I roll the ball of paper on the ground, and then stepped on it as I stood up. The students were not exactly the police and were totally unaware of what I was doing. Li was limping at the back as he was suffering from polio, and made his way to where I had left the note. He then also pretended to tie his shoelaces, and picked the note up.

That was how I gave Li the first message. Afterwards, I wrote a note for Qin Xiao telling him where to leave messages and gave it to him while handing him a slice of watermelon. The most difficult person to contact with was Wang Xiangrong. He looked tough, but he was actually quite timid, and he refused my attempts at passing notes to him. I eventually got somebody I trusted to speak to him and tell him not to mess around, because it concerned our well-being. A number of the mistakes we had made simply amounted to ideological problems. But opposing Lin Biao was a capital offense according to Article 6 of *Several Provisions on Strengthening Public Security Work in the Great Proletarian Cultural Revolution*. If labeled as counter-revolutionaries, we would be sentenced to death. The people who had arrested us were hoping us to admit our opposition to the Central Committee, Jiang Qing and Lin Biao. We had actually spoken out against them in the past, so I was keen to remind everyone to watch what they said and not to incriminate us.

We used the time we were let out for fresh air or to go to the toilet to exchange messages and get our story straight. This was indeed an effective way to get through the interrogations. I did not want them to find any hard evidence of us opposing Jiang Qing or Lin Biao. It was not a trial as such, just conversations. They asked if we had against Jiang Qing or her views, and we said things like, "Of course not. She's a proletarian revolutionary and a standard-bearer of the Cultural Revolution. Why would we oppose her? That's impossible!" They asked why we had said we needed to be alert to Khrushchev-style careerists and whom we were referring to. We answered, "We were simply stating that when Stalin was alive, Khrushchev shamelessly flattered him, when Stalin was dead, he then said the opposite behind his back. We must always be vigilant against the Khrushchev-style conspirators!" We swore to them, those were all what the article was about.

We were held at the school for about 40 days, but they were unable to pin any counter-revolutionary crimes on us, so they let us go.

From when we were released until the end of 1968, I did not take part in any substantial political activities. These events had forced me to the sidelines, and I found it difficult to stay energized. In the *Liberation of All Mankind* tabloid, we had often criticized the "carefree clique" as people without ideals and dawdlers, but I typically became one of them. Looking back now, being one of the carefree cliques was a happy time for me.

Once my friends and I were riding our bikes out of Beijing toward Zhangjiakou. Along the way we freewheeled while holding onto the back of trucks. It was of great fun. We followed the road until it reached Guanting Reservoir. The road to Zhangjiakou took a long detour around the reservoir, so we found two small boats, put our bikes and belongings in them and rowed to the other side. I was quite a strong swimmer, so my friend and I rowed the boats back to the other side, and then swam across the reservoir to meet up with the others. This was a very exciting experience. We felt like explorers forging our way over mountains and across rivers. We later went to a fishing village called Hangu, outside Tianjin. We stayed in the village and went out to sea on the fishing boats. As I remembered, Peng Zhen's son, Fu Liang, was also with us. During that time, I felt totally detached from the events going on. These days were my happy times.

"Sufferings" in Northern Shaanxi

Many young people of my generation were sent off to work in the mountainous areas or the countryside during the Cultural Revolution. It was our inescapable fate. In February 1969, I was sent to Yan'an in northern Shaanxi to work for the Gaojiachuan production team at the Angou Commune in Yanchang County. I stayed there until the end of 1972.

I had always lived a busy life, but often it has been involuntary. When I went to live and work in the production team, I did not have any choice over where I went. In late 1968, Mao declared that the urban youth should be "sent up to the mountains and down to the countryside", and it was already common for people to be placed in production teams when they got there. When this happened, I was keen to be sent to Shanxi province with my younger brother, Kong Dong. But the PLA propaganda team would not allow it. I then thought about going to Inner Mongolia with Qin Xiao and Li Sanyou, but the school still disapproved. Eventually I was sent to northern Shaanxi with my classmate from junior middle school, Han Song, and 11 schoolmates from other classes, including Liu Jiandang, Ma Weibo and Cai Danjiang. There were also nine female students in our production team who are from Beijing No. 36 High School. I later found out that the cadres in Beijing in charge of sending educated youth to the countryside had told the authorities in Yan'an to keep an eye on me.

When Kong Dong and I left Beijing, the last roots of our family had been totally removed. We were suddenly homeless. I remembered, as the train departed Beijing, everybody onboard began to cry, but I did not shed any tears. I felt there was nothing left for me in Beijing, and I did not care wherever I went. I was sure I would survive wherever I ended up. Nor did I have particularly strong emotions about being sent to the countryside for re-education. I did not really feel anything. I just assumed that was what life was like. Maybe it was because I had already been through so much, compared to other people of my own age. I already lacked strong emotions about new things. I was just resigned to going to the countryside and beginning a new life.

When we reached northern Shaanxi, the bus dropped us off in Yanchang County. The production team had sent people to meet us. The next day, we walked for four or five hours along a mountain path, which took us across two mountains on our way to the village. I remembered being impressed that having just arrived in the countryside, we had immediately climbed two mountains. I watched the villagers escorting us as they steadily plodded along, without changing their speed. Our pace, on the other hand, changed all the time. We were much slower than them despite our struggle of keeping up.

Yanchang County is next to the Yan River, about 150 kilometers away from Yan'an. The village of Gaojiachuan sits in a valley of a tributary of the Yan River, and it was 15 kilometers from the county along a dirt road, or 10 kilometers, if you took the path over the mountains. In our first year there, the government gave us 22 kilograms of raw grain, which was in fact not enough for us at all. To cook, we needed fire and the nearest firewood was from thorny bushes a couple of kilometers away.

The peasants were very honest and extremely hospitable. They had prepared house caves for us that had been hewn from the earth and could accommodate four or five people. I adjusted to my new surroundings faster than the others. I felt it was necessary for survival as well as something interesting. For example, I was the first to master the local dialect. I also dressed the same as the locals. In the local county, the men wore a white towel tied around their heads; clothes made from homespun cloth and locally made shoes with hard soles and sides. When my skin got darker, I was even mistaken for a local. The locals used to say, "Three layers of lined cloth are not as warm as cotton. Three layers of cotton are not as warm as a cotton belt", so in winter I also wore a cotton belt like the locals. I was a bit of a joker so I used to tease some of them. They knew that my father had been arrested and that my mother had committed suicide, so they felt sorry for me and often make quilts for me or help me patch my clothes.

Once we got to the village, we had to help with farm work. In my first year there, I picked it up quickly, so I was then awarded 10 work points for a day's work.[27] In spring, we planted corn, sorghum, millet, buckwheat and other fall crops. In summer, when it was hot and humid, we began hoeing and breaking up the soil. We then harvested the winter wheat by cutting and tying it in bundles. We used sharpened poles to skewer a bundle of wheat on each end, and carried it on our shoulders. Some of the students from the city struggled under the weight of the wheat, but I learned from the locals how to look natural and unrestrained by letting the pole move a little on your shoulder. I could even change shoulder during the mid-stride. In this way, I could carry it for two or three kilometers with ease.

After the summer harvest we went up the mountain to till the land. It was too hot for the oxen to work during the heat of the day, so we would get up around 3 am and lead the oxen up the mountain. After the land had been tilled, we planted wheat again. We mixed the wheat seeds with goat manure. The person in front would dig a small hole with a hoe, and the person behind would throw the wheat seeds and manure into the hole and step on it. In flat fields, wheat is planted in rows, but in the mountains of northern Shaanxi, it is planted in clusters. This is done because the land is so barren, and the limited amount of fertilizer had to be mixed with the seeds and planted together.

It was obvious that the villagers took a liking to me, because I was hard working and able to endure hardship. It was also because I was able to communicate with them. It was at that time that I learned how to smoke. The locals all smoked long pipes, which took a little time for me to get used to. The tobacco stuffed in the pipe was very strong. Like

---

27 At that time, people's communes implemented a system of work points, whereby a male laborer would receive 10 points for a full day's labor. When the educated youth first arrived in the villages of northern Shaanxi, they usually earned only 6-8 points per day.

the locals, I rubbed the pipe holder at the front of your coat, and then put it in my mouth. The first time I smoked, I almost passed out from coughing so much...

During those years, I always dressed like the people of northern Shaanxi, and my skin even turned dark, like that of the locals. I really enjoyed that period. It was a simple time. I did not think it was particularly tough. It was not like the TV show *Romantic Life*, where the educated youth did nothing except getting up to mischief and fighting with each other. I heard that some students were like that in Yan'an, but all the educated youth in our village were hard working. In my view, we were not pursuing an ideal, trying to integrate with the rural poor, tempering ourselves through agricultural work or seeking to profoundly alter our worldview. That was not us. I just considered myself a farmer and was trying to survive.

I was involved in all aspects of the works in the production team, including cutting grass and making sheep pens. On one occasion, I was almost crushed to death while carving a sheep pen out of the hillside. While half way through our work, we took a break, and just after we walked out of the cave, it suddenly collapsed. If we had not stopped for a break, I would be dead then. During my second year in Shaanxi, because I worked too much, I contracted lobar pneumonia and began coughing up blood. After I recovered, I still had very little strength and my feet were also infected. I was no longer able to do normal manual labor. The production team had a watermelon field next to the graveyard, and was usually looked after by two people, who were each given 10 points one day for the work, so I volunteered to work there on my own for earning 12 points. The team captain agreed.

There was a tree in the watermelon field, and I hung a rope from it to make a hammock to sleep in. It was a really pleasant life. During the day, I could eat watermelon whenever I wanted. At night I had an oil lamp that was used for reading. When I got tired, I would just blow out the lamp and sleep. The villagers were worried that I would be scared living next to the graveyard, so they brought over a dog to keep me company, and tied its leash around a tree. The next day, it had gnawed through its leash and run away. Besides, a stone tablet was unearthed one day, which said there was once someone hanged from the tree in the past. I just said that I was not bothered, which made the villagers thought I was brave.

We planted some buckwheat around the village. Between the end of summer and the start of fall, the pink flowers blossomed, and the stems turned purple. The mountains and plains merged into one. It was very beautiful. Sometimes we would pick some wild vegetables and herbs. We also kept a pig. The first time I slaughtered a pig, the knife did not stab on its heart. As a result, it managed to break free and ran around, while we chased it. It ran so fast that it took us quite a long time to catch it. On thinking of eating it, I then had the energy of chasing it. It was a short-lived joy amid the otherwise difficult life.

Travel on a Shoestring

Life in the production team went by day after day, and after a while, I got used to it. It was not what one would call an idyllic rural life; we still worried about getting enough food to eat and getting by. But relatively speaking, I still had some wonderful memories from my time there.

I later found out that Qin Xiao and Li Sanyou, who went to work in a production team in Inner Mongolia, lived a more comfortable life than mine. We were always concerned with getting enough to eat. In truth, most of the educated youth who went to work in the countryside always had some backup from their families. Their relatives and friends in the city would often send them food or money to buy food to keep them going. I did not have anyone to send me anything. After the first year in northern Shaanxi, I had earned about 30-40 yuan, so I returned briefly to Beijing that winter. The train ticket back and forth would cost me 40 yuan, and it cost more than 10 yuan for a bus, which I could not afford. So, I hitchhiked and snuck onto trains on the way back. It was not easy for members of production teams to return to Beijing. Upon my arrival in Beijing, I had no home to return to. I stayed with various friends, at a different place for each night. My best friend at the time was Zhang Haoyun, who was once in Grade Two at Beijing No. 4 High School. His father worked at the Second Ministry of Machine Building. I mainly stayed in his home at Sanlihe. I also stayed in Cai Danjiang's home for quite a long time that winter. He was a member of my production team, and lived in the dormitory of the Ministry of Railways.

During the slack season in the winter of 1971, my third year with the production team, I went "traveling" to the south of China with Qin Xiao, Li Sanyou, Feng Jianghua and Lu Shuqi, who all worked in Inner

Mongolia, and my brother, Kong Dong. We had a budget of 150 yuan per person for train tickets, accommodation, food and cigarettes while we were away. Kong Dong and I had no money, but luckily the boys working in Inner Mongolia had enough to lend us, so that we could go too. After we knocked off work that winter, we all met up in Beijing and set off from there. A lot of educated youth who took trains at that time did not buy tickets, but we tried an eclectic way by buying three tickets to Yingtan, a small city in the southeastern province of Jiangxi. Three people went first and got off at a small station just before Yingtan, and posted the tickets back to Beijing. Tickets back then were valid for six days, so they had not expired by the time the other three got them and boarded the train. We all met up again in Yingtan. That was how our trip had started.

Our first stop was the Jinggang Mountains. Despite already being winter (I remembered we arrived there on December 31, 1971), we swam in the clear, cold mountain pools. We then traveled to Mount Lushan, Mount Huangshan, Suzhou and Hangzhou. In total, we each spent 100 yuan, with 50 yuan remained for each. I remembered we smoked "Pujiang" cigarettes during the whole trip, which cost 0.22 yuan per packet. Lu Shuqi was the only one of us who did not smoke, while I was a heavy smoker. If he was given a cigarette, he always gave it straight to me. We had a great time despite our straitened circumstances, and took a lot of pictures. It was a wonderful experience.

Lin Biao was already deposed before we set off on our trip. We had suspected that it would happen sooner or later. Now we felt liberated, which was a reason for us to take our trip.

There was another interesting event on our trip after we arrived at Mount Huangshan. We had found a hostel and rented three beds for the six of us. There were not many tourists in winter back then, and the police did not have much to do. They kept watching on us as soon as we arrived. In a bid to save money, we were sleeping with two people sharing one bed. As soon as we had just turned in for the night, the police knocked on our door. They stormed in and took us away for questioning. It was said that the local governments regarded educated youths as vags, so such events were quite common in many places.

We six were separated, and each of us was questioned in turn about what we were doing, where we were from, how and why we had got there. The person who questioned me seemed to be the head of the local Public Security Bureau. He smoked expensive "Chunghwa" cigarettes. I smoked such a cheap brand that it made quite deep an impression on me. I suddenly had an idea. I pounded the desk and shouted, "Why are you still questioning us? You've still got Lin Biao quotes painted all over your walls up here. And you haven't erased any of them. Don't you know he's a traitor and died in a plane crash trying to defect?" His face suddenly turned pale as he stammered, "We…we… we had conveyed that…" "Are you still going to question us? This is enough to have you all arrested for being counter-revolutionaries. Do you know that?" I said. He was terrified at this suggestion and quickly handed me the packet of cigarettes. I lit a cigarette as I continued my rant.

During the Cultural Revolution, Wang Zhen worked for a time at the Fuzhou Red Star Farm in Jiangxi province, and a friend of ours, Wang Xing, went there too. To stay anywhere back then you needed the correct documents. So we got a letter of introduction from the farm through our friend Wang Xing. The head of the Public Security Bureau in Mount Huangshan had been afraid we might report on him, to show their friendship, they had written us another letter of introduction. This made the rest of our trip a lot easier. It was a great time. Lin Biao had fallen from grace, and things within the Party and in the society were slightly more relaxed. Our travel on a shoestring was such a carefree time.

Life in a Cave

My memory of being part of the production team is that it was a relatively stable phase in my life. There was very little pressure on me. In this sense, leaving Beijing was a kind of relief, which was probably very different to how the majority of educated youths felt. Moreover, I got on very well with the villagers and communicated with them openly and harmoniously, and they liked me as well. I am quite an open and relaxed person, so I used to sing to them. I even sang them some foreign songs they had never heard before. This led them to give me the nickname "golden voice". I also learned some local songs when I worked with the villagers. I still remember them clearly to this day.

Sometimes I liked to challenge the locals. On one occasion, I said that I could drink a quarter of a liter of wine in one go. One of the villagers said I was talking nonsense, so I challenged him. I said that if I could do it, he should give me three cartons of cigarettes. We then walked to a sales cooperative at a commune almost three kilometers away, arguing and talking all the way. When we got there, I took my rusty old mug, and asked for half a kilo of wine made of sweet potato. The person behind the counter filled it up, then I stood there and finished it in one go. I won the three cartons of cigarettes (they were cheap cigarettes, only 0.06 yuan per packet) and was very proud of myself. Then we walked back up the road to the village. I had lots of stories like that. I was living a simple life, just like the ordinary farmers.

I was very fond of cleaning, and despite I was living in an old cave, I used to sweep it clean. I also made a desk out of some stone with tree branches as legs, so we had somewhere to study at night. The only cost we had to spend was on kerosene for the lamp. We used to read whatever we could find, and all our books were brought over from Beijing. I felt at the time that I should continue my study. I had already finished studying all my high school textbooks, so I started reading some textbooks for science and engineering colleges, such as general chemistry, general physics and advanced mathematics. I also studied languages as a sort of hobby, because I was interested in them. I studied quite a few languages. In addition to Russian and English, I studied Japanese and even some German. After I returned to Beijing, I studied French, which became my second foreign language during my postgraduate studies. There was a certain rhythm in life. In winter, there was not a lot to do so except to occasionally work on irrigation channels, if I was not going back in Beijing, I would have lots of time to study.

I could not remember where all our books came from. I had read one book about farming methods in the US, which were highly efficient and intensive. Living in the countryside, I had a lot of time to think, and my mind was never at rest. Our production methods had already undergone the 1962 adjustments, and production teams were the basic units of all work. Communal canteens had already been shut down, and everybody ate in their own homes, but the production teams still worked together and earned together. We also held meetings together quite often. Whether you worked hard or not, everybody got the same. Labor productivity was low. It was just another version of the communal pot system. At that time, one *mu* of land in northern Shaanxi produced about 65 kilos of wheat, which was considered to be quite good.[28] During the years of famine, it could only produced 10-25 kilos, or sometimes none. In those years, people did not make any money from selling grain, and work points were worthless.

I later wrote an essay on rural issues that raised some questions about farming methods and argued which methods were the most effective. It was not an investigative report. Rather, it was just an outline of some of my ideas at the time. It was heavily influenced by the book I read on farming methods in the US and provided some suggestions

---

28 One *mu* is 0.0667 hectares. In other words, one hectare is 15 *mu*.

of improvements that could be made to our organizational methods. It did not go into nearly as much detail as the economic reforms and rural production responsibility system that followed. This revealed that even in the village, I still kept up my habit of studying, and my mind was still active. I studied books on culture, knowledge and theory, including the works of Hegel. This led Comrade Xi Jinping, when he was Secretary of the Shanghai Municipal Party Committee, to comment during a meeting with Chang Zhenming from CITIC, "You know Kong Dan, he was reading Hegel while living in a cave in northern Shaanxi!"

Our production team was involved in a Party membership drive on one occasion. A work group was sent to our village, having heard I was a Party member, they asked me to say a few words. I told them that I was still just a probationary member, and asked them if they could help me become a full member. I had joined the Party in 1965, but had still not been made an official member. They listened and enquired about it for me, but later replied that there was nothing they could do. I helped several villagers to write their applications of becoming Party members. They later became full members but I remained a probationary one. The head of the work group was an interesting guy. He knew I was from a big city, so he asked me if a general or a field marshal was of a higher rank. I teased him by saying that it was a general. I remembered he taught everybody to sing the Party song. We also had organized political study classes and read newspapers. We used to deliberately mispronounce words to make funny sentences.

Although I lived in northern Shaanxi for four years, it did not feel like a long time. The time flied fast.

My Views on the Youths' Being Sent to the Countryside

The days spent in the countryside was a kind of life experience. It was a chance for me to meet, interact and understand people from other walks of life. Though I had got in touch with peasant before, in these four years, I did start to experience their life as a member of them.

In the long history of China, there has never been another movement like this. Nor has there been anything like it ever after. The junior and senior high school students are quite an energetic group of people. If we had been allowed to continue with our normal studies, I wonder what would have happened. I sometimes wonder if the decision of sending us to the countryside was to do with employment, or if it was just because those in power wanted to get rid of us, because we were seen as troublemakers. Chairman Mao had undoubtedly the power and authority to do that. I wonder if the Party Central Committee was ever involved in the decision, whether the leaders at the highest rank had any say. Looking back, I believed we were sent to the countryside simply because of a Mao's command. He saw what we were doing and decided we should all go and work in the countryside. I believed that was his reasoning. He wanted the students who were causing trouble to be sent to the countryside, so that he could take over the whole chaotic situation in an instant.

Trying to trace his motivation nowadays, it would be hard to argue that he did it for economic reasons. We were a burden on these relatively economically backward places with limited production capacity. We contributed more than 17 million people to production teams, but I am sure we did not increase the production capacity to the value of more than 17 million people. Villages still cultivated the same amount of land and harvested for the same amount of grain. Our village had very limited resources. Originally it was home to no more than 200 people, but when we got there, 22 people were added to the population, resulting in an increase of more than 10%. When we first arrived, we needed to walk for two and a half kilometers to collect firewood. By the time we left, we had to walk for three and a half or four kilometers to find firewood. Wasn't that a depletion of their resources? Many people were moved to the countryside, but they added little or nothing to the productivity.

This was just a certain outcome that occurred under specific historical conditions and during a particular period. It was something driven by Mao Zedong within a particular historical context as well as a natural historical process. I say this because it was not something we could avoid. We had no choice at all.

Regardless of how it came about, it was a unique experience shared by my generation, and a training to our personality. It made us the people we became. According to the Japanese, Chinese Go player Nie Weiping was using a "Cultural Revolution" style, because he did not adhere to any conventional rules. He played in an unpredictable manner, which vexed his competitors. He led China to victory in the China-Japan Supermatches for three times, beating several top Japanese players along the way. He changed the way Go is played in China and has made an invaluable contribution to the game. Has his style been heavily influenced by his experiences during the Cultural Revolution, when he spent six years working in the countryside?

Take me for another example, the days working in the production team helped to temper my character, willpower, and traits, as well as my ability to communicate with ordinary people. I was not able to communicate like that before I went to the countryside. My vocabulary was so rigid, which meant I could not talk to those people. This ability to communicate stood my generation in good stead. We also gained an intuition for the suffering of others. It has been particularly beneficial for some senior leaders. That experience has been extremely valuable to them, and it has a very positive influence on their political careers in terms of the positive impact on their characters and their ability of communicating. For many of us, Mencius' words ring true: "When Heaven is going to give a great responsibility to someone, it first makes his mind endure suffering. It makes his sinews and bones experience toil, and his body to suffer hunger. It inflicts him with poverty and knocks down everything he tries to build. In this way, Heaven stimulates his mind, stabilizes his temper and develops his weak points."

The difficulties of working in the countryside for four years certainly improved my willpower. Although we never enjoyed any excessive privileges, there were some benefits as a child of senior cadres. For example, we went to the beach resort of Beidaihe every year, and my father would sometimes take my brother and me with him on work trips to other cities. Common people did not get to do these things. During the years of famine, although we had to eat sweet potato flour and sophora flowers, many people were much worse off than us. During the Cultural Revolution, my family suffered terribly, my mother was dead, and my father was in prison, but even then I had an allowance of 15 yuan per month to supplement the meals I was given, to buy some fried shredded pancake, for instance. Our family were certainly better off than most. The most difficult time in my life was those spent during the countryside.

Living with ordinary people, one directly sees the inequality that exists. I particularly felt this when I left northern Shaanxi. I realized that, whereas I could leave, they would always remain in those areas, on that land. Their whole lives revolved around getting enough food to eat, finding a wife, having children, and saving for a funeral. That is their life. And because of the hard life, their lifespan is much shorter. Their joy and sadness is tied up to the land. By listening to their songs, you realized that all the joy and sorrow is tied to it. This inequality is something that we must face and change today.

When the educated youth were sent to the countryside, they were suddenly brought face-to-face with the very lowest level of Chinese society – those among the peasantry living the hardest lives. This was a very rare opportunity for us to understand how people lived and what our own country was like. Looking at it now, I am convinced that the place I was sent to should not be inhabited. The people should be moved to somewhere more suitable. It suffered from severe soil erosion, the barren loess soil could barely support vegetation, and the raising of sheep had almost completely degraded what little scrubland there used to be.

Later on, when I worked at the CITIC Group, I traveled to Yunnan as part of an initiative by the central government to help people living in poverty. We drove for three or four hours along a mountain road from the Red River to a remote village. We gave money to the people there to build a tarred road, toilets and a primary school. The children there lived under very primitive conditions and had poor access to education. I thought to myself that these people would always be poor due to their natural environment. The children had virtually no academic opportunities and very little chance of going out by sitting the college entrance examination and going to college, so how could they be expected to improve their life? My time working in the countryside left me with strong feelings on the matter. There was a fatalistic helplessness about the peasants in northern Shaanxi.

My closest friends in the village were the Gao family. Mr. Gao had three children. The eldest was so mournful-looking. I also remember the other two well, and I can still picture their appearances clearly. The youngest married a beautiful girl from Mizhi County. There was a local saying that the boys from Suide County and the girls from Mizhi County make good couples, but she was reluctant to marry him because his family was poor. The problem was that her family was even poorer, so she had little choice. To communicate with rural people, one needs to be on their rank, which we were at that time. Although we live different lives now, it is impossible to erase our feelings and experiences from that time. What is more, it motivates us. I still believe in what the Communist Party is trying to achieve, but I do not think we have resolved the issue of inequality. How can we be worthy of them, since those people are still living like that even today?

This is truly how I feel. Perhaps a lot of Party members have already forgotten this purpose, and they are no longer struggling for the same thing. But I still think like this. Comrade Deng Xiaoping had once talked about common prosperity and adjusting the distribution of wealth. This is one of the major themes in economics for dealing with equality and efficiency relations. It is also demanded by the historical development of China. Conversely, it is the basis for the survival of the ruling Party. As such, our experience of working in the countryside also deepened our feelings toward the people there.

In a certain sense, the political status of educated youth at that time was below that of farmers. We were undergoing re-education, so we had a different political identity. For many of us, that was something of a mental scar at the time. In addition, a lot of people were physically damaged from their long-time working in the countryside. For example, I have been left with chronic obstructive pulmonary disease from having colds and coughs but no access to drugs back then. I also had lobar pneumonia and coughed up blood when I lived in the village. A lot of people suffered from liver and kidney diseases as well as muscle strain as a result of the harsh living conditions in rural areas back then. The living condition in those days is incomparable to that nowadays.

Many female educated youth in northern Shaanxi could not stand the intensity of the hard labor. One of the girls from our production team even married a local, because she found the work unbearable. Every day we walked three or four kilometers up the mountains to work, and then walked three or four kilometers back down. Our work usually involved mixing wheat seeds with sheep manure by our hands and planting the seeds in the ground. At lunchtime, we would spit on our hands and wipe them on our clothes before picking up our food. That was what the locals did, so we had to do the same. Some people just could not take it through, and I should not blame them. We were living in very basic conditions, and there were problems that even revolutionary romanticism could not solve.

Objectively speaking, I feel that during my four years in northern Shaanxi, I was converting negative situations into positive. Despite the tough work and living condition, life was stable politically, and I had an opportunity to think over certain issues. During that time, I also tried my best to expand my knowledge. Reading was a way of detaching ourselves from the realities of rural life. In the evenings, we could manage all our time after dinner. No matter it was summer or winter, we would retreat to our caves, pick up our books, and read for hours. We did not have lofty aspirations like some revolutionaries back then, who wanted to transform the society and the country. We just considered reading a natural requirement. I read a lot of books, which included all I could find. I read literature and politics, including *Trotsky: A Biography* and Milovan Djilas's *The New Class: An Analysis of the Communist System*. I started my postgraduate studies when I was 31 years old, despite a bachelor degree. Those days were like a fault in my life. It was also a heavy price for social progress.

Television series, such as *Romantic Life*, have romanticized the "up to the mountains and down to the countryside" movement. Many young people have watched these shows and said that they envied for such a romantic experience. In fact, it was not like that.

Personally, I believed that, in terms of its historical role, the movement was completely negative and should be widely recognized as such. However, there is no need to view the movement in completely negative terms. What it meant to individuals is a different matter, and that depends on their particular experience and whether they were able to take something positive out of a bad situation. This is something people still argue about regularly. The recent program on China Central Television called *Educated Youth* by Liang Xiaosheng has aroused a lot of controversy. When I meet up with old classmates from No. 4 High School, it has also become a topic for discussion. A topic for future studies related to the Cultural Revolution is whether or not the movement had a significant impact on the personalities of my generation, whether or not these impacts were positive or negative, and whether they were confined to the individual or affected the whole society.

There was no doubt that a lot of people had suffered from the movement. People's normal lives were completely disrupted. Their lives were changed forever. There are stories, for example, of children born of educated youth in Yunnan, who have gone to Shanghai in search of their mothers and fathers who left the villages when the movement ended. This also happened in Shaanxi. For those who married local villagers, some had children with them, while some divorced with them.

Return to Beijing

After four years of working for the production team, I returned to Beijing. In 1972, I was told that I could visit my father. Kong Dong and I immediately decided that one of us should move back to Beijing to look after him. When we went to see him, he was still being held, so he asked that I return as I had quick wits, knew more people, and was good at writing, so that I was more likely to secure his release.

A chance of moving back soon presented itself when I met Zhou Enlai's former secretary, Pu Shouchang, who was then Dean of Beijing Foreign Studies University. I explained the situation to him and asked him to deliver a letter for me to Premier Zhou. Pu agreed and told me to write my letter. Premier Zhou read it and approved my request. His office sent a letter to the Shaanxi Provincial Party Committee and I was given the green light to return to Beijing.

When I got to Beijing, I had no place to live, so I moved in with a nanny who had taken care of my grandmother. We called her Aunt Li. The Red Guard rebels had evicted my family from our home when they raided it. My grandmother had nowhere to go, so Aunt Li took her in. Aunt Li's family lived in a house made from rammed earth in a village called Weigongcun, which was then a rural area in northeast of Beijing. I lived there for a long time until Central Investigation Department permitted me to move into a block inside the Institute of International Relations.

I had returned to Beijing in an attempt to save my father. I arrived back to the capital at the end of 1972, and I spent most of the following year of 1973 trying to secure his release. Despite my visits being watched over by guards, my father also used those opportunities to give me confidential instructions on how I should proceed. He told me to speak to two people about his case. One was Premier Zhou, the other was Kang Sheng. He asked me to write a letter to Kang because, in his words, "whoever ties the bell to the tiger should be the one to take it off."

As I said earlier, my father was close to Kang when they were studying in the Soviet Union. But I did not know Kang's attitude when my father was named by Jiang Qing and imprisoned. I heard that, prior to the Ninth Party Congress, a list of names of people in the Eighth Central Committee had circulated and that Kang had written next to my father's name the words "traitor, special agent, maintains illicit foreign relations". This seemed very harsh and was difficult to understand. During the Nanchang Uprising, my father was part of the workers' picket. He had stood up bravely by the time of gunshot. Many people were so afraid and hidden themselves under the table. After the uprising had failed, they headed for Chaoshan, but had been dispersed along the way, and my father had then been detained by the troops of a local warlord. This was all in his file held by the Party as he had already told them all about it. But the Party took this sort of events very seriously, and had therefore examined whether or not he had been turned a traitor or was collaborating with the enemy. He explained to them that he had been released as he claimed himself a common people. As a "special agent", it was hard to explain. The only thing I can think of was that he was doing intelligence work. I can only assume that the claim of maintaining illicit foreign relations had to do with his intelligence work with the Soviet Union.

That was why my father had said, "whoever ties the bell to the tiger should be the one to take it off." I remembered his words so clearly that I wrote two identical letters to Zhou Enlai and Kang Sheng, asking for my father to be released, so he could receive medical treatment. Both of them responded after reading the letter. Zhou's instructions were that he was to be released for treatment, while the investigation continued. Kang's response was slightly more straightforward and lenient, perhaps because he already had cancer at the time. His instructions were that my father was to be released from custody and taken to hospital for treatment.

My father went to prison in 1967. A great many senior cadres had been put into prison by the Party. He had been imprisoned in a single cell with nobody to talk to, and could not talk well by the time he was released. He was 60 years old when he went in and 67 when he came out. Just before Kang Sheng died of cancer, my father took me to see Kang at his Diaoyutai residence. Kang could not speak by that time and was very thin but with a swollen face. My father thanked Kang for releasing him after reading my letter. Kang's eyes filled with tears on hearing this. As we left my father turned to me and said, "When a man is near death, he speaks from his heart". "He cannot say anything," I replied.

On October 1, 1973, my father was released from prison and was sent directly to Fuwai Hospital. On that day, Wang Hongwen was made Vice-Chairman of the CPC Central Committee and we could hear the announcement being made over loudspeakers outside. I remembered it very clearly. After spending some time in the hospital, my father moved to a house at No. 5 of Tieshizi Alley Zhangzizhong Road, where Soviet experts used to live. The experts had left during the Sino-Soviet split. Next to our building was a courtyard that had belonged to V. K. Wellington Koo, who was the minister of foreign affairs during the Beiyang period. Sun Yat-sen also lived there until his death. We lived there for a while until we were eventually given our house back.

After my father was released from prison, I was eager to get a job. I went to speak to my local sub-district administration. They wanted to place me in a local factory, but my father refused. He was adamant that I should stay and look after him, insisting that it was also a form of revolutionary work. I was aware that he really wanted to go back to work at the Investigation Department as a consultant, but the leaders were not keen for him to return. He felt that he was treated in an injustice way. He explained to me that while he had been in prison, he had never said a single word against the Party or the leadership, yet they still would not accept him back. I tried telling him that he was a victim of the circumstance, what he did was good, and it was a normal reaction for them not to want to take him back.

In the summer of 1975, Wang Zhen invited me to be his secretary. At that point, Wang Zhen was Deputy Director of the State Council Administrative Group, which was equivalent to the Vice Premier. Having spent a lot of time chatting with him at his home, I was clear on his political leanings. His old secretary, Wu Shaozu, wanted to leave, and Wang wanted me to take over. I worked in that post for almost three months. My first task was to help him organize his files. After that, I accompanied him on business trips. I remembered two incidents very clearly. The first was a trip to the outskirts of Beijing to inspect a humic acid fertilizer plant. He was mainly concerned with how to develop growth production, so he was interested in fertilizers. He was also the sort of person who enjoyed learning new things. Besides Ivan Michurin, he also read the Williams' works on pedology. The other was when he took my father and me to visit the gold mines near Qingdao, Weihai and Yantai on the Shandong Peninsula. On the basis of this trip, he promoted the establishment of an armed police force in charge of gold. By that time, I was already working as his secretary, but the State Council later disapproved that I was not permitted to work in that capacity, because the investigation of my father had still not been formally concluded. For that reason, I did not get the job. In turn, Zhan Aiping's son, Zhang Pin, replaced Wu Shaozu as Wang Zhen's secretary.

I therefore had no official employment in the first two years after I returned to Beijing. I simply took care of my father and fulfill my duty as a son. In 1975, when Deng Xiaoping came to power, my father wrote to Deng, telling him his ardent wish of returning to work and for the case against him to be dropped. Subsequently, Wu Xiuquan, who was the Deputy Chief of the PLA General Staff Headquarters and Chief of the General Staff Second Department, welcomed my father to work for him. That was how my father came to be political commissar at the Second Department of the PLA General Staff Headquarters. Having been a Minister of one of the five main central government ministries, he was going back in at a lower level within the military organizational structure. He saw this as something of an injustice, but by that time the campaign to "refute right deviationist views" had already begun. It was a rare chance for Deng to give this job to him. My father was extremely grateful. He was later given the perks of a Deputy Chief of Staff, and had his secretary, driver, bodyguards and staff. The treatment was much better than working for local governments. At this point, I was relieved of my duty to take care of him, and began looking for jobs.

I had originally thought about going to work in a local factory, but one day my father asked me what I wanted to do. Having lived through the Cultural Revolution, I wanted to make sense of the tortuous experiences the Party and the country had been through, and, in a way, to make sense of my own life. So I told him I wanted to be a theorist. He then spoke to his friend Song Yiping, who was in charge of the Philosophy and Social Sciences Department of the Chinese Academy of Sciences. Song arranged a job for me as a librarian at the Economic Research Institute. My father reminded me that I was lucky even to get that job, given that I only had a high school diploma. I was very pleased just to have the opportunity to continue my studies. I do not generally think of myself as someone who relied on contacts. But in that instance, my father's contacts certainly got me the job.

I joined the Party as a probationary member on July 1, 1965, and became a full member a decade later in 1975. I went myself to the Organization Department of the Beijing Municipal Party Committee. Li Ligong was in charge at the time. My mother had had a friend called Li Zengjie, who was the wife of Wu De. Li Zengjie and Li Ligong knew each other quite well, so she introduced me to him. I went straight to his office, and he listened patiently as I explained my predicament. Afterwards he told me that he would try to resolve the issue.

The year 1975 was very important for my family. In that year, my father went back to work, and I found a job. I also became a full Party member. Kong Dong had originally been working for a production team in the Yanbei region of Shanxi province, but was in this year transferred to a better production team near Nanchang, in our ancestral home of Jiangxi province.

At the Institute of Economic Research, I received my first salary of 38 yuan per month. With 38 yuan in my pocket, I felt that I was so rich. In those days, university graduates only had a monthly salary of no more than 56 yuan. At the institute, I was honored to be in the same Party branch as Sun Yefang.[29]

After I had been working there for a few days, Premier Zhou Enlai died. A number of major events occurred in 1976, which was an important year of Dragon in the modern history of China. Near the end of the campaign to "refute right deviationist views", my father was preparing to be re-arrested. He felt that if the campaign continued, he would be likely to be put into prison again. During that time, none of us dared to speak openly at home, in case there may be people monitoring us, so we went out to the courtyard to discuss over these matters. We talked about the fact that it would take an extraordinary intervention to solve all the problems. I later heard that Wang Zhen had used a hand gesture to express this meaning to Ye Jianying, by pointing his thumb up and then down, telling Ye it was "the only way".[30] When Zhou Enlai passed away, Deng Xiaoping was criticized again, we had no hope for senior leaders in the Party, because it seemed to lack a mainstay.

Around the time of the Tiananmen Incident on April 5, 1976, I visited the Square on several occasions to transcribe some poems and slogans, and then I went home to tell my father what was happening.[31]The Institute of Economic Research had issued a notice on behalf of the higher authorities, telling people they were not allowed to go to Tiananmen Square. I still snuck along through to watch the events unfold. When I told my father and others what was going on, they concluded that indignation and discontent were really widespread. High-ranking officials including my father felt sympathy with the people at Tiananmen Square. The April 5th Incident was about creating

29 Sun Yefang (1908-1983) was a prominent Chinese economist.

30 Wang Zhen and Ye Jianying controlled the army at that time and later led efforts to topple the Gang of Four.

31 The Tiananmen Incident occurred after police removed wreaths, flowers, placards and poems placed next to the Monument to the People's Heroes in Tiananmen Square to commemorate Zhou Enlai. Hundreds were arrested following widespread rioting.

a break from the Cultural Revolution. It was the people saying that they could not continue the Cultural Revolution any longer. Without the Tiananmen Incident it is hard to imagine how the Gang of Four would have been arrested, as there would have been no legal or judicial basis. The incident showed the people's fortitude and strength, and it made their wishes clear.

When Zhu De died, my father said to me, "Jiang Qing hated your mother, so she hounded her to death. If they come for me again, I might not have the chance to escape, but you must run away. You cannot go back to prison, and suffer the same fate as last time. If you go in again there's a good chance you will not come back alive." A lot of senior cadres had a bleak view over the matters. They knew Jiang Qing could do whatever to persecute them. They respected the Party discipline, but they first had to think of their survival. Many of them had held family meetings. The struggles had come to this point.

But just as people were preparing for the worse, things suddenly took a dramatic turn for the better. On October 7, 1976, senior cadres in the army were informed that the Gang of Four had been arrested. That day, my father came home, he hugged and kissed me. I asked him what was wrong, but he just told me to get him a drink. I knew something important had happened. All he said was, "Drink! They've been arrested!" "Which of them?" I asked. "Who do you think? Jiang Qing." "Can they arrest Chairman Mao's wife?" I wondered. "They already have! Along with Zhang Chunqiao, Wang Hongwen and Yao Wenyuan. The whole rotten lot have been arrested," my father exclaimed. We were ecstatic at that moment.

Deng Xiaoping once said, "Without Mao Zedong, we would still be groping in the dark today." I wonder where we would be if Hua Guofeng had not supported the Gang of Four. Chen Yun had pointed out that the problem could only be dealt with under special circumstances, because it was becoming a life and death struggle. Without this turning point, Chinese history would have been rewritten. All in all, it was an effective means of dealing with the situation. There were extraordinary measures taken during an extraordinary period in time. It was a last resort whereby the lowest price was paid for the most efficient outcome. The Gang of Four's views coupled with their power and brutality would have led to a dark time for China, had they been allowed to continue. It would have resulted in total collapse or an armed struggle. As my father and his colleagues said at the time, as soon as Chairman Mao was dead, they would revolt. The overthrow of the Gang of Four was a great event, because the weapon of criticism cannot replace the criticism by using weapons.

Evaluating the Cultural Revolution

The CPC Central Committee later published the *Resolution on Certain Questions in the History of Our Party Since the Founding of the People's Republic of China*. I heard the following story about something that occurred during the soliciting of opinions for the resolution. An early draft supposedly contained a section stating that Chairman Mao's basis for launching the Cultural Revolution was sound. But Wang Zhen's youngest son, Wang Zhi, read about this and argued that it was wrong and the Cultural Revolution should be condemned thoroughly, firmly and without reservation. This suggestion was accepted by Deng Xiaoping, which led to the Resolution's total condemnation of the basis for the Cultural Revolution, and its entire process.

Fundamentally condemning the Cultural Revolution naturally meant condemning the actions of Red Guards. The background of the Cultural Revolution was an adherence to a left-wing political line, and it was Mao's mistake to launch it. Some people wonder if some good did come out of it, and whether or not his intentions were good. I do not think history would remember whether your intentions were good or not, but what you actually did and what role it had played in history. Looking back now, it is clear that the entire decade was reactionary. Everything that followed in terms of the Red Guards, regardless of factions and groups, as well as the various workers' revolutionary rebel organizations all came out of this background. It is difficult for young people today to understand how several hundred million people could get swept up in such a devastating movement. Those that have not been through it wonder how it could have happened in China. It was a tragedy seen from the perspective of "scar literature", but literary works can do little to conceptualize or to make sense of it, so we should try to understand its context.

Mao was extremely powerful, and his speeches were like adding fuel to flames. He regarded the CPC Central Committee as the enemy and fanned the flames among the masses. As the Cultural Revolution developed, those from the top and bottom layers of society intermingled, and it became a broad mass movement. During the first six months or so, the children of high-ranking cadres acted as detonators. Their education, family background, political sensitivity, access to information and revolutionary fervor made them perfect for their historical role.

Within this context, the Xicheng District Picket Corps appeared only for a brief moment. Its voice was heard momentarily, just as an echo, but it resonated far longer than it actually existed. Because the sound it made was a discordant one, which was the sound of resistance. Meanwhile, it reflected what was actually going on in the upper echelons of the Party. In fact, the Picket Corps, the Red Guards and the "big-character poster" by Nie Yuanzi from Peking University, being seemingly spontaneous or obviously incited, were all tools used in the struggle taking place at the highest levels of the Party.

Within this period, some of us had good intentions, but were quite naïve. We were just trying to improve, but were too radical. We made mistakes, but only out of devotion. As leaders of the Red Guards, we should have a basic understanding of the role of the Cultural Revolution. We should completely negate the so-called Red Guard movement. Our wildly popular mass movement was in fact an integral part of the Cultural Revolution. Therefore, we should not have reservations in our evaluation of the Red Guard movement and positively affirm it just because we were honest, with good intentions, and wanted to do something for the country and society. I believe this is the view that we who experienced the Cultural Revolution should adopt.

Moreover, I do not think people should condemn us for superficial mistakes, although this is also necessary. Superficial mistakes include criticizing school Party committees, treating classmates unjustly, beating people and participating in destroy the Four Olds campaign and other extreme movements. I thought we should reflect more deeply on our involvement in the Cultural Revolution and recognize that, as the Party's supreme leader, Chairman Mao manipulated the Party towards class struggle based on his own ideas. Following the founding of the People's Republic of China, Mao's ideas developed step-by-step from the anti-rightist movement, to the struggle against right deviationists, the socialist education movement and finally the Cultural Revolution. Even when people at all levels of society grew tired of and resisted the Cultural Revolution, he insisted on continuing the revolution under the proletarian dictatorship and suppressing dissenting voices within the Party, by labeling anybody who disagreed with him as a reactionary or class enemy.

A more profound reflection leads one to conclude that there is a need, as Deng Xiaoping once said, to establish a system to prevent it, or something similar, from ever happening again. This is something that my generation – the people who lived through it – should agree on.

Within the Cultural Revolution itself, Mao acted as the driving force, propelling the revolution under the proletarian dictatorship, while others played various supporting roles. What was my role in it at all? Let me keep a record of my thoughts for those who would study the Cultural Revolution in the future.

I believed in Chairman Mao. He was a great figure who managed to seize political power. In the course of studying from the Soviet Union, he criticized some of the ideas behind the Soviet planned economy, and wrote *On the Ten Major Relationships*. But just as China had the opportunity to progress along the correct track, he swerved off. He felt that the Chinese revolution would not come to an end just because the CPC had seized power. Internationally, he got into a fierce debate with the Soviet Union, and domestically, he was convinced of the existence of "two headquarters" and he criticized the eight-grade wage system, which later led him to the theory of continuing the revolution under the dictatorship of the proletariat. Nevertheless, we still believed he was a man of great insight that stood at a commanding height above us all, directing the Chinese revolution. So we tried our best to keep abreast of him ideologically. In those days, we never doubted him for a moment.

In all honesty, I was aware of the purpose of the Cultural Revolution from quite early on. I knew that it was not simply aimed at school Party committees and Party branch secretaries. It could not be. Each of Mao's speeches was directed at senior Party members. He believed there were forces opposing him, which were the target for continuing the revolution under the proletarian dictatorship. He later labeled them as "capitalist roaders". On September 13, 1966, *Red Flag* magazine proposed that the people should "overthrow capitalist roaders".[32] Also, Liu Shaoqi was demoted from second in the Party leadership to seventh, and the Standing Committee of the Political Bureau expanded from seven to eleven. All these events were unusual. Having witnessed these things, it was difficult to believe that the whole thing was just about school Party committees and branch secretaries, or that it was just a struggle in the areas of culture and education.

This was the basic context to the emergence of the Xicheng District Picket Corps. We were called the "protect-Mom-and-Dad faction" because people thought we opposed the mass movement and were trying to block the revolution to protect our parents, who were being targeted. But who was the revolution directed at? At first it was directed against a small number of problem Party cadres, but it quickly spread to being directed at the whole of the Party's backbone — the entire corps of officials.

It was inevitable for Mao to adopt such measures during the Cultural Revolution. He had to do things that way to resolve the problems he faced within the Party. He could have just called a meeting or convened a Plenary Session of the Central Committee to voice his opinions, but he had to carry out the movement the way he did. As it was a revolution continued under the proletarian dictatorship, it had to

32 The term "capitalist roaders" was first used in January 1965 in *Some Problems Raised Recently Regarding the Socialist Education Movement* (also known as Article 23) and later seen in the *Notice of the Central Committee of the Communist Party of China* published on May 16, 1966, but it did not draw widespread attention until it appeared in *Red Flag* magazine on September 13, 1966.

be a violent one in which he lived and his enemies died. This is what led to large-scale struggles and even violence between the masses. Society descended into chaos and all control was lost. That was beyond Mao's expectation. So at that point he tried to recover the situation by calling in the military to take control. At that point, we still believed wholeheartedly in him.

Later on, we were sent to work in the countryside. After the "Seven Thousand Cadres Conference"[33] in 1962, the system of people's communes was adjusted to consist of "three levels of ownership with production teams as the cornerstone". Things were constantly being adjusted to fit with the local realities in rural areas. While in the countryside we also encountered some of the specific problems people faced, but we could only study or investigate specific issues one at a time. We did not study the rural system as a whole. We did not doubt Mao's authority or veracity. We were far from the point of doubting him.

Moreover, we did not allow Mao's targeting of us as individuals or our families during the Cultural Revolution to affect our view of him or our belief in his theories. Those things were separated in our minds, just as we separated Mao from Jiang Qing and the Cultural Revolution Group. It was not just me that thought like this. I know a lot of old cadres who thought the same way, and it was something that kept them going during the Cultural Revolution. People saw Jiang Qing and Mao as two separate people. In times of crisis, we looked for Mao, not Jiang. Nobody was looking for Jiang to save them. Although I resented the Cultural Revolution at times, I never wavered from my fundamental belief in Chairman Mao.

Jiang Qing was another matter. In our minds, Jiang never truly gained our respect. Her conduct and her arbitrary and emotional actions meant I had direct antipathy towards her. When she read out my parents'

33 Held from January 11 to February 7, 1962, the Seven Thousand Cadres Conference was called as such due to the number of attendees. The conference was held during the post-Great Leap Forward reform process and was notable for repudiating the Great Leap Forward and implementing policy proposals drawn up the previous year.

names at that meeting at the Workers' Stadium on December 16, 1966, it led directly to the breakup of my family. One sentence from her had the power to destroy us. Did my mother deserve to be punished like that? Did my father deserve to be treated like that? From the bottom of my heart, I do not believe they did. People put Mao up on a pedestal and treated him like a god. Was Jiang just carrying out his wishes or acting in accordance with his policies? At least Mao gave some instructions on cadre policies and said there should be way out for them. He also said we children of capitalist roaders can be reformed through education. But Jiang only gave my mother one way out — the dead end, which was the same for the rest of my family. I still think that Jiang was a unique character in the Chinese history.

It was the same for all the other members of the Cultural Revolution Group. We resisted them, especially during the period of the Xicheng District Picket Corps. The Capital Red Guards Joint Action Committee also directly resisted them. I was in prison at that time, so it's hard to say whether or not I would have got involved with the Joint Action Committee, but there is a good chance people would have asked me to get involved because of my influence among the students.

From the start, Lin Biao had a very obvious role as the deputy commander-in-chief next to Mao, but his behavior aroused people's suspicions. Why did Wang Jun offer us money for the newspaper if we would write articles that opposed Lin? It was because he understood our views on Lin from things we had said in the past. When I was rearrested in 1967, my greatest concern was things we had said about Jiang Qing, and then things we had said about Lin Biao. I think it is more accurate to say that we were unsure about Lin at that time, and were not convinced by him. We directly opposed Jiang, so there was a difference between the two.

As for Premier Zhou Enlai, he was simply our beacon of hope. Through all the crises and huge problems we encountered, Zhou gave hope to me and a large number of people. We believed that if we could speak to Zhou and get his attention, then one would have the attention of Mao himself. During his speech at the Great Hall of the People that day, Zhou told us that he was releasing us because Chairman Mao had said we should be released to continue our revolution. He even took responsibility for the mistakes that we had made. He was taking responsibility for not educating us correctly. We were deeply moved by that.

Some senior cadres later criticized Premier Zhou's methods during the Cultural Revolution. In my view, one can understand why he did the things he did. Some claimed that if it had not been for Zhou, senior cadres would have had a worse time of it during the Cultural Revolution, and it would have only lasted between three and five years before it collapsed. I believed Zhou should be treated justly, because he did a lot to protect the senior cadres. A lot of people like my father were under his guardianship. If they had not been and were left to fend for themselves, they simply would have been attacked by rebel groups, and it is likely that many of them would have died.

Kang Sheng was a very capable person. He made some contributions to the history of the Communist Party of China, especially in the area of intelligence work. He also played a very significant role in establishing Mao in a position of authority during the Seventh Congress of the CPC. He always came to Mao's aid when he was mostly needed.

During the course of the Cultural Revolution, a number of powerful politicians who had been well regarded were pulled into the sphere of the Gang of Four. Xie Fuzhi was a classic example of this.

During that time Liu Shaoqi and Deng Xiaoping were considered by Mao to be the architects of the forces that opposed him. I met Liu when I was young, and I have a lot of respect for him. In addition to Mao's works, I often read Liu's *How to be a Good Communist*. When I joined the Party, I wanted to be an obedient tool of the Party. I later decided that I wanted to be an enthusiastic and obedient tool of the Party because I felt that it was important to also have some initiative. *How to be a Good Communist* had a huge influence on my way of thinking by instilling in me an interest in the works of Confucius and Mencius and teaching me the importance of the principles of cultivating one's moral character, putting one's house in order, running the country well and letting peace prevail on earth.

When I was imprisoned by the school and brought out for public criticism, the whole audience was shouting "Down with Liu Shaoqi!", but I did not raise my arm and shout it with them. Afterwards I was asked why I did not join in. I explained that I thought we should only shout it if the Central Committee said we should. They had not issued any orders condemning Liu Shaoqi and he was still a member of the Standing Committee, so we should not shout slogans like that. That was how I viewed things. I was not going to join in just because they were struggling against me. I later wondered maybe it was also because I respected Comrade Shaoqi.

For those who experienced the Cultural Revolution, especially those who played an active part at various stages, it is important to reflect on the events of that time. I once said to Deng Pufang (Deng Xiaoping's son), "Without the Cultural Revolution, there would not have been Reform and Opening Up." He immediately said that that is how his father felt. I was very gratified to know that our great leader Deng Xiaoping saw things the same way as me, an ordinary Party member. In a certain sense, the logic of history involves regeneration and things going from bad to good. If China had not experienced a century of suppression to the point that it was left poor and weak, then there would not have been a national revival movement. If it had not experienced this pain and disillusionment, history and the people would not have chosen the Communist Party of China. If not for the fact that 95 percent of the Red area and almost 100 percent of the White area were lost during the leftist line, then Mao's correct line would not have been established. If not for the decade-long catastrophe of the Cultural Revolution that so impacted the high-level leadership and the masses, then the country would not have reverted to the ideological line of seeking truth from facts from which it had so greatly deviated, Deng Xiaoping would not have come up with and promoted the policy of Reform and Opening Up, China would not be the way it is today and it would not have the future it will have tomorrow. If the Cultural Revolution had not taken place, we would not be as adept at abandoning misguided ideological, political, economic and cultural doctrines and ideas. That is how history transformed an unprecedented national disaster into a great national revival.

Skipping Undergraduate Studies

After the Gang of Four had been toppled, a wave of condemnation of the Cultural Revolution surged forth from the people and the Party Central Committee, but Hua Guofeng (Chairman of the Central Committee), failing to grasp the sentiment of the people and this historic shift, still insisted on promoting his "Two Whatevers" policy,[34] which stood in stark contrast to the ideological emancipation that subsequently took place.

During the putsch against the Gang of Four, Geng Biao was in charge of China Central Television and other forms of mass media. At the end of 1976, Geng was ordered to resurrect the Propaganda Department of the CPC Central Committee. Other members of the department included Zhu Muzhi from Xinhua News Agency, Hu Jiwei from *People's Daily*, Deputy Director of the General of the CPC Central Committee Li Xin, and General Editor of *Red Flag* magazine Wang Shu. Being short of suitable staff following the overthrow of the Gang of Four, the department was looking for politically reliable young people. Geng therefore contacted me through his son Geng Zhiyuan, who had been a classmate of mine, and asked me to go and work for him. I had never directly spoken to Geng Biao before, so I was surprised to be invited, but I agreed and was transferred from the Institute of Economic Research to the propaganda office where I was made a secretary. I worked there from January 1977 until the summer of 1978 when I sat the entrance examination for postgraduate students. The office was located in Building 17 at Diaoyutai, which was the largest

34 Refers to the statement, "We will resolutely uphold whatever policy decisions Chairman Mao made, and unswervingly follow whatever instructions Chairman Mao gave".(Study the Documents Well and Grasp the Key Link, *People's Daily*, published on February 7, 1977)

building there.

It is my impression that the Propaganda Office tightly controlled public opinion through the *People's Daily*, *Red Flag* magazine and important messages from Xinhua News Agency. Our office held meetings with them to convey instructions. During my time there, I continued to reflect on the Cultural Revolution. We had previously tried to understand positively the theoretical system and practices of continuing the revolution under the dictatorship of the proletariat. But now that the political situation had been completely reversed, how were we going to view this theory? In the eyes of the Propaganda Office, the main task was to control or prevent criticism of Chairman Mao and uphold the "Two Whatevers". This was very clear from the files of the Propaganda Office.

Geng was later made Secretary-General of the Standing Committee of the Central Military Commission, but I was not asked to go with him as his secretary. By that time the Central Propaganda Department had been restored, and I continued to work there. The former Party Secretary of Hunan Province, Zhang Pinghua took over as Minister, and I regularly escorted him on business trips.

An important event occurred in 1977 changed the fate of many people and even the development direction of Chinese society. That was the restoration of the National College Entrance Examination. It was a turning point in history. Despite the fact that my class at No. 4 High School and Grade Three students at the No.1 High School for Girls had been the ones who advocated its abolition, I was extremely disappointed when it happened. I felt like a hero with no place to display his prowess. I had spent ten years honing my skills and was sure that I would get into any university I wanted. After the examination was reintroduced, I thought about sitting it. Unfortunately, all my time was taken up by my work that year, so I missed my first opportunity to take the examination. The next year, as I was studying for the examination, I was approached by a famous economist from the Institute of Economic Research, Wu Jinglian. He told me that he was going to recruit his first batch of graduate students, and asked if I would like to sit the examination. He explained, however, that he would be unable to help me prepare for the examination. I would be on my own.

One might ask why Wu was interested in me. I supposed it was because he knew who I was as I had worked at the Institute of Economic Research. While working there, I had attended a number of small seminars and discussions on economic theory. Other people who attended these events were economists and researchers, whereas I was just a librarian. I knew my place among them, so I just sat in the corner of the room. But it did not stop me from expressing my opinions on certain occasions. I do not remember exactly what I said during any of the discussions, but I must have made an impression on Wu. He mentioned to others that he thought I had the ability to think theoretically and was smart. That was how I managed to skip undergraduate studies and sit the postgraduate entrance examination.

I worked during the day, and stayed in the office to prepare for the examination at night. There were five examinations on *Das Kapital*, political economy, politics, foreign language, and Western economics. *Das Kapital* is an obscure book that contains a lot of Hegelian philosophy. Fortunately, I had read Hegel before; otherwise I would not have been able to grasp it so quickly. I only slept for three or hours each night back then.

I sat the examination in July 1978. That was the first year graduate students were admitted after the reintroduction of the National College Entrance Examination. Unfortunately, I pushed myself too hard and let myself get too rundown, so I had a stomach ache every day. I used to dig my elbow into my stomach, so I could carry on studying and working. Soon after I had sat the examination, I was working in the office at Diaoyutai, when I suddenly collapsed on the floor in pain. My colleague immediately arranged for a car to take me to Fuxing hospital, which was the nearest. The doctor there diagnosed me with duodenal perforation, which is when the abdominal cavity floods with stomach acid, so he began preparing for a surgery. My abdomen felt like being cut open with a knife, and by the time I got to the hospital I was completely unable to speak. I wrote down my father's phone number, so that they could ring him and let him know what was happening. He arrived and immediately called one of China's top specialists, Dr. Wu Weiran. Dr. Wu asked me if it had happened before or after I had eaten. I told him that I had not eaten, and he was relieved slightly because it meant there was not too much food in my stomach except acid. He tapped on my stomach and told me it was hard, because the muscles were tense. He suggested trying a conservative therapy first and only resorting to surgery if it did not work.

The hospital was ready to perform surgery, because a duodenal perforation can be lethal if not treated properly. While I was in northern Shaanxi somebody suffered from the same thing and died because they were not treated in time. But Dr. Wu was an expert, so when he suggested conservative treatment I listened to him. I had secretly been hoping that I would not need surgery. Although the examination results had not yet been published, I was confident that I would soon be attending interviews. Before that, however, I would need to have a physical examination like all the other candidates. If I needed a surgery, I would not pass the physical examination needed to get into the graduate program. Nowadays, the physical examinations before entrance are not that strict, but back then, you could not be accepted if you failed.

Dr. Wu said that the conservative treatment would take six or seven days, and I told him I would be able to take it. He then inserted a tube in my stomach, which he used to remove yellow-green digestive juices each day. I am a fairly hardy guy. I had managed to live in the village without drugs or a doctor, so I was confident I would be able to stick it out for the week until the perforation healed. To this day, I have still never gone under the knife. People used to say that this meant no air had escaped from one's body.

Three hundred students sat the examination to become Wu Jinglian's graduate students. A student called Shen Shuigen scored the highest mark. I had the second highest mark. We were interviewed and Professor Wu picked the two of us as his graduate students. I later found out that I almost failed because I only scored 61 on politics. I found it hard to believe I had scored so poorly. To tell the truth though, I had been so confident of passing it that I had not bothered preparing. In the end, I had lost points for getting certain wording and dates wrong. If I had scored just two points less I would have been disqualified, which would have been a disgrace to the Propaganda Department. I had been expecting to struggle with the English paper, and the translation section was indeed very difficult, but I still scored 80.

The Dean of the Graduate School of the Chinese Academy of Social Sciences at the time was Wen Jize, who had previously worked in news media. The Graduate School was still without a home, so we lived in dormitories on the campus of Beijing Normal University, four in one room. Professor Wu lived on the same campus, which meant we could seek him out to ask questions whenever we needed to. After I was admitted, a number of my old classmates decided to give it a try too. The next year, Ma Kai was accepted onto an economics graduate program at Renmin University, and Li Sanyou was accepted to study law. In the following year, Qin Xiao went to the Mining Institute to study economic management. That reflects the mentality of people who studied at No. 4 High School. If you work hard, I am going to work hard. If you are successful, I am going to be successful too. We inspire each other, and everyone wants to be the best.

1978 was another unfortunate year for my family. That year my 45-year-old half-brother, Chen Mo, died at home suddenly from a myocardial infarction. My family's living situation had only just improved before he passed away, as we had moved into a large courtyard home with PLA general Wu Xiuquan. My father lived in the building in front of the courtyard, and my half-brother lived in the building at the back. That was where he fell ill. He had been a Navy captain before the Cultural Revolution, and had worked on nuclear submarines. He had high blood pressure from an early age. At a denunciation meeting during the Cultural Revolution, he had been standing on a chair when somebody kicked it out from under him. He hit the ground hard. That was the root cause of his illness. When he passed away we were all very upset. He left behind a wife of only 40, and a son of 10, and a daughter of 8. Despite his grief my father turned to me and said, "Several members of Li Jingquan's family died during the Cultural Revolution. Our family lost only two. Compared to them, we faired quite well." At first I wondered how he could say such a thing, but then I realized he was simply trying to comfort himself. It was heartbreaking. I then thought of Li Jingquan's son, Li Mingqing, whom I had been imprisoned with. He had a very round face and was very kind. He had been released before me, so I had asked him to deliver a message to my younger brother. He agreed and said he hoped I would be released soon. I learned soon afterwards that he had been beaten to death by a rebel faction of the Beijing Aviation Institute Red Guards. Similar to my mother, his mother, Xiao Li, also committed suicide.

Another major event in that year was the Third Plenary Session of the Eleventh CPC Central Committee. After I went off to the countryside, I took a large step back from social and political life as I did not have the opportunity to participate, and was not sure of what was going on behind the scenes. When I read memoirs or articles about struggles within the Party at that time, I realized that there were a lot of things I did not know. At that time, I knew little except Lin Biao's death, various campaigns to criticize Zhou Enlai and Deng Xiaoping, as well as Mao's directives. After I went to work for the Propaganda Office, I began paying close attention to political life again. But this had been interrupted once more, as I started the graduate program. However, being based in Beijing and studying political economy meant that I was close to the ideological struggles taking place within the Central Committee.

Just before the Third Plenary Session of the Eleventh CPC Central Committee, my father was asked to prepare a speech, and he asked me to help him write it. An ideological storm was blowing through the Party in an attempt to completely expunge any remnants of the Cultural Revolution. There was a lot of resistance from some individuals, however. The Plenary Session was therefore being convened as part of a coordinated attack on the "Two Whatevers" and to echo Deng Xiaoping's call to liberate people's minds. My father had been an alternate member of the Sixth CPC Central Committee and deputy head of the rear delegation. Ye Jianying was head of the rear delegation. My father had been an alternate member of the Eighth CPC Central Committee, but was in prison for the Ninth and Tenth CPC Central Committees. He was then made a member of the Eleventh CPC Central Committee. At the Third Plenary Session, he was asked to give a weighty speech that echoed the main points of the meeting.

Having been persecuted by the Gang of Four, my father and others like him had a deep-seated hatred for the ultra-leftist political and ideological line that prevailed during the Cultural Revolution. Similar to the people of the nation, our family suffered in that period and reflected deeply on the events of that time. The more one tries seriously rather than perfunctorily to understand Mao's theory of continuing the revolution under the proletarian dictatorship, which was a development of the traditional theory of class struggle, the more one keenly feels the importance of profoundly criticizing it. After the Cultural Revolution, my father devoted a great deal of thought to what had happened, and I could see the changes and progress his generation made. Both my father and I were strong supporters of greater ideological freedom and of Comrade Deng Xiaoping. This made it easier to help him with his speech. After the meeting, Chen Pixian (Secretary of the Hubei Party Committee) asked me who had written the speech. I told him I had helped my father write it. He replied that it did not seem like my father had written it himself, because it was so systematic.

My graduate studies took place at a time when people's thinking was becoming more liberal. I was studying economics, and although Western economics was very much our point of academic reference, the concept of reform had begun to enter our minds. This major turning point was the result of Deng Xiaoping's ideological line of "seeking truth from facts".

I was one of Professor Wu's first students, and he always had a high opinion of me. I thought I was the favorite of his first two students. It was Professor Wu who helped me decide on my research topic and research area. He told me about comparative research, and suggested that I look into it because my English was quite good. I gladly accepted. CITIC Group currently published a magazine called *Comparison*, which compares economic systems and research on economic development. My particular area of research was economic systems. This was a specialist subject, and nobody in China was doing it at that time. I read a lot of literature in English, including the works of a number of reformist writers and scholars, such as the Czech reform economist Ota Sik and Polish economist Włodzimierz Brus. It is no exaggeration to say that I was one of the pioneers of research into comparative economic systems in China, along with the likes of Zhao Renwei and Rong Jingben. In accordance of my research area, the title of my thesis was "A Preliminary Study of Socialist Economic Models".

In my thesis, I highlighted the relationship between the plan and the market, and proposed a system of mixed ownership. My thesis contained some original ideas, and I was asked to reduce the article from 60,000 words to 10,000, so that it could be published in an influential Chinese journal called *Economic Research*. However, just before it was due to be published, a number of people high up in the Party expressed views that ran contrary to my ideas. Editors at *Economic Research* felt that my thesis was too market-oriented, which did not fit with the views of the CPC Central Committee, so it was not published. If it had been published, I may have continued on the path of theoretical research and become an economist. The opportunity was there, but the timing was not right.

Worked as Zhang Jinfu's Secretary

I graduated with a Master's degree in economics in 1981, and was assigned to work at the Institute of Economic Research as an assistant researcher. And my salary rose from 38 to 62 yuan per month. After I graduated, Professor Wu was keen for me to study abroad. At the time, the Ford Foundation provided a grant each year for a group of Chinese scholars to study in the US, which included US $8,000 for living expenses. A number of us were therefore sent to the Beijing International Studies University for intensive English learning. I was honored to be among a group of scholars, including Dong Fureng (deputy director of the Graduate School of the Chinese Academy of Social Sciences), Wu Jinglian and Liu Guogang (deputy director-general of the National Bureau of Statistics). We were all there to improve our English, and we lived together in one dormitory. Regardless of the differences in their theoretical perspectives, they were all top Chinese economists.

This time, however, a transfer order appointing me as a secretary arrived. In 1982, Zhang Jinfu received orders to establish a National Economic Commission on the foundations of five existing ministries, which would be responsible for running the entire national economy. Zhang had been the Minister of Finance during the latter period of the Cultural Revolution. I had met with and spoken to him a number of times. He was very interested in the views of young people, and he had taken a particular interest in me. While setting up the National Economic Commission, he had decided he needed another secretary like me. He was looking for somebody who could help him communicate with the young people, so I was approached about the job.

When I was first asked, I felt conflicted. I had already decided that I wanted a career in the field of economic theory, and was confident that I was capable of some meaningful research. This made me hesitate. After a while, Zhang Jinfu asked me to meet him for a chat. He told me that it was a good opportunity because, although I was involved in theoretical research, the point of it was to solve practical problems, and the job would give me the experience of practical situations, and expose me to all aspects of state affairs and people from various fields. He also explained that he wanted me to help him communicate with young people. Afterwards I discussed the matter with Professor Wu. He told me that it would be good for me, as I would have direct dealings with social economic reform and could understand the relationship between planning and the market in practice, which would be helpful when I returned to work on the theoretical front. After speaking to them both I decided to accept the job. It seemed I was predestined to work as a secretary. Things had not worked out when I wanted to become a secretary for Wang Zhen or Geng Biao, but this time I would work for Zhang Jinfu instead.

People have a lot of choices to make during their life. We may choose to head in one direction for a time and later in another. But when one reaches a crossroads, one rarely has the chance to go back to the point where the road splits. That is one reason I greatly admire my old classmate Qin Xiao. While working as director of a large state-owned enterprise, he took time off to study at Cambridge University, and eventually earned a PhD in economics in five years between two congresses of party representatives. In a sense, he really did return to the theoretical front.

I, on the other hand, have continued along the road I chose back then. I worked with Zhang Jinfu for a short time, from June 1982 to September 1984. During that time, I had dealt with many areas of economic work, mainly through reading and preparing large amounts of information, attending meetings and carrying out visits. I traveled all over the country, and visited the No. 2 Automobile Factory in Hubei Province in Central China, rode in a helicopter to inspect the forestry industry in Northeast China, and visited many other industries and enterprises.

I have stayed in close contact with a number of people of my generation that I met during the 1980s. It was a period that produced young elites as well as a period of active thinking. A lot of people look back fondly on that time. The Rural Policy Research Department contained many well-known figures, including Weng Yongxi, Wang Qishan, Huang Jiangnan and Zhu Jiaming, who were collectively known as the "four men with noble character". When we met up, we discussed every aspect of China's economy, as the Central Committee was exploring market-oriented reform in both theory and practice at the time. In terms of price reform, overcoming major existing obstacles within the system became one of the priorities for the central government. It was my impression that CPC Vice-Chairman Chen Yun placed greater emphasis on the role of planning and thought that the market should operate within the cage of planning. He was also relatively cautious when it came to price reform. The head of the Leading Group for Financial and Economic Affairs was Zhao Ziyang. He was also in charge of the Leading Group on Price Reform, of which Zhang Jinfu was the deputy leader. My role in Zhang's work was to use my contacts to introduce him to young scholars with new ideas and theories. The meeting at Mogan Mountain was an important event in this regard.[35] In the summer of 1984, I accompanied Zhang to Hangzhou, together with Zhao Ziyang's secretary, my old schoolmate Li Xianglu.

It came about because I told Zhang that a group of young people were meeting at Mogan Mountain to discuss issues related to price reform. I suggested that I should go and listen to their ideas to see if any of it would be valuable or beneficial to our work. Zhang agreed so I suggested I take Li Xiangyu with me given that he worked for Zhao

35 The Mogan Mountain Meeting took place on September 3-10, 1984, at Mogan Mountain in Deqing County, Zhejiang Province. This national seminar, which was the first of its kind for young economists, was attended by more than 100 people. It was later referred as a seminal event in the history of economic thought reform, and it was the first time the collective voice of young economic workers was heard. The meeting not only brought a new group of economists to the fore, but also contributed important ideas to the reforms of the 1980s, which the CPC Central Committee sat up and took notice.

Ziyang, and Zhang was doing this work on price reform for Zhao. After Zhang agreed, Li and I went to Mogan Mountain.

We barely slept that day at Mogan Mountain. As soon as we got there we found a room and started the meeting. At the meeting, there were Wang Qishan,[36] Chen Yizi,[37] Zhang Gang[38] and Huang Jiangnan.[39] My initial impression of Chen Yizi was that he was slightly manic and not very rational at times. He did not give me a good impression. Wang Qishan took more than just a theoretical approach, and he consistently demonstrated to me a strong ability for a government advisory or decision-making role. After our discussion, I suggested they set out their ideas in a document for me. I told them that, if possible, I would then arrange a meeting in Hangzhou between them and Zhang Jinfu. They quickly drafted a document which I took with me and left. In total, I had spent just one day at Mogan Mountain.

In these days, I hear a lot of people debating who invented or first suggested the concept of the dual-track pricing system and whether price reform should have been completed in one step or using the dual-track system. At the time, my main concern was to integrate the ideas and results of this research with social realities by getting Zhang to promote them. In truth, I was not heavily involved in core discussions on this issue. I felt that it was up to Zhang to decide whether there was any real value in it.

I handed the document to Zhang, and he read it carefully. Afterwards he said he would meet with the young economists. I cannot remember now who exactly was invited. I remembered Lou Jiwei,[40]

---

36 Wang Qishan went on to become Mayor of Beijing and is currently (since 2014) a member of the seven-man Politburo Standing Committee.

37 Chen Yizi later became a well-regarded academic and was, at one time, the head of the China Society of Economic Reform.

38 Zhang Gang later opted to work in the private sector and (since 2014) is the CEO of one of China's largest chain restaurants.

39 Huang Jiangnan received his Master's degree in applied economics from the Chinese Academy of Social Sciences in 1981, and later moved to the United States where he enjoyed a successful career in business.

40 Lou Jiwei was director of the Institute of Finance and Trade of the Chinese Academy of Social Sciences at the time and (since 2014) is currently the Minister of Finance.

Xu Jingan, Zhang Gang, Hua Sheng[41] and Huang Jiangnan there, while Ma Kai and Wang Qishan were absent. The economists have all expressed their views during the meeting. Thinking about it now, it seems to me that some of them have exaggerated the importance of the meeting at Mogan Mountain. Those students and scholars were not the only promoters of price reform. It was already on the agenda as part of China's market-oriented economic reform and development. As far as I know, the head of the Price Bureau, Cheng Zhiping, had been researching this issue and was trying to decide whether it should be done in one fell swoop or split into two steps. A variety of ideas were being discussed, with the advantages of each being weighed against its disadvantages. It seemed to me that Zhang was also listening to the views of Chen Yun on the matter, as Chen Yun held a lot of sway within the Party.

After the summary of the meeting in Hangzhou were released, Zhang issued instructions stating that he thought the views expressed were valuable and they should be sent to Zhao Ziyang. Zhao wrote some comments in approval, but I did not locate the document. People nowadays attribute the comments to the leader of the State Council, but they were actually the comments of Premier Zhao and Zhang Jinfu regarding price reform. They are important suggestions for continuing to promote reform. In reality, reform is not the individual idea of one person, but rather the natural historical process of a state and of a nation at a particular stage when all conditions are met at every level.

In my opinion, allowing scholars and students to communicate directly and express their opinions to those at the heart of the decision-making process on reform was taken to an unprecedented level at that time. Despite having left the circle of theorists, I still played a communicative and promotional role that involved liaising between different parties. The meeting at Mogan Mountain served to strengthen the confidence of the Central Committee in the policy of price reform.

---

41 Hua Sheng was studying for a Master's degree at the Graduate School of the Chinese Academy of Social Sciences at the time, and is currently a renowned economist.

Considering that liberalizing prices all at once would be too great a shock for society, the more prudent system of dual-track pricing was eventually adopted, whereby some prices would be liberalized first. In one respect, then, the meeting provided a theoretical contribution, as the views of the young scholars were taken on board. Another important outcome of the meeting was that the people who attended it received greater attention, and they each went on to be successful in their respective careers. This was a very important outcome. Among them was Ma Kai, whose research was on price reform.

I later saw a collection of works about that time. Apart from some recollections of Zhu Jiaming about me and Li Xiangyu, I found it interesting because everybody seemed to be seeking recognition for certain ideas. Luckily, I am not the sort of person who gets jealous. My role was that of a go-between. All the people involved were far more accomplished than me. I merely passed on any ideas that I thought were useful. That was something positive I did at that critical time of reform to promote decision making between the government and members of the public in my capacity as secretary. Integrating advanced research results with the realities of Zhang's work was precisely the role he had hoped I would play.

In 1984, while still working as secretary for Zhang, I was asked by Chen Yun to establish a study group made up of Zhu Jiamu[42], Xu Yongyue[43], Chen Yuan[44], Ren Xiaobin and me. We were to study classical Marxist works, with the list of books chosen by Chen Yun from among the 30 original works on the Party's reading list. Chen Yun asked us to read the books, take notes and discuss them once in a week. He used it as a way of encouraging us to temper each other, straighten out our thinking, and strengthen our Party spirit.

42 Zhu Jiamu is currently Vice President of the Chinese Academy of Social Sciences.

43 Xu Yongyue was Chen Yun's secretary at the time, and went on to become the Minister of State Security.

44 Chen Yuan graduated with a Master's degree from the Postgraduate Research Institute of the Chinese Academy of Social Sciences, and later served as governor of the China Development Bank.

The Purge of "The Three Kinds of People"

In 1979, I wrote an article about the Xicheng District Picket Corps. Yang Shangkun was interested in the matter at the time, so we discussed it, and I wrote the article at his request, which was later published in Volume 1107 of *Compilation of State of Affairs*, the internal reference of *People's Daily*. It was not written as a historical textual criticism, and did not focus on any details. Rather, it described the general background that led to the establishment of the Picket Corps. It contained some analysis of what happened during the early stages of the Cultural Revolution, and some of the things we did as part of the Picket Corps. The article reflected my thoughts in 1979, and provided the basis for a public rehabilitation of the Picket Corps.

In 1984, the central government decided to consolidate the Party by purging "the three kinds of people",[45] which meant those who had ties with radical factions during the Cultural Revolution. I remembered my father returned home one day, and told me the central government's decision. He was very happy, even excited. He explained that the people who had turned on us during the Cultural Revolution would be exposed and purged, and we shall never let them hiding in our team. I asked him to tell me everything about the meeting that had reached the decision. Then I knew I was in trouble. I asked him how he could be so naïve and explained that, according to what he had just told me, the spearhead of the attack would be aimed at people like me. He said I was being

---

45 The three types were as follows: first, rebels who "had seized political power 'in rebellion,' rose to high positions and committed evils with serious consequences"; second, people who were "factionalists in their ideas," namely those guilty of vigorous propagation of radical ideology, factional ties with Lin Biao and the Gang of Four, and continuation of factional activities after the fall of the Gang; third, anyone who "had indulged in beating, smashing and looting".

ridiculous, because I had been persecuted as well. But I explained that based on their plan of targeting Red Guards involved from the start of the Cultural Revolution, including high school students, it was not ridiculous to assume I would be a target. I said I could understand why senior cadres were keen to deal with people that persecuted them during that time, but using the expression "three kinds of people" ran the risk of purging some people who did not deserve to be purged. My father assumed I was being overly concerned. But I believed my concerns were justified and knew that it was likely for me to run into problems.

The document that was produced as a result of the Central Committee meeting stated that an investigation was to be held to determine who was to be included in "the three kinds of people". As expected, people were quickly rounded up for investigation by the army. Leaders of rebel groups, such as Kuai Dafu and Han Aijing, heads of the Tsinghua University Red Guards, such as He Pengfei and Qiao Zonghuai, and those in charge of the Xicheng District Picket Corps and the Capital Red Guards Joint Action Committee were investigated, and people across the country in a variety of positions began experiencing problems.

At that critical moment, I decided to write a letter to the CPC Central Committee. Given that the letter was related to a major policy issue, it did not seem appropriate that it should only carry my name. As such, I discussed the matter with Ma Kai and Qin Xiao and asked if they would be willing to sign their names on the letter. After consideration, they felt it would not be appropriate given their positions as deputy chief of Xicheng District and Song Renqiong's secretary respectively. I then asked my old schoolmate Dong Zhixiong, the son of a well-known translator Dong Qiusi. I told him I wanted to inform the Central Committee that the boundaries of this policy were ill-defined and asked if he would be a cosignatory. He told me that he had complete faith in me, and duly agreed to sign the letter without reading it.

I addressed the letter to Chen Yun. In general terms, the letter stated that a purge of the "three kinds of people" was necessary, but distinctions needed to be drawn. Then I talked about my views on

Red Guards as a former Red Guard. I told him that the original Red Guards had committed leftist errors, such as the Destroy the Four Olds campaign during the early stages of the Cultural Revolution, but most were general errors, and we had later struggled against the Gang of Four when we realized what they were doing. I told him that serious cases, such as people who committed murder, should be dealt with accordingly, but they should not be talked about in the same breath as "the three kinds of people". I explained that if no distinction was made between the Red Guards in the early stage and the rebel groups that were set up later, then there was a significant risk that some innocent people would become targets of the purge.

Chen Yun issued a statement on February 27, 1984, the details of which are included in his chronological biography. He had very clear views about this. The gist of his statement was that he agreed with me, and he wanted the relevant departments to look into it. He stated that some Red Guards did not belong to "the three kinds of people", with many also belonging to the "third echelon".[46] He concluded that a purge of the "three kinds of people" was a political struggle, and people should avoid muddying the waters. Chen forwarded his statement to the Politburo Standing Committee, and asked that it be forwarded to the Politburo, Secretariat, Central Party Consolidation Guidance Commission, and Central Organization Department. Later on, Hu Yaobang (General Secretary of the CPC) issued a statement agreeing with Chen's assessment, and asking Deng Xiaoping, Zhao Ziyang and Li Xiannian to read Chen's statement. At Hu Yaobang's request, Qiao Shi (head of the Organization Department) gathered all relevant statements into a Politburo document, and sent it to each member. Li Xiannian, Deng Xiaoping and Zhao Ziyang all supported Chen's statement.

The Central Committee later produced a specific policy document regarding the purge of "the three kinds of people", which was aimed at preventing everybody being treated in the same way. As there were differing views regarding to the purge, especially regarding to who

46 The term "third echelon" refers to third-generation leaders or potential leaders.

should be the target, I knew that the stakes were high, which was why I tried hard to stop the spotlight falling on me and those like me.

I believed we were a positive force during the Cultural Revolution, or rather there were some positive elements to us. But it is very clear that our entire mind-set was inclined towards the leftist political line. We naturally accepted those ideas, and we personally and willingly promoted them.

During that long period of turmoil, we were like two sides of a coin. On one side, we appeared socially responsible and rational; on the other side, we were inadvertently implementing the leftist Party line. These different sides were manifested under different circumstances. We began by opposing the school's Party committee, and later clashed with the rebel factions. But all these were related to our basic understanding of the Cultural Revolution. In 1975, we began to completely reject the Cultural Revolution, and condemn continuing the revolution under the dictatorship of the proletariat. However, our theoretical condemnation of the Cultural Revolution did not take place until Deng Xiaoping promoted ideological emancipation in 1978.

We made mistakes during the Cultural Revolution, and we should review those mistakes and reflect on them. But we should also be given a chance. There were fundamental differences between us and the rebels. I wrote that letter to prevent a group of people from receiving the undue punishment, which helped, and may even have saved some individuals. Nevertheless, writing that letter to Chen Yun came at a considerable personal price. I had already prepared myself for a backlash, but I had not imagined that the reaction would be so strong and so direct.

Despite the fact that Chen Yun and the Politburo Standing Committee agreed with my letter, things quickly changed. Other leaders stated that although I was not one of the "three kinds of people" I did not deserve to be part of the third echelon either.

When I heard that it hit me hard. That was the price I paid for putting my head above the parapet. My letter had come at a price and required sacrifice. For a long time afterwards, I had a heavy heart whenever I thought about it, and I was feeling very bitter. At the start of the Cultural Revolution, I was relatively conservative, or perhaps moderate. I was also relatively rational. But I was rational at a time when the whole society had succumbed to erroneous ideological trends. The tide of the Cultural Revolution swept me into the position that I then occupied, and I felt I had to protect people from house raids, from being beaten or even being killed, as well as to ensure people's property was not stolen and protect senior cadres from being attacked. We helped a lot of people in that way, but I paid a heavy price. I naturally came to Premier Zhou's attention, and he wanted to make use of me. This resulted in my mother becoming a channel between us and ultimately led to events unfolding in a way I never expected.

The things I did implicated my mother, and with just a few words from Jiang Qing, my father became embroiled as well. The Xicheng District Picket Corps could be said to be the fuse that led to my mother's suicide. There was no doubt about that. If it had not been for that, my mother probably would not have committed suicide, and there might be a chance that she would have survived the decade-long catastrophic Cultural Revolution. My father was mentally prepared for the Cultural Revolution. He knew it was just a matter of time before he became a target, though he did not think he would be imprisoned so soon. At that time, suicide was seen as a betrayal of the Party. Even the question of where to place people's ashes became a thorny issue. Every time my father and I discussed these things at home, we got very upset. Yet, my father never blamed me for what happened. But I have carried that feeling with me during my whole life. And occasionally, my father would say things like, "Well, had not been for the event... If your mother were alive today...."

I often feel a deep sense of remorse for what happened to my family. Looking back now, I thought that even if the Xicheng District Picket Corps had not existed, the other picket corps would still have. If it was not us, then it would have been somebody else. But the difference would have been that my family and I would not have been affected in the same way. I should have learned my lesson much earlier, but I still felt that I had to do what I thought was right. The result was that I come forward and exposed myself again.

Once more I had become a participant visible to those at the highest levels of political power. That was clear from the documents of the CPC Central Committee. Senior cadres as high up as the Politburo Standing Committee knew who I was, and they each had differing opinions of me, as one would expect. So, even though Chen Yun agreed with my letter and stated that I should be considered among the third echelon rather than "the three kinds of people", some people disagreed. They did not agree that I should be included in the third echelon and groomed for leadership. I stuck my head above the parapet again. I should have a clear understanding of this limitation of mine.

During the Cultural Revolution, many old cadres had problems with people they employed. Many secretaries of senior leaders had turned on or betrayed them at critical moments. As a result, they had learned to take greater care over their choice of staff. As son of a senior cardre, I was considered as trustworthy politically. That was why I was asked to work as secretary to Wang Zhen, Geng Biao and Zhang Jinfu. I was also later recommended as the secretary to Wan Li. At the time, Wan was an important reformer, and I knew him well because my father, my brother and I used to play bridge with him. I spent a lot of time among the older generation of leaders, and people generally thought of me as a promising youngster who was capable, humble, reliable and practical. They were therefore keen on choosing me as their secretary. However, secretary could only be a transitory job, so I faced another career choice at that moment.

My friends thought that I should seek a career in politics. They thought that I had the ability, the correct qualities and the right image. I felt that my abilities and willpower had been tempered by the Cultural Revolution, but I also thought I may have peaked too early. Though I was only on the political stage for one or two months, I was finding it extremely difficult to leave behind the problems it had brought me. After I wrote that letter to Chen Yun, I saw more and more clearly that my future lay outside officialdom.

Work for the Everbright Group

Zhang Jinfu was a State Councillor. In addition to his supervisory work, he was also in charge of the CITIC (China International Trust and Investment Corporation) Group and the China Everbright Group. He once lived together with Rong Yiren in a courtyard in Beijing, and the two of them were close. Rong set up the CITIC Group in 1979, and Wang Guangying set up the China Everbright Holding Company Limited in 1983. When Everbright was established, it received greater funding from the central government than CITIC did. It was given RMB 2 billion as well as US$ 200 million as working capital to import advanced technology and second-hand equipment from abroad. During that period of transition, a lot of things were driven by the Party leadership. Deng Xiaoping specifically entrusted Rong to set up CITIC, and it played a role the old system could not achieve.

I had spoken to both Rong and Wang before through my work, and I had made a good impression on both of them. As a result, Wang wrote to Zhang explaining that, having just set up Everbright, he was in need of talented people. He told him that he thought I was an outstanding young man who understood economic issues, and asked if he would consider allowing me to be transferred to his company. I therefore faced another choice in my career: whether or not to take the plunge into the "sea of commerce", as it was known back then.

I have been familiar with Wang Jun since I was young. We often played chess together, and around that time we would sometimes play through the night. We would start at seven in the evening and play until about five the next morning. He would then give me a lift home on his motorbike and I would cycle to Zhongnanhai to start my work. Wang had been involved in setting up CITIC, so when I told him I had been offered a job at Everbright he told me that I should work at CITIC instead. He said he would speak to Rong and find me a good position within the company. He asked what Everbright had offered me. I told him that they had offered to put me in charge of a department, and he offered to do the same. Wang Jun was the deputy general manager of CITIC's business department, so he sought out Rong to talk about my joining CITIC. Rong pointed out that Wang himself was only a deputy general manager and that I was still very young, so he suggested I be made an assistant manager in the business department. I was 37 years old at the time, and I was considered a young deputy section chief. The business department was CITIC's core department, so it was quite something for me to be offered a position as the department's assistant manager. Wang Jun came back and tried to persuade me to join, saying that they had various good opportunities for future development.

I told Zhan Jinfu about the job offers, but he was not keen for me to take either of them. He thought that with my political, theoretical and working experience I should work in the government. I then unexpectedly received another job offer. My old classmate Duan Cunli, the son of the Beijing Municipal Party Secretary Duan Junyi, told me that his father admired me and wanted me to work for the Beijing municipal government. He asked me about my rank and told me that they needed a deputy chief for Haidian District, saying that they were seeking to put young people in positions of importance.

Zhang Jinfu also told me about a vacant post for a deputy director of Shanghai Municipal Economic Commission. At that time, Chen Guodong was Party Secretary and Wang Daohan was the mayor in Shanghai. Both were old comrades from eastern China, and Zhang Jinfu knew them both well. Being introduced through him would have stood me in good stead for the job.

I had been offered some excellent opportunities in the goverment, but I still felt I was not the right person for politics. What was more, in the early 1980s, people's minds were active and the economy was in a period of exploration. CITIC and Everbright were new organizations seeking to explore and innovate. After much consideration, I decided

I wanted to work for a private enterprise. Both CITIC and Everbright had expressed an interest in me, so I now had to choose between them. Wang Jun wanted me to work for CITIC, while Wang Guangying's assistants, Li Xinshi and Liu Jifu, were trying to persuade me to go to Everbright. I felt that CITIC had more talented people than Everbright, and concluded that I would have more space to grow at Everbright. In September 1984, seeing that I had already made up my mind, Zhang Jinfu reluctantly agreed me to leave, so I went to work for Everbright.

After taking that first step, I was there for a long time before I moved again. I worked at Everbright for 16 years, and then at CITIC for 10 years. When I eventually moved to CITIC, Wang Jun joked that I had taken such a circuitous route to get there, and asked if I had not joined originally because they had not offered me enough. But I told him it had nothing to do with that.

Following the June 4th Incident in 1989, the Central Committee decided at a meeting in Beidaihe. For the five companies directly under the central government, they would only keep CITIC and dispose of the other four. We therefore wrote to Yao Yilin (Vice Premier) expressing our concerns. Everbright had already established many business contacts in Hong Kong, and we were worried that it would lead to social instability in Hong Kong if the company was sold or shut down. Wang Jun also joked at the time that I should have gone to CITIC, as Everbright faced the risk of being shut down. Fortunately, the Central Committee took on board our concerns and retained Everbright.

I had felt bad for Wang Jun after making my original decision, so I recommended my old classmate Qin Xiao. I told him that Qin had been with me during the Cultural Revolution and was more capable than me in many respects, especially in foreign language, as he had worked as deputy director of the Foreign Affairs Bureau. Wang took my recommendation seriously. Before long, Qin went to CITIC where he worked as Wang's assistant for a long time, until Wang was made company president and Qin became General Manager.

I like to do things for other people, and I often recommend people for having capabilities that exceed mine. I like to put people in touch with each other. I held Qin Xiao in high regard, which is why I recommended him to Wang Jun. I also recommended Ma Kai to Chen Yuan, who was then the Xicheng District Party Committee Secretary. Ma often tells me that he would not have a job in Xicheng District or been a politician without my recommendation. I just see that Ma has brought his abilities and expertise to bear on our nation's development. And he has always been an upright and sincere pragmatist.

16 Years at Everbright

I worked at Everbright from 1984 to 2000. My time there was eventful due to the company's ill fortune. Both CITIC and Everbright were unique in that they did not have a specific area of operations. The central government had not told them to work in a specific sector, so we used to say that we did anything that made money. As such, we were highly innovative. Wang Guangying, who had the backing of the central government, went to Hong Kong and made deals with some of the major players there, and under his leadership the company enjoyed a unique status.

From the start, CITIC and Everbright had very different ways of doing things. Both were established as ministerial-level institutions, but while CITIC's seal contained the national emblem, Everbright was only allowed to use a five-pointed star on the seal with the same size as that of CITIC. Nevertheless, when Everbright was established, the Central Committee document issued on the matter clearly stated that it was a ministerial-level agency. As I had been working in these two companies for a long time, so I could describe and compare them.

CITIC's business model reflected Rong Yiren's belief that it should not be run like other state-owned enterprises or companies overseen by ministries and commissions. Nevertheless, Rong was still a pragmatist. He knew it would be difficult to expand the company without government support. He therefore filled his board with leaders of ministries and commissions, including Zhu Rongji, and also employed a group of older business people. Wang Jun and the group of talented people he was in charge of were the backbone of business development at CITIC.

Wang Guangying took a different approach. He established

Everbright's headquarters in Hong Kong and employed a group of relatively young talents, including my friends Li Xinshi and Liu Jifu, both of whom played a crucial role in the company's development, and later myself as well. I did not really know Wang when I joined the company as they had convinced him to hire me. Before I started to work at Everbright, they sent me an application for importing second-hand equipment. They asked me to make changes to it, before it was handed in to the higher authorities, so I helped improve it slightly before submission. Bo Yibo was in charge of the Machinery Committee, so the application landed on his desk. He read the application and underlined some parts. When it came back, they saw what Bo had highlighted were all the parts that I had written. I explained that this was because I was familiar with the style of leadership reports and how to request things. Wang therefore decided to make use of my experience of working for the State Economic Commission and my connections with people in ministries and offices. It also helped that I knew Zhang Jinfu so well, given that he was directly in charge of overseeing both CITIC and Everbright. To play to my strengths, Wang also set up a coastal business department and put me in charge. He then arranged for the 14 coastal cities opened up to foreign investment by the State Council[47] to dispatch representatives to our headquarters in Hong Kong to provide business services of opening-up to their cities. These people were all later put in charge of organizations set up in Hong Kong by their respective cities.

The two CEOs, Wang and Rong, also had political roles. Rong was first of all appointed Vice-Chairman of the NPC Standing Committee, and later promoted to Vice President of the nation. Wang started off as the Vice-Chairman of the Chinese People's Consultative Conference and was later appointed Vice-Chairman of the NPC Standing Committee. A few years after Everbright was established, the Central Committee appointed the former deputy governor of the People's Bank of China, Qiu Qing, as Wang's successor. That was the start of a period

47 These cities include Dalian, Qinhuangdao, Tianjin, Yantai, Qingdao, Lianyungang, Nantong, Shanghai, Ningbo, Wenzhou, Fuzhou, Guangzhou, Zhanjiang and Beihai.

of strong links with the People's Bank, and Qiu was followed by two more deputy governors — Zhu Xiaohua and Liu Mingkang. The current company chairman, Tang Shuangning, was previously vice-chairman of the China Banking Regulatory Commission.

After the June 4th Incident in 1989, the five companies directly under the central government were reduced to two — CITIC and Everbright. It was also shortly after the June 4th Incident that Wang Guangying was replaced by Qiu Qing. After that, a number of section chiefs were transferred from the People's Bank to Everbright, including director of the State Administration of Foreign Exchange, Tang Gengyao, as well as Liu Jiyuan and Li Shucun. I got on very well with Qiu while she was in charge. She is a fine person, and I developed under her tutelage. In 1993, the Central Committee appointed Wang Xuebing and me as vice presidents of Everbright Group. Qiu had high expectations for the company's young talents, but Wang Xuebing was transferred to the Bank of China not long after.

CITIC stands for China International Trust and Investment Corporation. At that time, every province set up a trust and investment company as a financing platform. Everbright also set up Everbright International Trust and Investment Corporation, which was managed by Wang Yake, a former section chief at the State Administration of Foreign Exchange. In a relatively short period, he increased the company's investments from RMB 0.9 billion to 14 billion. However, his foreign exchange trading ran into problems, and he quickly lost US$ 40 million. Nowadays, US$ 40 million is not a lot to a large company, but it was a huge amount for us at the time. He then invested a considerable sum in an attempt to recoup his losses, but ended up losing another US$ 40 million. Around the same time, CITIC lost a considerable amount of money investing in copper futures.

Qiu Qing came to me one day, and told me Wang Yake was struggling under great pressure. She asked me to take over from him, and report to her after three months. I had previously been involved in trade and industry investment in Hong Kong, but I was happy to take on this new task. China Everbright International Trust and Investment

Corporation was located next to Tiantan Hotel in Beijing, and I immediately headed there to take up my new post. I was shocked to learn what had actually been going on.

China Everbright International Trust and Investment Corporation had a total of seven offices nationwide, but none of them were independent subsidiaries. In just three or four years, the company had racked up a huge amount of debt by offering extremely high rates of interest to depositors. These rates ranged from 22-24% on RMB accounts to 12% on US dollar accounts. They had then invested most of the money in projects in various provinces, while some money had been lent to other people. I discovered that the money was largely irrecoverable. I therefore wondered how the books were still showing the company to be in profit. After further investigation I saw that Wang had been giving a false interest margin. It took less than a month for me to figure out what had happened, and I went straight to Qiu Qing to tell her what I had discovered. I estimated that in one year we would owe RMB 2.2-2.4 billion on deposits of RMB 10 billion, and about US$80 million on US$600-700 million of deposits, which was the equivalent of about RMB 500 million. In total, we were facing an annual loss of RMB 2.5-3 billion.

Qiu Qing asked me if I were telling her the truth. I said that I knew how much she trusted me and that I would tell her only the truth. Qiu then called in Tang Gengyao, Liu Jiyuan and Li Shucun, and I told everything to them. I laid the data on the desk for them to have a look, and explained what had happened. Tang Gengyao's face even turned pale. He then asked me whether I was certain about it. I gave him my solemn guarantee that there were serious problems with Wang's accounting standards. Tang replied, "In that case, we're finished." I then pointed out that it was not just Everbright International Trust and Investment Corporation that was finished, but Everbright Group. I explained that our debt was a living tiger that would devour billions every year.

This all occurred in the mid-90s, by which time Zhang Jinfu had retired and Vice Premier Li Lanqing was in charge of foreign trade at the State Council as well as overseeing CITIC and Everbright. Qiu suggested we report the situation to Li, and asked me to do the talking as she felt I could explain things more clearly. I explained to Li the ins and outs of what had occurred. When I had finished, he said he would be unable to deal with the situation, as it largely concerned financial matters, so he phoned Zhu Rongji, who was Vice Premier and Governor of the People's Bank (Li Peng was the Premier). Li told him that Everbright was in trouble and he needed his help. Zhu seemed unfazed and immediately agreed to deal with the matter. From that moment on, the affairs of CITIC and Everbright were placed under Zhu's jurisdiction.

Zhu also sent Dai Xianglong and Chen Yuan from the People's Bank. I spent the whole day explaining what had happened to them. When I had finished reporting to Dai, he pointed out that it was a blatant case of false accounting. I told him that I knew it was false accounting, but we could not stop it, because it had already happened. The deputy governors of the People's Bank at the time were the current chairman of the People's Bank Xiao Gang, the current vice-chairman of the China Banking Regulatory Commission Cai E'sheng, and Xie Ping, currently working at China Investment Corporation. The three of them later arrived at Everbright to investigate the matter. The whole thing was considered quite incredible in the financial circle at the time.

Not long before, a forex trader called Nick Lesson had lost about £500 million at British bank Barings. He was also guilty of false accounting, which meant his losses had been hidden for a time. He had pulled the wool over the eyes of inspectors by telling them he had money with Citibank and BNP Paribas, but eventually he was unable to continue the charade and the 200-year-old bank folded. He was imprisoned in Singapore, where he wrote a book called *Rouge Trader: How I Brought Down Barings Bank and Shock the Financial World.* I thought to myself at the time that Wang Yake could have written a book called *How I Almost Brought Down Everbright.*

I have always had a great deal of respect for Qiu Qing for her dignified manner. She suggested that we write a report for Zhu

Rongi, which I drafted and she amended. At the end of the report, she added a note that said, "I am to blame for this and willing to accept any punishment, as long as Everbright can be saved." I asked her if she really wanted to include those words, and she insisted that she did. Zhu Rongji took decisive action. He appointed Secretary of the Central Political and Legislative Committee Luo Gan to shake up the management team. Following some discussions, Qiu was removed from her post, but was not held responsible. In 1996, deputy governor of the People's Bank Zhu Xiaohua was appointed the new chairman of Everbright, and I was appointed the general manager.

Soon after Zhu Xiaohua took up his new post Zhu Rongji asked to see us. I was sitting in the car outside Everbright's office in Beijing, waiting for Zhu Xiaohua to arrive in his car, so we could set off together. My driver had not seen Zhu Xiaohua's car left yet, so we continued waiting. We had been waiting for a long time, then I told my driver to leave, because I was afraid of being late for the meeting. When I arrived Zhu Rongji's office at Zhongnanhai, I saw that there were nine seats around the table and only one empty seat, which was kept for me. Luo Gan, Dai Xianglong and the others were already there. It made a spectacle of myself. Nevertheless, when the meeting started, Luo announced the new appointments and dismissals. Zhu Rongji then turned to me and said that he had recommended me for the post of general manager, and he hoped me to lend help and support to Zhu Xiaohua.

After the meeting, we put together a rescue plan. After we had drawn up an initial plan, Zhu Xiaohua and I took hard seats on a train to Beidaihe for a work meeting of the State Council. We took a bundle of materials that I had prepared with us. After I finished my report to Zhu Rongji, he told me that I would have to take responsibility for the report, and if total losses were found to be less than RMB 2.5 billion, then he would consider it false reporting on my part. I agreed to take responsibility, and insisted that total losses would certainly exceed that amount. A specialist auditor from the Auditing Administration later confirmed that total losses for only one year would be RMB 2.5-

3 billion, and would continue in the subsequent years. Zhu Rongji was furious on hearing this, he immediately phoned Premier Li Peng, and had Wang Yake arrested.

The State Council then convened another work meeting on the problem at Everbright, where we presented a report on the details of the rescue plan. The meeting was chaired by Li Peng, but Zhu Rongji constantly interrupted proceedings. Our first proposal was a debt-for-equity swap, because we knew we would be unable to pay our debts. This meant that anyone we owed money to would directly become shareholders. Everbright International Trust and Investment Corporation would be owned by everyone. Several deputy premiers were anxious about the idea. Li Lanqing stated that we had owed some money to his foreign trade section, and that we must pay it back. Qian Qichen complained that his diplomatic agencies did not have much money, and had invested some with us in the hope of earning some interest. He told us we had to pay the money back. Li Lanqing was also in charge of education and insisted that any money for education should be protected and paid back. I told them all that we would pay a small amount of the debt back, and we would do everything we could, but we needed money to continue operating, and they would still need to send some money to us.

It was a very long process. I often described it at the time as like being in a castle under siege, with no provisions and no reinforcements. It was a hopeless situation. In the end, at a State Council work meeting in Beidaihe attended by Chen Yuan and deputy governors of the People's Bank, we settled on the approach of returning a small amount of money and swapping the rest of the debts for equity.

After the meeting in Beidaihe, Zhu Xiaohua asked me to handle future meetings regarding specifics of the rescue plan, to which I agreed. So I attended a meeting of creditors at the People's Bank chaired by Chen Yuan. I remembered the meeting clearly. Zhou Yongkang, the new general manager of the China National Petroleum Corporation (CNPC) was also there. Chen Yuan asked me to run through the plan that had been approved by the State Council. I therefore proceeded to talk to everybody through the plan. When I got to the US$ 300 million owed to CNPC, Zhou Yongkang turned to his finance director and cursed him for having lent so much to us. Back then in 1996, that was a huge sum of money. CNPC had given us their spare cash to invest in an interest-bearing account. Afterwards, the company's CFO phoned me repeatedly at all times of the day, even at nights, begging for the money back. I used to answer the phone, and tell him that even being killed, I still had no money for him.

If the debt-for-equity swap had been completed entirely, as I advocated, it would have been the equivalent of a stop-loss measure, because we would no longer have had to pay any interest on the debt. Our RMB 14 billion debt would have become RMB 14 billion of stock given to the original creditors. In fact, Everbright Trust and Investment Corporation's assets only amounted to RMB 2-3 billion. We had calculated that if Everbright Trust and Investment Corporation were liquidated, then each share would be only worth 0.1 or 0.2 yuan. Later on, though, problems arose during the debt-for-equity swap, and it encountered strong resistance. That meant the debts still needed to be repaid with interest. In the end, Everbright Group had to repay 90% of the total RMB 14 billion assets.

Ultimately, a compromise was reached, which gave Everbright more time to repay the debt, but this meant we needed to raise funds. Zhu Xiaohua had worked at the People's Bank before, so he reached out to the heads of the four major banks (Industrial and Commercial Bank of China, Agricultural Bank of China, Bank of China, and China Construction Bank) for help. Each of them lent Everbright part of the funds it needed, while the People's Bank lent us RMB 2 billion. With their help, Everbright raised almost RMB 10 billion, a huge amount at the time.

Everbright was desperate to deal with the payment crisis, but I felt that the deeper problem was the crisis in its operating condition brought about by investment mistakes. It seemed to me to be even more serious than the payment crisis. The payment crisis could be resolved by improving the company's cash flow, but the operational crisis could only be resolved by making money for the company to shore up its losses.

Thanks to his rich experience of working in the industry, Zhu Xiaohua was well placed in this respect. He had excellent connections with various ministries and commissions as well as the provincial governments across the country. By the time Zhu Rongji appointed him as Everbright's chairman, he was quite ambitious. Zhu Xiaohua worked very hard, and was very capable. When China Mobile was listed on the Hong Kong stock exchange, Everbright acquired a 1.5% stake in the company, while CITIC was only able to secure 0.5%, which was a reflection of Zhu Xiaohua's influence.

Zhu was aggressive and eager to expand the business. Prior to the Asian financial crisis, he was often referred as having "golden fingers" in the Hong Kong press, because everything he touched turned to gold. When Everbright bought an asset, its value went up. When Everbright bought a stock, its value went up as well.

I, on the other hand, was not very optimistic about all these, and was always willing to offer my views. At one meeting, he spoke for a long time about all the good news from Everbright's investments, and was very excited. I then poured cold water on the moment, by suggesting that we should quickly realize those gains, so that we could return the money to Everbright Group. I proposed three suggestions using a military analogy: firstly, to pull back so as to reduce the front on which we were fighting; secondly, to concentrate our troops, so that we were not too dispersed and stationed in only a few key areas; and thirdly, to create reserves, because one can never be sure about the economic trends. This, needless to say, was at odds with Zhu Xiaohua's strategy.

We had three companies listed in Hong Kong: China Everbright International, China Everbright Technology, and China Everbright Financial. My specific proposal was to take advantage of the favorable market conditions to consolidate two of the companies, so that the cash would be returned to the group by realizing profits. We then made a big move by injecting part of the equity of Everbright Bank into

Everbright Financial, and the move caused its share price to rise from five or six yuan to 15 or 16 yuan in one day. I pointed out that this was an opportunity to reduce our holdings and "to eat twice from the same dish". In other words, we could demutualize Everbright Bank, and realize gains from the increase in the share price of Everbright Financial.

But, as soon as the Asian financial crisis came, the share price fell sharply. This was the rollercoaster effect. For a few days, conditions were perfect, and we could have made a profit by cashing out. Ultimately though, Zhu did not cash out, and we missed the opportunity. Zhu was full of regret. I told him that if he had done it, then his fingers would really be "gold fingers". After we lost this opportunity, Everbright's investments under Zhu began to encounter problems. From the perspective of a group of companies, one company cannot solve every problem, and one must make use of capital markets.

I was convinced Everbright missed business opportunities because Zhu was overconfident and overly optimistic. An example of this was in 1996, when Rong Yiren's son, Rong Zhijian, and others bought a 20% stake in CITIC Pacific, and CITIC Group made about RMB 10 billion. That happened before the Asian financial crisis. The company's profit would be around RMB 5-6 billion. Everbright had lost that chance.

Everbright operated in Hong Kong as two groups: Group A and Group B. Group A consisted of Zhu Xiaohua and several other members, and Group B consisted of me and several others. Zhu was very clever, but he had no self-restraint. In the end, he had too many hangers-on. He was surrounded by too many people. He lent money without consulting me, and avoided me even though I was the general manager. For my part, I thought he was acting so suspiciously. All I could do was to ask if the borrowers would be able to pay it back. I must come across as an upright person, because irregularities always seem to bypass me.

Later on, the head of Everbright's discipline inspection team, Zang Qiutao, became suspicious of Zhu and some other business people and reported them to the higher authorities. Zang was a very honest man, and he wrote to Jiang Zemin to tell him what he had discovered. The Central Commission for Discipline Inspection then contacted me to ask what I knew. The investigator naturally found it odd that I, the general manager, knew nothing about almost US$ 200 million transferred from Everbright's accounts. The prosecutor's office also questioned me about the missing money and whether I was involved, so I had to explain the company's operating model of having two independent teams.

Prior to that, the Central Organization Department had also talked to me, and I had told them what I thought of Zhu Xiaohua. I explained that I had tried to tell Zhu himself the same thing on several occasions by various means. As I said, I hoped that, as representatives of the Party, they would try to get through to him and bring him in line, but I was only his general manager so I had no authority. In 1999, Zhu Xiaohua was taken in for questioning. Vice governor of the People's Bank Liu Mingkang replaced Zhu as chairman of Everbright, and I continued in my role as general manager.

To some extent, these problems at Everbright were inevitable. It was quite tough to work in that type of environment, where we lacked a clear industrial strategy, did not receive strong state capital support, and were allowed to develop independently in the process of transforming from a planned economy to a market economy. If it had been a fully competitive market economy, we would have had to fend for ourselves. But that was not the case at Everbright. We were considered too big to fail. We faced the pressures of a monopoly enterprise as well as competitive pressures. I have yet not seen a comprehensive summary of the highs and lows of Everbright. There are already two books on the history of CITIC, but I still have not seen a book that systematically summarizes the history of Everbright.

Visit to Japan

While I was working at Everbright, there was another event worth mentioning. In the aftermath of the June 4th Incident in 1989, Western countries imposed sanctions on China, so did Japan. In the spring of 1990, I was asked to join a group with five other people for a trip to Japan as part of an Asia-Pacific symposium organized by CITIC and a non-governmental organization supported by the Ministry of Foreign Affairs of Japan.

Among the six members in the group, there were Wang Qishan — vice president of China Construction Bank, Ma Kai — deputy director of the State Price Bureau, Qin Xiao — director of CITIC Group, me as managing director of Everbright Group, Zhu Yuening — deputy mayor of Shenzhen, and Tang Ruoxin — deputy mayor of Qinhuangdao. At the meeting, Ma Kai gave a keynote speech about China's economic development as well as reform and opening up. The rest of us discussed matters in our respective areas. I remembered Wang Qishan getting into a heated debate with Japanese officials from the Ministry of Foreign Affairs and the Ministry of International Trade and Industry. As always, Ma Kai was calm and assertive. In response to Japanese criticisms of China's investment environment, I admitted that we could do better, but retorted that if China's infrastructure was as developed as Japan, and its economy was as advanced as that of Japan, then Japan would not have the same opportunities to invest and make money in China.

During our exchanges with Japanese officials, politicians and businessmen, we came up against strong opinions and attitudes, and had shown our strength to them. This supposedly came as a shock to the Japanese side. On one occasion, we met with Minoru Kobayashi, who was chief economist at the Industrial Bank of Japan and economic advisor to the Japanese Prime Minister. While talking about the opinions in the book *The Japan That Can Say No*, Kobayashi was very worried that Japan's economic strength was hollowing out Japanese industries, as young people flooded into the financial sector. We also talked at the meeting about whether or not China would one day learn to say no.

Twenty years later, after Minoru Kobayashi had passed away, his fears became a reality. In the 1990s, Japan fell into a long-term economic slump, while China became one of the world's largest economies, with a greater voice in international affairs. The lives of the six of us also took very different paths. Wang Qishan and Ma Kai became Party and state leaders, with both now playing important roles in China's national development. Qin Xiao and I continued to work for government-owned companies in front-line positions, and tried to make some achievements. Zhu Yuening and Tang Ruoxin went on to work for the China Travel Service Group and a foreign insurance company respectively, but both ended up being investigated and punished for violations of the law and Party discipline.

The six of us had very different personal experiences and careers, but all of us were involved in some way in China's reform and opening up.

Transfer to CITIC, Renaming and Restructuring

When I went to work at CITIC, Wang Jun was the chairman of the company. He was CITIC's third chairman and had been in the position for five years. In my opinion, a major difference between CITIC and Everbright was that the former had a stable development.

During job transfer in 2000, I moved to the CITIC Group. By that time, Qin Xiao had been working as general manager alongside Wang Jun for five years. In those five years, CITIC had experienced a number of ups and downs. Director of the Central Organization Department — Zeng Qinghong told me that CITIC had a larger scale than Everbright, and I was going to be transferred to CITIC, because they thought I would work well with Wang Jun. Meanwhile, Liu Mingkang became the chairman of Bank of China, while the former chairman of the Bank of Communications Wang Mingquan became the chairman and general manager of Everbright. Not long after, Qin Xiao became the chairman of China Merchants Group.

When I arrived at CITIC, I was confused from what had been happening at Everbright. Liu Mingkang had been against mixing financial and non-financial business. He advocated withdrawing from non-financial business and concentrating solely on finance, including banking, securities, insurance and trustee functions. Therefore, Everbright had gradually withdrawn from its original investment projects.

CITIC also had a diversified development model. In 2009, the supervisory board noted that CITIC involved in more than 50 of the 90 industries mentioned by the Development and Reform Commission. That meant despite a long period of trying to concentrate its activities in fewer areas, CITIC still involved in more than half of those recognized by the commission. When I arrived, the former director of the Industrial and Commercial Bank of China, Zhang Xiao, who was still the vice-chairman of CITIC, told me that the company was like a smaller version of SASAC (State-owned Assets Supervision and Administration Commission). Chang Zhenming later said the same thing. It really was like SASAC, because we had so many companies across so many industries that they had become difficult to manage. CITIC's development strategy therefore needed to be clarified, and the management structure needed to be adjusted to meet its development requirements. So when I got there, I helped Wang Jun to make further adjustments to the business structure and management model of CITIC based on the philosophy of "doing some thing while setting others aside".

As we know, there were considerable differences in the subsequent development of Everbright and CITIC. Whether from an internal or external perspective, I think everybody agrees that CITIC's development has been better than that of Everbright. There are stark differences in terms of total assets, net asset growth, profitability increases and management improvements. A very important reason for this has been the stability of CITIC's leadership, which means it has not suffered from the short-termism that Everbright has. Everbright has six chairpersons since it was founded, namely Wang Guangying, Qiu Qing, Zhu Xiaohua, Liu Mingkang, Wang Mingquan and the incumbent Tang Shuangning, all of whom came from the banking sector. Everbright was founded four years after CITIC, but it had replaced its top leader more frequently, and all of them have been transferred from elsewhere. CITIC has been relatively stable with only five chairpersons, namely Rong Yiren, Wei Ming, Wang Jun, me, and the incumbent Chang Zhenming. What was more, Wang Jun, the third chairperson, held the post for 11 years. Wang was one of the founders of CITIC and played an important role in the company's development, which means he knows a great deal about the company's history, the challenges it has faced in its development, how to deal with them, and the lessons learned from them. The relative stability of CITIC's leaders has certainly been a factor in its sustainable development.

Deng Xiaoping once described CITIC as "a bold innovator and great contributor", while Jiang Zemin encouraged us to "pioneer and innovate, work diligently, and manage CITIC well". These two generations of leaders took a personal interest in the development of CITIC. CITIC is notable for its many "firsts". These include having the first commercial business premises in China — International Building, being the first Chinese company to issue foreign bonds (Japanese samurai bonds and US Yankee bonds), being the first Chinese company involved in a satellite launch, and being the first non-state-owned commercial bank, later followed by Huaxia Bank and Everbright Bank. This last point changed the banking landscape in China. As such, CITIC has lived up to the role Deng Xiaoping hoped it would have, namely experimenting with reform and opening up within the original planned economy under the leadership of Rong Yiren.

CITIC's role in China's economic development was originally that of a window for opening up and a pioneer of reform. CITIC was a window for China's opening up when it was established, then it is fair to say that the external walls to the national economy have now been torn down. Being open to the external world has become the new norm. But back then, CITIC was the only Chinese company carrying out market-oriented cooperation with overseas business institutions, while others were still restricted in many ways. Everbright later followed in CITIC's footsteps, though it started from a different point by establishing its headquarters in Hong Kong. By the time I moved to CITIC, it already had 20 years of development, and it was already a huge organization whose importance had been repeatedly affirmed by the central government. Naturally, it still suffered from some problems associated with the way the company was formed. During the period that Wang Jun was the chairman and Qin Xiao was the general manager — a period referred as the Wang-Qin era within the company — many problems were identified and work was been done to rectify them, mainly in terms of focusing on fewer industries and projects. It was a relatively difficult process, however, getting management and staff of a 20-year-old company on the same page and putting it into practice. When I got to CITIC, I spent my time trying to implement this objective of Wang and Qin.

Soon after I arrived at CITIC, I raised the question at a Party committee meeting whether or not the company should withdraw from non-financial business as Everbright did and concentrate solely on finance. In fact, I raised this question to resolve my own confusion regarding what was being done at Everbright, and not because I thought it needed to be done at CITIC. Indeed, CITIC had no intention of withdrawing from non-financial sectors.

The non-financial sector was an important foundation of CITIC's development, and the company was seeking to develop comprehensive financial services on that base. With dealings in such a complete range of industries, CITIC had developed into a full-service financial institution within its original framework, with services in the areas of banking, securities, trusts, insurance, funds, asset management, financial leasing and futures. Prior to the financial crisis, this was a trend in international finance, with these types of institutions referred as universal banks in Europe and financial holding groups in the US.

At the time, we were seeking to maintain diversified operations and to strengthen our financial services, and the key was to develop CITIC into a full-service financial institution. The first thing I involved at CITIC was restructuring China International Trust and Investment Corporation into the CITIC Group. Following eventual approval from the State Council, CITIC, which used to be a non-banking financial institution, finally became a non-financial institution, an investment company. CITIC Group would not directly engage in financial services, however, as this and the trust business was placed under a subsidiary. Ma Kai was the Deputy Secretary-General of the State Council at the time, and had worked extremely hard on the restructuring. It was destined for him to be related to CITIC.

I was then working on projects aimed at blazing new trails, in line with the Central Committee's hopes for the company. I was also involved in the decision to rename and restructure the company. People were initially reluctant to change the name, given that it was already a well-known name in the country, and the one given by its founder, Rong Yiren. But an analysis of our business structure showed that it made sense to change it, so we settled on CITIC Group. Looking back now, this laid an important structural foundation for the company's development.

This occurred in 2002, while Zhu Rongji was Premier of the State Council, and after I had taken over as the general manager. We had previously been seeking to maintain both financial and non-financial business, while concentrating on strengthening and expanding the financial business. To do this, we had to distinguish ourselves from the major state-owned banks. CITIC's strength was that it offered clients a complete range of financial services, so we proposed a framework based on this by establishing a financial holding company. We then attempted to place the controlling stake of all our financial operations within this company, though this failed due to poor operability.

There had been a lack of regulations or a specific regulatory framework for companies engaged in a number of different business operations. Only in these days had the Banking Regulatory Commission issued a consolidated supervision proposal. But this was inadequate for a business such as CITIC, because there were overlaps with the Securities Regulatory Commission and the Insurance Regulatory Commission. To this day, there is still no regulatory body in China capable of implementing regulatory conditions for the whole of CITIC.

What is CITIC's biggest asset? In the preface to the book *Thirty Years of CITIC*, Wang Jun wrote that CITIC holds a huge amount of wealth and is extremely profitable, but its greatest asset is its ability to innovate. This ability is down to the fact that it developed within a competitive market environment. I therefore disagree with Qin Xiao's statement that state-owned enterprises (SOEs) are not market-based businesses in the true sense and that SOEs possess no genuine entrepreneurs.

CITIC developed amid market competition. When I joined CITIC, I involved in helping Wang Jun to carry out structural and management reforms as well as to reform incentive mechanisms. I have long believed that SOEs are in competition with foreign-invested and private companies in China. We both had our advantages, but our greatest disadvantage had been that our incentive and restraint mechanisms are not suited to market competition. Traditionally, working for an SOE meant low pay, regardless of whether one worked long hours or not or whether one worked hard or not, so there was a lot of waste and inefficiency. People did not see their personal interests as being tied up with the interests of the company. When I got to CITIC, Wang Jun encouraged me to change this, and look at worker remuneration. The first thing I did was to separate finance management from personnel management, and set up an incentive mechanism that links remuneration to business performance. I also strengthened our auditing system to prevent people from pursuing false profit.

I got the idea for this from visiting historical financial institutions in Shanxi province. They used a simple incentive mechanism of allocating "personal shares" to workers based on their position and duties. Personal shares had no capital value, but entitled employees to a share of the company's profits. These are known nowadays as "performance shares". When I read about this, I thought the merchants in Shanxi had a very effective way to get people pulling in the same direction, because their performance would directly decide how much they earned, which in turn affected how well the company did. If the employees prospered, the company did too. We then called in a human resources company to help us implement a new remuneration system to closely align the personal interests of employees with the interests of the company. Within this system, for every RMB 1 of profit that an employee made for the company, the employee would receive RMB 0.1 from the company. This incentive mechanism is now used throughout the company, in every field and every enterprise. It has gone a long way in solving the major drawback of SOEs, and has played an important role in CITIC's stability and development. CITIC has never received much resources or capital from the state, nor does it have a monopoly in its field. Rather, it has grown up amid fierce market competition at home and abroad. It therefore needed an appropriate incentive and restraint mechanism.

CITIC Bank Went Listed

As the general manager of CITIC, I was facing a major challenge, which was the restructuring and listing of CITIC on the stock market. Like other large banks, CITIC had accumulated a lot of problems as a result of defects in the formation and development of its operations management systems during China's Reform and Opening Up. Banks also took on a large number of financing functions in local economic development, even though many local projects had little chance of making money, and therefore with repaying capability. This meant banks were accumulating large amounts of bad debts.

I had not been at CITIC long when I met the manager of the Shenzhen branch of CITIC Bank. I asked how the branch was doing, and was shocked to hear that it had RMB 10 billion of non-performing assets. I asked if he had got his numbers right, as it seemed inconceivable to me that such a small branch could have such an astonishing amount of bad debt. Sure enough, after some investigations I discovered that the initial estimate of bad debt for the whole of CITIC Bank amounted to RMB 28.3 billion. After further investigation, it was concluded that the actual amount exceeded RMB 30 billion. CITIC Bank's capital amounted to only a few billion, so CITIC was already insolvent according to accepted accounting principles. CITIC Bank's problem had suddenly become the biggest crisis CITIC Group had ever faced.

It was a very grim situation. As I remembered, not long after I joined CITIC, I explained to Chang Zhenming how difficult it was to work at Everbright due to our operating losses and liquidity problems. Then, Chang had reassured me that those days were long gone, yet I was faced with another serious banking crisis involving a severe liquidity shortage. The Banking Regulatory Commission gave us only three years to get rid of our non-performing assets and raise sufficient capital.

Wang Jun and I spent a long time deciding how to solve the problem. One option was to reach out to the government for help, just as the four major state-owned banks (Industrial and Commercial Bank of China, Agricultural Bank of China, Bank of China, and China Construction Bank) had done. During his time as Premier, Zhu Rongji removed RMB 1.4 trillion of non-performing assets off the four banks, and set up four asset management companies. During their restructuring, the state again stripped them of non-performing assets and provided large amounts of capital during their process of being listed on the stock market. Moreover, another option was to finance by ourselves, carry out a large-scale recapitalization of CITIC Bank, dispose of the bad debts, increase loss provisions, consolidate assets, meet regulatory standards, become a joint-stock bank, and choose a suitable moment to be listed on the stock market.

I played a relatively important role in this event. At the time, Ma Kai was the director of the National Development and Reform Commission (NDRC), so I asked him whether he could approve us to issue bonds. He told me that I should speak to the People's Bank or China Banking Regulatory Commission (CBRC), as the NDRC could only approve the issuing of bonds for projects. I explained that CITIC Group's efforts to resolve the capital base of CITIC Bank could be seen as a type of project, and issuing bonds with the NDRC's approval was a type of reform and innovation. After our discussion, in 2003, the NDRC submitted our approval to the State Council, and we issued RMB 10 billion of bonds, RMB 6 billion of which was earmarked for recapitalizing CITIC Bank. In 2005, we used the same procedure to issue another RMB 9 billion of bonds, while RMB 8.7 billion of which was used to recapitalize CITIC Bank.

In addition to issuing bonds and retaining earnings, we also borrowed RMB 1 billion, but this later became a problem in auditing, as the State Council had not given its permission for the loan. In total, CITIC Bank received more than RMB 20 billion in capital, and RMB

20 billion of the bank's RMB 30 billion of non-performing assets were written off. This immediately resolved our capital adequacy ratio crisis, and basically created the conditions for the bank's healthy development. Then, on March 31, 2006 – within three years – we started restructuring CITIC Bank. In the July of the same year, I took over from Wang Jun as the chairman of CITIC Group, and soon afterwards I was also appointed the chairman of CITIC Bank. In the following year, on April 27, the A-share and H-share of CITIC Bank was listed on the Hong Kong and Shanghai stock exchanges, which signaled the end of the bank's capitalization problems.

We reformed at our own expense, as our H-stock was listed abroad. CITIC Bank raised a total of US$ 6 billion through the flotation, with shares more than 90 times oversubscribed. That really made me excited, even until today. During the road show, I took a team to the US, while the president of CITIC Bank, Chen Xiaoxian traveled to Europe, and Chang Zhenming stayed in Beijing to coordinate with the Securities Regulatory Commission. Since I left, after only three or four days, the subscription rate increased 10 fold. I am not sure about other industries, but I am sure that is still the highest rate of overseas oversubscription for any Chinese bank.

As soon as CITIC Bank was listed on the two stock exchanges, the company's crisis ended. We had turned the crisis into an opportunity. People at CITIC now firmly believe that every crisis represents both danger and an opportunity. We transformed the crisis into an opportunity for rapid growth. In the year we raised our capital, we expected to make an after-tax profit of RMB 5.7 billion, but we actually made a profit of RMB 8.3 billion. Achieving such large growth was not easy, however. It was something that could not have been conceived of at CITIC in the past unless it was a one-off, but this became the new norm. As the general manager, I had worked hard to assist our chairman Wang Jun, and when I became the chairman, I completed my task.

During the night that Wang Jun stepped down as chairman, we held a party for him. At the party, I was slightly drunken, and told him that CITIC was a mystery to outsiders and that I felt there was a need for greater transparency. What I meant was that CITIC's development model, in terms of its industrial strategy and management, is successful but little understood. When I took over as the chairman in July 2006, I stated that I wanted stability and continuity but also development and innovation. I summarized my mission in the following statement: "We must continue to push the company to a new level. Founded by Rong Yiren, and led by Chairmen Wei Mingyi and Wang Jun, the company was at a new historical starting point due to the joint efforts of the whole staff." I also set myself a clear mission, which was "to plan strategies, promote key areas, unite the workforce, and improve management".

During my second year as the chairman of CITIC Group, we listed CITIC Bank and the group's after-tax profits jumped to RMB 16 billion. This represented an extraordinary increase in a short period of time. We had originally faced a host of problems and a great deal of risk, but we had seized opportunities in the midst of a crisis. Although CITIC had a sound business structure, it also had a poor long-term annual profitability of approximately RMB 1-2 billion. Prior to that, CITIC Group's most profitable year was the time when it was sold at 20% stake in CITIC Pacific to Rong Zhijian. That was profit-making, as we could get high non-recurrent profit. While talking with foreign clients, I was reluctant to talk about our balance sheet or profit and loss income statements, because they were still not of a sufficient scale. Business people outside China tend to talk in terms of billions of US dollars or euros, and if you are not talking in billions, you would not be considered a serious player. In the past, our profits had not reached a billion dollars, but by the time of 2007, the bank was on a better footing and other parts of the business were doing well. We had made a profit of US$ 2 billion.

When I arrived at CITIC, I was impressed by its image and reputation of never having repudiated a debt. During the 1990s, loan and trust companies faced a number of crises by never paying back the money it borrowed. Everbright International Trust and Investment Corporation had both defaulted on debt payments and wrote-off huge amounts of debt. CITIC paid all money back, due to the business ethics and standards by Rong Yiren and Wang Jun. I find it truly remarkable that CITIC has never failed to pay a debt. Despite this, though, CITIC was not profitable enough, and it lacked a competitive edge. I therefore focused my efforts on promoting my strategy in this regard. When the company announced a net profit of RMB 16 billion in 2007, the morale of the entire staff had completely changed. It encouraged them and gave them confidence.

What Would Happen in the Next Year?

The year 2007 marked a turnaround for the company, and 2008 was as good a year as we expected. In the first half of 2008, the financial crisis struck. I remembered I had dinner in Beijing around that time with Goldman Sachs' CEO Lloyd Blankfein. A number of Wall Street investment banks had already suffered heavy losses dealing in derivative products, but Goldman Sachs was still making profit. So I asked Lloyd how he was still making money when others were losing so much. He told me that he was always in a high-state of alert, and he had sold those products when he felt they were no longer profitable. But other financial institutions, such as the old Wall Street banks Bear Stearns and Lehman Brothers, both of whom we came close to doing business with before they collapsed, were still buying them. He then asked for my views on the matter, and I told him that my philosophy was "money is king". I always like to have reserves of cash. If you are unable to deal with the impact of a crisis, you will be brought down by a monetary chain reaction. I believed that we should have enough cash in reserve to deal with any potential crisis.

In 2008, I felt that the CITIC Group was in a positive position, and I was feeling good about myself. In the autumn of that year, I visited North America. On Monday September 22, I flew from Canada to New York. On the last Monday, September 15, Lehman Brothers filed for bankruptcy, and Bank of America announced its acquisition of Merrill Lynch. I had originally planned to meet the CEO of Lehman Brothers, Dick Fuld, on Tuesday September 23, but I was told that the company had already filed for bankruptcy. On Sunday, Goldman Sachs and Morgan Stanley were forced by regulators to become bank holding companies. Afterwards, I paid a visit to Lloyd Blankfein — CEO of

Goldman Sachs, and John Mack — CEO of Morgan Stanley, and they both talked about their worry about the business conditions. That was when the financial crisis was starting in earnest. I said sardonically that CITIC was just a small, weak company that could not handle losing so many billions of dollars. I told them that their companies must be much more powerful, because they both made and lost in billions. I concluded that our business was on a much smaller scale, but at least we were still operating. I was just being mischievous, because I felt that they were facing much bigger problems than CITIC.

To solve the problems faced by Morgan Stanley, they decided to attract Japanese investors. I had been scheduled to meet with John Mack at 4pm that day, but I was almost 40 minutes late due to the traffic between uptown and downtown Manhattan. John had a global meeting scheduled at 5pm, so I only talked with him for 15 to 20 minutes. I could tell that he was under a great deal of stress. In comparison, we were still stable. But I was completely unaware of the major crisis looming around the corner.

On October 20, 2008, the Australian dollar futures contract crisis at CITIC Pacific was exposed, and the company's stock price plummeted. In a nutshell, the crisis occurred as the result of CITIC Pacific entering derivatives contracts to fund an iron ore project in Australia. A particular feature of these contracts was that the amount the company stood to gain was capped at US$ 3 million, but they were not subject to a minimum guarantee. This meant that losses that started out as HK$ 800-900 million in October gradually increased to HK$ 12-13 billion and reached HK$ 15.4 billion by the time we implemented a solution. I had not expected to be eating my words so quickly. In total, we suffered direct losses of about US$ 3 billion. When Wang Jun came to my office one day, I asked him whether it was the biggest loss CITIC had sustained throughout its history. He replied simply, "Of course it is the biggest".

The most direct problem posed by the crisis was that our losses were in billions. A more serious problem, however, was the damage to our reputation. If we were unable to repay money we owed to the banks due to the losses sustained by CITIC Pacific, the banks would stop lending their money and stop its original credit line. With approximately RMB 60 billion of debts, if any issues arose, then CITIC Pacific would likely go under. I was starting to wonder if CITIC Group would be able to solve this on its own.

Chang Zhenming later told me that he was having difficulty to sleep every night. Although I am usually quite a calm person, I too was feeling the strain, and was having difficulty thinking clearly at night. Then, one early morning I suddenly awoke wondering what would happen to CITIC within a year. I was truly wondering, because it was so difficult to predict the outcome. I wondered how I would face the others if CITIC went the same way as Lehman Brothers.

I quickly conducted some emergency researches and called a meeting of the Party committee as well as the executive board of directors in that weekend. My main aim was to stabilize the situation, so I formulated a package of solutions, which consisted of two parts. The first part involved CITIC Group taking on two-thirds of CITIC Pacific's Australian dollar futures contracts at an exchange rate of one Australian dollar to 0.7 US dollars. The remaining one-third of the futures contracts would remain the liability of CITIC Pacific. It would have to sustain the losses from those contracts, regardless of their scale. This meant that CITIC Group and CITIC Pacific would share the losses. The second part was concerned with shoring up CITIC Pacific with sufficient capital to get it through this difficult time. The idea initially was that CITIC Group would simply buy shares in CITIC Pacific. But there was a significant shortfall, as a large value of foreign exchange funds was required. It was therefore proposed that we should seek a loan from the Agricultural Bank of China. This was a big task as the Agricultural Bank of China was undergoing a restructuring before it went listed. Someone high up in the bank heard that CITIC was looking for a handout and went on the defensive, but it was later made clear that we were just looking for a loan. The bank eventually agreed, on the provision that it did not affect the bank's flotation. That was how we ended up borrowing US$1.5 billion from the Agricultural Bank of

China.

CITIC Group already held a 29% stake in the CITIC Pacific, and CITIC Pacific's management, led by Rong Zhijian, held a 20% stake. The rest of the company's stock was held by institutions and the public. We proposed a rights issue at a price of HK$8 per share. The value of CITIC Pacific's shares calculated according to net assets was almost HK$16 per share, but they were trading for only HK$4 at their lowest on the stock market. We were offering HK$8 per share, a price considered appropriate by small and medium-sized investors. However, this transaction affected a lot of parties, so the CITIC Group had to be sure that it was offering a suitable price. We could not simply dictate to people. We therefore called a shareholders' meeting to vote on the matter. Some Hong Kong investors claimed that we had not followed the correct procedures, but the vast majority of minority shareholders felt that the CITIC Group was taking responsibility and offering a reasonable price of buying stocks worth HK$4 at HK$8.

Given that the share price based on net assets was HK$16 per share, so we were offering half of that, and were not losing out. The important thing, though, was that the investors felt like they were getting a good deal. They felt we were responsible to help CITIC Pacific pull through wholeheartedly. On December 19, 2008, the plan was accepted by 99% of the shareholders. On that day, a number of us in charge of the CITIC Group were in Hong Kong to oversee the situation, and we appointed Chang Zhenming the CEO of CITIC Pacific. This case could be used in future textbooks as an example of how to deal with such a crisis.

Afterwards, we all watched the foreign exchange markets intently. Every RMB 0.01 change in the exchange rate equated to more than HK$ 200 million. I remembered bumping into Ma Kai one day, and he told me that the exchange rate between the US and Australian dollars had swung in our favor by RMB 0.71. I was touched that even he was keeping an eye on the exchange rate.

At the Party committee meeting on the last weekend of 2008, I explained that achieving profits of RMB 10 billion was a major psychological barrier for CITIC employees. Its increase to RMB 16 billion had required tremendous effort, which once made all our staff excited. We therefore should not just let that fall away.

Around that time, the CITIC's staff and managers were in low spirits. They complained that despite our efforts on management and constraints, CITIC Pacific had still got itself into trouble. They felt that all their good work had been undone. All I could say was that we needed to continue working hard and maintain our normal operations to help the CITIC Group. Then, in the same year, CITIC Pacific resumed normal operations, and in the following year, the company posted profits of HK$ 5.95 billion. In 2010, CITIC Pacific's net profit had reached HK$ 8.9 billion. The CITIC Group had helped CITIC Pacific through the crisis, and meanwhile maintaining and increasing the Group's value. It had also helped maintain the stability of Hong Kong's financial markets. In 2008, following all our hard work, we managed to keep the CITIC Group's net profit at above RMB 10 billion. In the end, the Group made RMB 14.2 billion net profit in that year.

Two Brothers Working in Two Central Enterprises

Before I finish this oral autobiography, I would like to say something about my brother, Kong Dong.

We had a half-brother, Chen Mo, who was the son of my father and his first wife, Zhang Yuexia. His surname was the same as my father's original surname. My elder brother, Chen, died tragically at the age of 45.

We also had a sister. A 1941 photo of her in my mother's arms shows that she had huge eyes and was very pretty. Because of my mother's work commitments, my mother left my sister in a family in northern Shaanxi when she was still a baby. She later went back to look for the baby, but the family said that she had died at a young age. I still sometimes wondered if that was just a lie, so they could keep her there. She may still be alive today, living a life completely different from ours.

Therefore, it means that there are only two children in our family — Kong Dong and I, and the two of us are extremely close. I am one year and three months older than him, and we were both born in Northeast China. When he was young, we called him Dong Dong, which means the northeastern region.

In our childhood, I was surly and stubborn, whereas Kong Dong was well-behaved and likable. We grew up together during the difficult period of the Great Leap Forward in the 1950s and the 1960s, and I became his example when I was admitted to No. 4 High School. He failed to be admitted for junior high school, and went to No. 6 High School instead. But he studied hard and eventually won a gold medal from the Beijing Municipal Bureau of Education, which was even one level higher than mine. That meant he could choose which school he went to except No. 4 High School, which was reluctant to accept recommended student. So he decided to sit the entrance examination and was eventually accepted to No. 4 High School on his own merit. That was a happy moment for our family.

Afterwards, we attended senior high school and experienced the start of the Cultural Revolution together. During that period, our destinies intersected for a relatively long time. I was considered an outstanding student leader and Kong Dong also strived for excellence. I was appointed the leader of the Xicheng District Picket Corps during the Cultural Revolution, and he was appointed the leader of a brigade in the picket, which meant we both took part in several clashes with the rebel groups. However, our darkest day also came during that time, on December 23, 1966. In the afternoon, I was imprisoned and my father was arrested and interrogated, and that night my mother passed away. My mother's suicide was considered a "betrayal of the Party" at the time. Kong Dong had no choice, but to single-handedly arrange her funeral despite the intense political pressure. He later personally carried her ashes to the production team he joined in Shanxi Province, where the ashes were kept with him until 1975, when my mother was posthumously rehabilitated and her remains were laid in the Babaoshan Revolutionary Cemetery. When Zhang Jinfu, who was a student of the great educator Tao Xingzhi and has great respect for China's traditional culture and morals, heard that my brother had carried our mother's ashes to Shanxi, he remarked, "Your brother is truly a dutiful son."

In 1969, I was forced to join a production team in Yan'an, while Kong Dong was in Shanxi. This marked the start of almost a decade of separation, during which time we both struggled to get by. We would only meet occasionally. One circumstance had moved me greatly, and would be carved in my memory forever. It was in the spring of 1971, and I had contracted lobar pneumonia, and was very weak physically. Kong Dong therefore made the long and difficult journey across the Yellow River from Shanxi to northern Shaanxi to visit me and help me complete my work, so that I would still receive work points. Despite the hardships of the time, we never lost our fighting spirit, and we always supported each other through the tough times and sought to better ourselves. After the Lin Biao incident on September 13, 1971, we enjoyed a wonderful trip around the country together with several friends from production teams in Inner Mongolia.

At the end of 1972, when Zhou Enlai approved for either Kong Dong or me to return to Beijing to look after our father, we both felt the other should be the one to return, but he insisted that his health was better than mine, and I should leave the countryside first. Our father ultimately insisted that I should return to Beijing, but I still greatly admired my brother's selflessness. He was later transferred to a commune in Jiangxi Province, while I took care of our father in Beijing.

In 1974, Kong Dong was recommended from among workers, peasants and soldiers to study at the Jiangxi Institute of Technology, which meant he had taken up formal education again four years earlier than me, while I had to wait until 1978 to be directly admitted to graduate studies. As such we leapfrogged each other in terms of our higher education.

Kong Dong graduated in 1978 and returned to work at a research institute in Beijing. Before long, he was made secretary to the Minister of Light Industry, Song Jiwen. In 1983, he went to work for the Shenzhen-based China Offshore Helicopter Company, which marked the start of his career in aviation.

For a long time, we lived together with our father in happiness. We were all obsessed with playing bridge and used to sharpen our skills with our father's friends, such as Wan Li and Lü Zhengcao. We had achieved our victory for many times. Because of our fame for playing bridge, during a period of about three months, Uncle Deng Xiaoping also invited my brother and me to play bridge with him twice a week. That was a truly special experience.

The Deng family all addressed Deng Xiaoping as "grandpa". Deng's usual partners were Ding Guangen and Wang Hanbin. Deng had an excellent feel for the game, while Ding Guangen was the best at calculating points. This made them a formidable team. Deng said in a low voice when he played, so we used to whisper when bidding. We had a deep respect for the great man, and it was interesting to closely observe his focused demeanor when playing cards, as well as his joy at winning and disappointment at losing. I remembered one time Kong Dong and I completely forgot where we were and quarreled during a game. Deng suddenly turned to us and asked what we were fighting about in his Sichuan accent. Although he said it quietly, it still shook us to our cores. There was great authority in his words despite his calm demeanor. The two of us immediately stopped fighting and stayed silent. When we played cards, Deng's son, Deng Pufang, would often sit in his wheelchair beside us and watch. Deng's daughter, Deng Nan, would sometimes come over to give suggestions; though I remembered one time she gave Deng a wrong suggestion that resulted in him losing the game and in our victory. That was the first time we saw him losing his temper.

Sometimes we would stay for dinner and continue playing after the meal. There were always a large number of people at the table, which made us very shy, but Deng would considerately say to us, "All are welcome. Do not stand on ceremony. Eat as much as you like." After that he would not say much, but it made us slightly less nervous.

I worked at Everbright for 16 years and at CITIC for 10 years during the period of Reform and Opening Up. The two companies were both windows for Reform and Opening Up, as well as diversified amalgamated corporation. During that time, Kong Dong worked in several positions within the aviation industry and always made distinguished achievements.

From 1983 to 1991, Kong Dong worked as an assistant to several leaders of China Offshore Helicopter Company, including the general manager, Wang Bing (Wang Jun's elder brother), where he played an important role and experienced the difficulties and obstacles faced during the development of China's general aviation industry.

In 1991, he was transferred to the Shenzhen Airport Group, and was later promoted from deputy general manager to general manager and Party committee secretary. He excelled at airport management, and helped Shenzhen Airport become the fourth largest airport in China within only four years. This resulted in the rapid development of business at Shenzhen Airport and helped accumulate his valuable management experience.

On the back of the recognition he received for his work at Shenzhen Airport, Kong Dong was put in charge of the project to expand the Beijing Capital Airport in 1995, which involved building a second terminal. Having worked elsewhere for more than a decade, he returned to Beijing once again. By that time, I was the general manager of Everbright, and I regularly flew between the company's offices in Beijing and its headquarters in Hong Kong, so I was able to see for myself how the new terminal was progressing. I was slightly worried about Kong Dong's lack of experience of large construction projects, especially given the size and importance of the building and the fact that it was designated a "gift to the nation" to celebrate the 50th anniversary of the founding of the People's Republic. I reminded him that if done well it would be considered a national monument, but if done poorly then it would be considered a national disgrace. By 1999, I was relieved when the new terminal was completed on time and accepted as an excellent project, even was awarded the Luban Prize.[48] In the same year, I experienced crises and setbacks at Everbright, and was appointed general manager of CITIC Group, which meant I also returned to Beijing.

Having worked in general aviation, airport management and airport terminal construction, Kong Dong moved in 2001 to another area of aviation — civil air transport. Afterwards, during the 10 years I work at CITIC, he reached the pinnacle of his career in this high-risk industry, before stepping down from frontline management positions in November 2011.

It is a coincidence that, having leapfrogged each other throughout our careers, we each came to be in charge of our respective companies (CITIC and China National Aviation Holding Company (CNAH)) at the age of 59, both weathered the storm of the 2008-2009 financial crisis, both took our companies to the highest stages in their histories, and both

48 The Luban Prize is China's highest award for construction engineering.

retired at the age of 63, in line with the government regulations. During this period, our two companies also engaged in major cooperation and significant transactions. I cherish a photo taken of the two of us at a ceremony to mark the launch of a joint credit card between CITIC Bank and CNAH. In addition to this, CITIC Pacific transferred shares held in Cathay Pacific to CNAH, which was a major transaction in the strategic restructuring of the two institutions and reflected the strong cooperation between enterprises owned by the central government.

I have also kept a newspaper from 2009 with a picture of "the most valuable business leaders" from the Chinese Annual Management Conference, which includes Kong Dong and me.

Under Kong Dong's leadership, CNAH became the country's leading civil aviation company and a global leader in the industry. In 2010, CNAH became the world's largest airline in terms of market capitalization and profits, and Kong Dong was named one of China's top ten businessmen. All of this made me very proud of my brother. I often told the others that I am the brother of one of China's top ten businessmen! In the same year, I went to the United States to receive an international business award from the Asia Society. The other who received awards that day included Cisco's CEO, the Minister of Women and Children's Affairs of Bangladesh, and the Chairman of the US Joint Chiefs of Staff — Admiral Mike Mullen.

Some people have looked at our family and remarked that we have all worked in senior positions for the Party and the country. In fact, my brother and I were just leaders of central government enterprises and could be regarded merely as senior cadres without any administrative rank. In any case, our whole family has always done its utmost for the causes of China's revival and prosperity, and we have contributed what we could.

A Perfect Ending

In 2009, both Chinese and foreign economies were busy dealing with challenges posed by the US financial crisis. Within the same year, by confronting the crisis affecting CITIC Pacific, the CITIC Group took a significant step in its development. The CITIC Group is particularly adept at dealing with crises and spotting business opportunities. We were constantly looking out for opportunities and seizing profits where we could. As such, the group's profits jumped again the next year to RMB 18.9 billion, marking the end of the crisis.

Despite the significant risks brought by the financial crisis, we still managed to seize the opportunities. In terms of market capitalization, the value of the US$1.5 billion stake we bought in CITIC Pacific with the loan from Agricultural Bank of China at least doubled in its value. We also earned US$500-600 million (almost several billions of HK dollars) on the US-Australian dollar futures contracts we took on.

Everyone said we should summarize what we have learned from the lesson. But I thought that we should not assume that we were out of the woods. We thought we were fine before, but in truth things were not fine at all. We have worked very hard to get where we are today, but that only accounts for about 30 percent of our success. The other 70 percent is good fortune. An old saying in the countryside goes like, "If people work hard, and policies are correct, fortune will lend a helping hand". I would change that into, "If people work hard, and leaders are good, fortune will lend a helping hand". We certainly worked hard. And the leadership, including CITIC's executive leaders, Vice Premier Wang Qishan and other leaders of the State Council, as well as those in charge of various government departments, all helped in dealing with

CITIC's problems. Fortune lent a helping hand because the Australian dollar strengthened throughout the year. Of course, it was also fortune given by China. If China's economy was not growing, there would have been less demand for minerals from Australia, and the Australian economy would have collapsed. However, since the Australian dollar strengthened, it was a big help for us. It seems fortune favors the brave.

The CITIC Bank crisis was handled so well that our profitability actually increased significantly, and the CITIC Pacific crisis was also handled so well that our operating capacity actually improved. As a result, the CITIC Group's profits increased considerably. In 2009, I summarized the company's operating condition as "the three 'threes'": assets of US$300 billion, sales income of US$30 billion and net profit of US$3 billion. Such would guarantee our development in a larger scale.

In 2010, which was my last year of my tenure at the company, our net profit was RMB 33.2 billion. That made us one of the most profitable centrally managed financial institutions and SOEs in China, except, of course, for the five major banks, CNPC (China National Petroleum Corporation), Sinopec, CNOOC (China National Offshore Oil Corporation), China Mobile, and Shenhua Energy, which were all with huge amounts of state investment that we could not be compared to.

For CITIC, more strategically significant than increased profitability is its overseas expansion. CITIC is a window for China's opening up, and it has long invested in projects and companies abroad, such as lumber production bases in the US and aluminum production companies in Australia, to exploit resources overseas as a pioneering Chinese company. Over the years, CITIC has implemented China's overseas strategy through overseas projects and investments with outstanding results, and these have become important routes into overseas markets, spanning to regions like Africa, Latin America, Central Asia, Australia and Europe. In Africa, there were the East-West highway project in Algeria, social housing projects in Angola, coking and gold projects in South Africa, and manganese projects in Gabon. In Latin America, there were social housing projects in Venezuela, a thermal power plant and niobium production project in Brazil and subway vehicles in Argentina. In Central Asia, there were the Karazhanbas oilfield and bitumen projects in Kazakhstan, potash and soda ash production projects in Uzbekistan and a bus project in Turkmenistan. In the Middle East, there were the Tehran subway and Zarand coking projects in Iran. There were also aluminum, coal and iron ore projects in Australia; and in Europe, a cement plant in Belarus, heavy machinery project in Spain, auto parts project in Germany, and other projects, some worth as little as a several hundred million dollars and others worth as much as several billion dollars.

We have also developed a solid working relationship and friendly exchanges with politicians from many countries. This reminds me to an interesting story. In January 2008, President Nursultan Nazarbayev of Kazakhstan traveled to Hainan Island in China for a holiday. I met him there for a round of golf. On the par-three seventh, he hit a hole in one. He was very happy and told me that it was his first ever hole in one. I later gave him a special trophy to commemorate the moment. That afternoon, we chatted as we played, and he told me that he hoped CITIC would not only invest in projects completed with resources like oil, but also invest in non-resource related projects. We later did just that. CITIC invested in an oil development project, which included processing bitumen, but also set up funds with Kazakhstan in non-resource related fields. This helped us win the trust and support of President Nazarbayev and encouraged economic exchanges between the two countries. Since then, President Nazarbayev always spares time to meet with CITIC leaders during his visits to China. I and several other people at CITIC had been very well treated when we visited Kazakhstan.

It can be said that CITIC's overseas expansion has not only been supported by the Chinese leaders, but also held in high regard by leaders of other countries. It holds strategic significance not only for the company's development but also for China's relations with other countries.

After the crisis at CITIC Pacific, the CITIC Group faced other major issues: Is its development sustainable? Can it continue to expand? Is its business model, in terms of industry strategy and management model, able to meet the requirements of overall economic development? In truth, I had been thinking about these questions for a long time before the financial crisis, which is why I suggested the group should go public.

Normally the whole group would go public together. But due to the competition, if we had not first listed our affiliated organizations and strong assets, we would not have survived.

Then, CITIC Securities went public on its own. At the time, Wang Dongming told me that he wanted me to speak to Zhou Xiaochuan, chairman of CSRC, to try to get his support for the move. Without his support, CITIC Securities would not have become the largest securities company in China. When I joined CITIC, CITIC Securities and Everbright Securities were of a similar size, but CITIC Securities seized the opportunities and grew more quickly, which was also a reflection of our competitiveness.

There is also CITIC Bank. The CITIC Group owns 60 percent share of CITIC Bank, while China Merchants Group owns less than 10 percent share of China Merchants Bank. Once during my chat with Qin Xiao, he told me that China Merchants Group had profits of more than RMB 10 billion. I then told him that the CITIC Group had slightly more than that, which was more than RMB 30 billion. He asked how we were making so much money and I explained that a large part came from our stake in CITIC Bank. One of the reasons we still own such a high proportion of the bank's equity is because we issued bonds to raise funds for a capital injection. Those funds are now worth ten times as much.

Even though the CITIC Group's profits have been good in recent years, I still feel that its business model is unsustainable. This is because, if it continues the way it is going, it will no longer be a carrier fleet, but become a number of independent battalions. The bank struck out on its own, and is increasingly profitable, with recent net profits of RMB 30 billion. At its peak, CITIC Securities had net profits of RMB

10 billion, which fell as low as several billion. So how should the CITIC Group position itself?

I think the CITIC Group's development should always be considered in relation to the country's national and economic development strategy. It is the foundation of our corporate strategy. Without a definite corporate strategy, it will become a pure investment company. It will simply be about selling any investments that perform well — buying and selling, and buying again. Should we take that path or create our own type of business instead?

For example, because of its pace of development, CITIC Bank constantly requires additional capital. If the CITIC Group has a strong financing capability, then we can continue to provide the bank with capital. When CITIC Bank performs a capital increase, the CITIC Group has to bring out ten billion or tens of billions. Although it creates huge profits, it also requires huge amounts of money. If the CITIC Group cannot invest that much, then it would inevitably lead to equity dilution. As such, after CITIC Bank listed in 2007, I considered whether the CITIC Group as a whole should be listed, and I wrote a report to Vice Premier Wang Qishan. He then passed my report onto the CSRC, who came back to us and told us that we could not be listed as A-stock on the Shanghai stock market, because companies within the group had already done so, and it is illegal to have overlapping listings. I told the CSRC that we had conducted research on the issue, and we could be listed on the Hong Kong stock market following a restructuring, that is what we intended to do. If the whole CITIC Group listed on the Hong Kong stock market, it could expect to raise RMB 60-70 billion in financing.

Another implication of the whole of CITIC Group listing on the stock market is that it would enhance its ability to allocate resources. Without this foundation and strength, what direction would CITIC take? What would be its focus? How could it develop? How could it develop the industries it wanted to? The business strategy we had decided on was to be a leader in several fields with clear comprehensive advantages. This included a major focus on the financial sector, and another focus on the non-financial resource industry. But to be involved in resources, you need a lot of money. Where was CITIC going to get that money? We had already spent US$2 billion to acquire a medium-sized oil field in Kazakhstan, which had stretched us to our limits. The mining industry is an asset-heavy and capital-intensive industry. Listing the whole group would give us a financing platform that would allow us to allocate resources and develop in that direction.

Another consideration, however, was that with the expansion of industries, the CITIC Group would be hard to manage. In the end, it is about whether you can cope with it or not. The CITIC Pacific crisis was a major problem. Despite the fact that we were able to save the situation, it was a major emergency at the time, and it simply could not be allowed to happen again. We could not afford another major crisis that left more people unable to sleep at night. As such, the model of having a number of "independent battalions" was no longer suitable.

Based on these considerations, I strongly backed the idea of the whole CITIC Group listing on the stock market and slowly went round the houses communicating this to people. Chang and I then set about promoting the issue. In 2009, we once again reported our plan of listing H-stock on the Hong Kong stock market to the State Council and sought the views of dozens of government departments. Finally, on May 19, 2010, the State Council gave its official approval.

It was very gratifying that on December 27, 2011, exactly one year after I retired, the CITIC Group underwent a formal restructuring to become CITIC Limited. This was another major step in the company's history. This structural adjustment was undertaken, so that the group could be listed. It cost a huge amount of efforts. It has become a joint-stock company, but it is hard to say when it will eventually be listed. It will take a lot of work and some fortune, as well as waiting for the market environment to improve.

I would not say that I was proud of the last 10 years working there, but I did have a sense of accomplishment. What did CITIC mean to me? It had given me a platform to display my talents.

Wang Jun once said, "CITIC's most valuable assets are its ability of innovation, and its competitiveness in the market." One could say that I inherited CITIC's traditions, and strove to use them while making some primary achievements. I think our experiences and lessons could be used in textbooks, though they could never be replicated, and were specific to CITIC. In the course of building socialism with Chinese characteristics, we established a development model with CITIC's own characteristics.

I served as the chairman of the CITIC Group during the Party's 11th Five-Year Plan period (2006-2010). During that period, the company had completed the following tasks: built on its excellent development during the 10th Five-Year Plan period; resolved the long-standing problem of non-performing assets; restructured key businesses and subsidiaries; developed a group of dominant financial and non-financial enterprises; dealt with the impact and fallout from the international financial crisis; resolved the Australian dollar futures contract problem affecting CITIC Pacific; continued improvements in the main business indicators; achieved and exceeded the development goals set for the 11th Five-Year Plan period; significantly improved asset quality, profitability and competitiveness; developed the scale, quality and efficiency of the group by leaps and bounds; and changed the period with the best financial situation, highest quality of assets, fastest development and greatest profitability in the CITIC Group's history. In 2009, CITIC Group ranked the 415th in the *Fortune* 500 for the first time. In 2010, it moved up 161 places to the 254th, and in 2011, it moved further up to the 221st (based on the group's performance in 2010).

We have achieved a significant return on state-owned assets. Since it was founded, the CITIC Group has received a total of RMB 8.27 billion of state investment, including a RMB 250 million cash disbursement, RMB 2.34 billion in asset transfers, and RMB 5.68 billion in tax rebates. By the end of 2010, the CITIC Group's consolidated net assets increased 20 times the amount of state investment, and had the RMB 3.9 billion paid in tax in the two previous years been excluded, then it would stand at 38 times the amount of state investment.

The CITIC Group's Main Business Indicators 2006-2010
(in billions of RMB)

Items	2006	2007	2008	2009	2010	Growth during 11th Five-Year Plan Period	Compound Annual Growth Rate
Total Assets	927.2	1,318.8	1,624.1	2,153.8	2,529.8	1,747.1	26%
Net Assets	45.6	98.5	108.7	135.2	172.9	129.5	32%
Operating Income	80.6	109.4	157.0	188.4	260.8	180.2	34%
Net Profit	6.5	15.9	14.2	18.9	33.2	26.7	51%

CITIC's net assets currently total more than RMB 200 billion, ranking CITIC 194th among Fortune 500 companies in 2012. This is simply incredible for many, but this is the CITIC that was born at the start of the Reform and Opening Up period, and has flourished to the benefit of the country and its people.

Judgement Made Before I Leave This World

Times flows like water, and the days glide swiftly by. By the end of 2010, having turned 63, I formally retired from my post. On the Christmas Eve of that year, which was a Saturday, I was in Hong Kong, and I suddenly received a phone call from the Central Organization Department asking me to return to Beijing before 4 pm that day for a meeting with a central leader. I hurriedly bought a plane ticket, but the flight was delayed and I hit a traffic jam when I got to Beijing. Because of all this, I did not arrive until 5:30 pm in the evening. When I got there, I was informed that Vice President Xi Jinping was waiting for me. He had originally intended to talk with me first, and then with Chang Zhenming and Tian Guoli. But because I was late, Xi met the others first and then talked to me.

When I went into the meeting I apologized for being late. Xi asked if I had been caught in a traffic jam, then I explained that I had rushed up from Hong Kong for the meeting. Upon hearing this, he turned to look at the vice minister of the Central Organization Department, Wang Ercheng, who was also in the room and admonished him for giving me so little time instead of rescheduling the meeting for a later time, but I quickly responded and assured him that it was not a problem. We then sat down at a long table. Xi sat at the head of it with his notes in front of him. I sat to the side of him, and Wang was opposite me. In 2006, while I was appointed chairman of the CITIC Group, it was He Guoqiang, Politburo member and minister of the Central Organization Department that talked with me. I had originally thought that I would be meeting with the then minister of the Central Organization Department, Li Yuanchao on that day rather than meeting Xi himself. It was a reflection of CITIC's importance as well as their special care to me. Xi proceeded to give a detailed presentation affirming and praising of my achievements on behalf of the central government. He pointed out that I had worked at two of China's windows for Reform and Opening Up – CITIC and Everbright, and had worked fruitfully at both places. I was gratified by this summary of my work. The meeting reminded me of a visit Xi had made in 2009 to the CITIC Luoyang Heavy Machinery Company (formerly the Luoyang Mining Machinery Factory), where his father, Xi Zhongxun, had been transferred to work. I had been at the reception, and as soon as he saw me he told everybody there that his father and my mother had been colleagues at the State Council. I quickly responded that they were not at different ranks, as my mother was just a deputy secretary, while his father had been Deputy Prime Minister and Secretary of the State Council. He smiled and assured me that they were still colleagues. During the visit, he also took the time to meet with some of his father's workmates and thanked them sincerely for caring for and helping his father when he had been in difficulty. It was a heartwarming moment.

My retirement was officially announced on December 27, 2010. In the following year, the central authorities conducted a comprehensive audit that was officially referred as the Economic Responsibility Audit. The audit covered all those in charge of central government financial institutions as well as some who had recently retired. It included, for example, the incumbent chairman of ICBC, Jiang Jianqing; people in charge and retired heads of SOEs such as Qin Xiao from China Merchants Group; incumbent leading cadres such as the mayors of Shanghai, Tianjin and Beijing; and the Minister of the State Administration for Industry and Commerce. A central government regulation stipulated that the heads of all government departments, provinces, centrally owned enterprises and centrally managed financial institutions had to be audited. Given the size of CITIC and the number of industries it involved in, as well as the crises and setbacks I had dealt with during my time in charge, the 2011 audit was a relatively lengthy and complex affair. The National Audit Office has a total of 20 commissioners nationwide, and 13 of them arrived at CITIC for the audit, accompanied by hundreds of staff. The audit was unprecedented in the history of the CITIC Group in terms of its breadth, depth and intensity. The thorough and in-depth on-site audit took four months, and put a lot of pressure on me and the company. I viewed the audit as a final judgement to my work, and for a while, I felt it was a significant full stop over my career.

Ultimately, the National Audit Office's audit report provided suggestions on how to achieve the sustained, coordinated and healthy development of the group as a whole and implement state policies and decision-making arrangements; deepen structural reforms and improve management decision-making mechanisms; improve corporate governance and strengthen internal control and risk management; integrate the group's business and organizational structure to optimize overall business performance; and strengthen financial management and improve operational efficiency levels. The report also fully affirmed the economic validity of my work and clearly indicated that, according to assessment results, since 2006, the group's state-owned capital performed better than the overall average for the financial sector and preserved or increased the value of state-owned assets. As the audit report stated, "During his tenure, Kong Dan constantly promoted the development and reform of the CITIC Group to make it a modern integrated operating business and gradually form the structure of a group holding company with specialist subsidiaries. The group's overall business size, profitability and competitiveness have significantly improved as a result." It should be said that this was not just a recognition that I had performed my duties responsibly, made achievements and conducted myself professionally; it was also a recognition to the staged achievements of the CITIC Group over the past 30 years, in which it had often seen as an "exceptional" central government enterprise.

I was therefore able to retire with my head held high, with the central government having affirmed the value of my life's work. The entire audit took almost a year to complete. I was very happy that the results of the audit were consistent with the evaluation of the central government.

I have experienced some difficulties as well as some magnificent moments in my life, and this decision meant I was finally able to rest easy. There had been so many ups and downs: from being a student leader at No. 4 High School, to leading the Xicheng District Picket Corps in the 1960s; from being put in jail, to my family suffering a bereavement and subsequent separation; being sent to Shaanxi to work for a production team, getting in touch with the common people, and honing my body and mind; cramming day and night to study for a Master's degree and once more building up a good foundation; working as a secretary for two years and broadening my horizons; challenging difficulties and appealing to the higher authorities; working at Everbright for 16 years and at CITIC for 10 years; and suffering repeated setbacks but being unremitting in my endeavors. During these decades, I think I have shown my character and made use of the life experiences I have accumulated.

I do not care about success or failure. Life is merely a process. A sense of accomplishment comes from simply feeling that you have done something meaningful. The important thing is to do something for society and to make a difference. I believe that people should not set themselves unattainable goals by biting off more than they can chew. The key is to tackle things in a down-to-earth manner, and be conscientious. The most fundamental thing in life is to stay pure and act rationally. It is important to proceed from reality in everything one does, and not blindly follow dogma and doctrines. In that way, even if one gets lost along the way, he will still be able to get back on the right path.

Only by assimilating oneself with the great rising and falling tide of the Chinese nation over the centuries, can the successes and failures of an individual have any real social value. Our sages and martyrs have worked diligently and assiduously and dedicated themselves to difficult explorations. Only by taking China's realities as their starting point could they progress along the right path, be that in revolution, construction, reform or development. As soon as one deviates from

China's realities or proceeds from some imported dogma or simply copies the templates of others, one will go astray and get lost. "Chinese characteristics" is the product of the summary of Deng Xiaoping's excellent wisdom, and it is the starting point for China's century-long pursuit of the path of national revival. In contrast to this is the mindset of ethnic and historical nothingness that is popular today and comes from worship of Western fundamentalist, political and economic values. This has always and will, for a long time, continue to present a severe challenge and test to generations of people.

As witnesses of this special era, who have lived through the difficulties of the previous era, I feel that we have a responsibility and obligation to record our experiences and actions as well as our thought processes and reflections. Mi Hedu has done a significant task in recording the oral histories of the people in my generation, and I hope that more people will leave their own records. In that way, we will have left an account for history, and for future generations to evaluate us by.

I knew the recently deceased Nan Huaijin for many years. He used to say that I have a bold spirit, with grace under fire, fulfilled my duties faithfully and energetically, always willing to take up for a challenge, worked conscientiously, avoided doing what I could not handle, and did everything properly as long as I could handle. In 1999, he gave me a piece of calligraphy. It was an excerpt from a poem by Xin Qiji titled *Pozhenzi*, which says: "Half drunk, I stir the wick of the oil lamp to inspect my sword, Calling to mind the bugle call of our former camp. If only I could allay the Emperor's concerns, And win fame for ever to last. It's too bad, my hair has turned grey, alas!" Despite the inherent sadness of the poem, it is about ambition, and encourages people to make a contribution to improve the nation's position. Today, I can forget about fame, as I am aware of my capabilities. But one thing I can say is that I have given my all.

On my 65th birthday, Ma Kai sent me the following poem he had written. I feel it is fitting in terms of my personality and experiences, though it flatters me. Now, let me conclude the whole book with it:

Half a glorious life of a high achiever shines,

With his rare talent mirrored in what he writes,

Unswerving persistence in everything taken,

Cherishing true qualities prevailing in heaven.

Appendix 1

Xicheng District Headquarters of the Capital Red Guards Picket Corps

General Orders
(No. 1-10)

September 1966

Quotations from Chairman Mao

We are advancing.

We are now engaged in a great and most glorious cause never before undertaken by our forefathers.

Our goal must be attained.

Our goal can unquestionably be attained.

Let the 600 million people of our country unite and strive for our common cause!

You should concern yourself with the affairs of the state and see the Great Proletarian Cultural Revolution through to its conclusion.

The Chinese people will see that, once China's destiny is in the hands of the people, China, like the sun rising in the east, will illuminate every corner of the land with a brilliant flame, swiftly clean up the mire left by the reactionary government, heal the wounds of war and build a new, powerful and prosperous people's republic worthy of the name.

...Therefore, man has to constantly sum up experience and go on discovering, inventing, creating and advancing. Ideas of stagnation, pessimism, inertia and complacency are all wrong.

Foreword

For convenience of reading and learning, and in response to demand from Red Guards and the revolutionary masses, we have brought together the General Orders (1-10) issued by our headquarters and related documents in this volume for publishing.

Chairman Mao has taught us that we should educate ourselves, liberate ourselves, and stand up to start our revolution amid the great storm of mass struggle. We are publishing these General Orders (1-10) in compliance with this great teaching.

In this unprecedented Great Proletarian Cultural Revolution, we must act in accordance with Mao Zedong Thought, the "Sixteen Points" and the Party's policies and strategies at all times, in whatever we do, and wherever we go. Though we will inevitably fall short in our endeavors and make mistakes, encounter resistance and setbacks, and take a circuitous route to our intended destination, we must remember that errors are often the precursors of correct actions. In this rich and vivid environment of the Cultural Revolution, we must always uphold truth, rectify our mistakes, sum up our experiences, keep moving forward and believe that we will undoubtedly achieve ultimate victory.

Given our modest understanding of Mao Zedong Thought and lack of experience of revolutionary struggle, we sincerely hope that workers, peasants, soldiers, revolutionary masses and Red Guard soldiers will point out the shortcomings and errors in our work. This would be of the greatest help to us.

In the future, we would compile and publish further batches of our General Orders and related documents. We have also made a few textual changes in this reprinted version.

Xicheng District Headquarters of the Capital Red Guards Picket Corps
September 17, 1966

Contents

Note: The page numbers above refer to the page numbers of the original documents.

Declaration of Establishment (of Xicheng District Detachment)

Quotation from Chairman Mao

"It is up to us to organize the people. As for the reactionaries in China, it is up to us to organize the people to overthrow them. For everything reactionary, if you don't beat them, they would never fall. It is like sweeping the floor; where the broom does not reach, the dust would never vanish by itself."

In order to defend Mao Zedong Thought, support the Red Guards and their anti-bourgeois resistance, complete the glorious tasks entrusted to us by the Party Central Committee, Chairman Mao and workers, peasants, soldiers and the masses, and carry the Great Proletarian Cultural Revolution through its end, we hereby declare the establishment of the Xicheng District Detachment of the Capital Red Guards Picket Corps.

This decision was discussed and passed by the 31 schools in Xicheng District on August 25th.

The Picket Corps is an organization of the Red Guards, and its members consist of the outstanding individuals and hard core of the Red Guards.

The Picket Corps is a rebellious team, a tool of the proletarian dictatorship, and a close ally of troops of the People's Liberation Army stationed in Beijing.

The Picket Corps is a propaganda team of Mao Zedong Thought.

The establishment of the Capital Red Guards Picket Corps is a happy occasion for all Red Guards, and it once again shows that the Red Guards is a red revolutionary organization that applies Mao Zedong

Thought as its weapon. It is a rebel vanguard that is not afraid to think, speak, revolt and rebel, as well as a fighting force that resolutely implements the Party's policies and bravely defends Mao Zedong Thought.

Our duties and authorities include:

1. To study, faithfully implement, enthusiastically disseminate and bravely defend Mao Zedong Thought;
2. To resolutely assist the revolutionary and rebellious actions of the Red Guards;
3. To resolutely suppress the anti-revolutionary actions of landlords, rich peasants, counter-revolutionaries, bad elements, rightists, capitalist roaders and their progeny;
4. To confiscate and ban any promotional materials not consistent with Mao Zedong Thought;
5. To inspect the red movements of schools, organs, factories and work units;
6. To detain hooligans and those who impersonate Red Guards;
7. The Xicheng District Picket Corps shall be responsible for defending a number of important state organs and important streets prior to the establishment of picket corps in other municipal districts.

This order is effective since 10:00am on August 26th.

We request workers, peasants, soldiers and the masses as well as public security organs in every district to assist us in our work.

Long live the dictatorship of the proletariat!

Long live Mao Zedong Thought!

Red Guards from Beijing No. 3 High School

Red Guards from Beijing No. 1 High School for Girls

Red Guards from Beijing No. 4 High School

Red Guards from Beijing No. 3 High School for Girls

Red Guards from Beijing No. 6 High School

Red Guards from Beijing No. 6 High School for Girls

Red Guards from Beijing No. 7 High School

Red Guards from Beijing No. 8 High School for Girls

Red Guards from Beijing No. 8 High School

Red Guards from High School for Girls Affiliated to Beijing Normal University

Maoist Red Guards from High School for Girls Affiliated to Beijing Normal University

Red Guards from "East is Red" (Beijing No. 28) High School

Red Flag from "East is Red" (Beijing No. 28) High School

Red Guards from Beijing No. 10 High School for Girls

Red Guards from Beijing No. 29 High School

August 18th Red Guards from Beijing No. 29 High School

July 1st Red Guards from "East is Red" No. 4 High School (Huajiasi High School)

Red Guards from Beijing No. 30 High School

August 18th Red Guards from Beijing No. 30 High School

Maoist Red Guards from Beijing No. 30 High School

Red Guards from Beijing No. 31 High School

Red Guards from Red "February 2nd" High School

Red Guards from Beijing No. 33 High School

Red Guards from Red Eagle in Air Force

Red Guards from Beijing No. 35 High School

Red Guards from Beijing Construction Engineering School

School Beijing No. 39 High School

"February 7th" Combat Team from Beijing No. 39 High School

Red Guards from High School Affiliated to Chinese People's Anti-Japanese Military and Political College (Beijing No.13 High School)

Red Guards from Chinese People's Anti-Japanese Military and Political

College No. 4 High School (Temple of the Moon High School)

Red Guards from Chinese People's Anti-Japanese Military and Political College School of War (Beijing No. 41 High School)

Red Guards from Erlong Road High School

Maoist Red Guards from Chinese People's Anti-Japanese Military and Political College High School (Beijing No. 34 High School)

Maoist Red Guards from Taipingqiao High School

Red Guards from Beijing No. 40 High School Red Guards from Capital Jinggangshan (Beijing No. 98) High School

Red Guards from Beijing No. 110 High School

August 25th, 1966

Note: After the Xicheng District Detachment of Capital Red Guards Picket Corps was established, various Red Guards and other red organizations from 19 schools in Beijing's Xicheng District also joined it. The 19 schools include Xisi High School, No. 2 High School Affiliated to Beijing Normal University, Ande Road High School, No. 38 High School, No. 77 High School, Foreign Languages Faculty of the Foreign Trade Institute, Fengsheng School, No. 106 High School, Shehui Road Middle School, School of Foreign Languages, No. 32 High School, High School Affiliated to Institute of Nationalities, No. 2 Railway High School, No. 23 High School, No. 86 High School, Behai High School, No. 53 High School, No. 37 High School and No. 29 High School.

The Six-Point Rules of Capital Red Guards Picket Corps Members

1. Act firmly in accordance with the instructions of Chairman Mao. Dutifully study, faithfully implement, passionately disseminate and bravely defend his supreme instructions.
   Act firmly in accordance with the "Sixteen Points". Study them, be familiar with them, understand them and apply them.
2. Learn from the PLA. Vigorously promote and implement the "Three Eight Work Style": assemble when called, and be capable of fighting and winning.
3. We must resolutely implement the "Three Main Rules of Discipline and the Eight Points for Attention". Beating and insulting people and corporal punishment in any shape or form are strictly prohibited.
4. We must be modest, cautious, prudent, and serve the people wholeheartedly, so as to be the people's loyal servants. We must also resolutely prevent from becoming privileged.
5. Armbands may only be worn while on duty, and must be removed when not on duty. Armbands shall be kept by class monitors.
6. We must conduct in-depth investigations and research, and act in a calm and controlled manner in order to prevent class enemies from seizing opportunities to cause trouble.

Xicheng District Headquarters of the Capital Red Guards Picket Corps

The Six Major Tasks of Capital Red Guards Picket Corps Members

1. Strenuously promote Mao Zedong Thought and the "Sixteen Points".
2. Defend all important state organs and enterprises as well as state secrets.
3. Resolutely assist the revolutionary rebellion of the Red Guards.
4. Assist state public security organs to firmly suppress counter-revolutionary acts.
5. Monitor the behavior of all red organizations and detain hooligans and those who impersonate as Red Guards.
6. Actively assist the revolutionary masses and serve the people.

Xicheng District Headquarters of the Capital Red Guards Picket Corps

Xicheng District Headquarters of the Capital Red Guards Picket Corps

General Order No. 1

The order by the "East is Red" No. 1 High School concerning the ban on selling of works and images of Chairman Mao is hereby revoked.

From this moment on, every Xinhua Bookstore shall be permitted to sell large quantities of the works and images of Chairman Mao.

This General Order is immediately in effect.

Xicheng District Headquarters of the Capital Red Guards Picket Corps
August 26, 1966

Xicheng District Headquarters of the Capital Red Guards Picket Corps

General Order No. 2

No organization or individual may intercept the vehicles or search the dwellings of senior officials. Offenders shall be arrested by the Capital Red Guards Picket Corps. Knowing offenders shall be severely punished.

This proclamation is issued in all sincerity and earnestness.

Xicheng District Headquarters of the Capital Red Guards Picket Corps
August 26, 1966

Xicheng District Headquarters of the Capital Red Guards Picket Corps

General Order No. 3

Eight Comments on Some of the Existing Problems:

The Xicheng District Detachment of the Capital Red Guards Picket Corps was officially established in the evening of August 25, 1966, and it officially started its work on August 26, 1966.

We have already stated that we have the right to confiscate and ban any publicity materials that are not in accord with Mao Zedong Thought. We shall also resolutely oppose any behaviors that are not in accord with Mao Zedong Thought.

We have therefore made the following decisions:

1. At the height of the Cultural Revolution, in order to meet the urgent needs of the masses of workers, peasants, soldiers, ordinary people and revolutionary Red Guards, large volumes of Chairman Mao's works must be sold. They are our weapon, our sustenance and our compass. All sorts of Chairman Mao images and medals should also be made and sold. Chairman Mao is the reddest of red suns in our hearts. We shall wage a resolute struggle against, and thoroughly defeat, anyone who dares to prevent the masses of workers, peasants, soldiers, ordinary people and revolutionary Red Guards from studying Chairman Mao's works or who dares to remove the red sun from our hearts.
2. Without the permission of the CPC Central Committee, a directive from a municipal Party committee or instructions from the Picket Corps, no organization or individual has the right

to enforce martial law or intercept and inspect pedestrians and vehicles, particularly those of senior officials.

3. Nobody is permitted to arbitrarily inspect state organs or search the homes of senior cadres. We must defend state secrets, and we must ensure the safety of old revolutionary officials.
4. Nobody has the authority to order an old revolutionary official to move home, dismiss their housekeeping staff or turn in their belongings, including TVs, sofas and vehicles. We must resolutely stamp out class revenge by our enemies and firmly oppose absolute egalitarianism.
5. In order to facilitate the transport needed for the revolutionary activities of Red Guards during the Cultural Revolution, there is no need to use headlights on vehicles traveling along illuminated roads.
6. Any goods currently in stores with brands that are not considered reactionary shall not be forbidden, and may continue to be sold. Nobody may prevent their sale, and bad elements shall not be allowed to opportunistically destroy state property. In the future, production departments shall remove all old brands and establish new, revolutionary brands. Red Guards are not permitted to take any old branded products from factories.
7. It is forbidden to harass foreigners, returned overseas Chinese or compatriots from Hong Kong and Macao. It is necessary to ensure their safety and allow them to go about their business.
8. When searching the homes of landlords, rich peasants, counter-revolutionaries, bad elements, rightists and capitalist roaders, groups must notify the local Red Guard headquarters, contact the local police station and neighborhood committee. All seized property shall go to the state. When searching homes, be vigilant and only conduct verbal struggles. Let others expose themselves before taking action, and prevent bad elements from making trouble or taking advantage of loopholes.

The Red Guards Picket Corps shall actively publicize and strictly follow the above decisions. Every Red Guard shall take the lead in their implementation. Those who violate these orders without good reason shall be subjected to criticism. We shall resolutely fight against counter-revolutionaries with ulterior motives.

Only the Left could revolt, while the Right is not allowed to cause any chaos!

Long live the proletarian dictatorship!

We swear to defend the Party Central Committee!

We swear to defend Chairman Mao!

Xicheng District Headquarters of the Capital Red Guards Picket Corps
August 27, 1966

(The contents and gists of General Order No. 1 and General Order No. 2 are fully contained in General Order No. 3. This order shall be effective on its promulgation.)

Xicheng District Headquarters of the Capital Red Guards Picket Corps

General Order No. 4

"Policy and tactics are the lifeline of the Party; leading comrades at all levels must give them full attention, and must never on any account be negligent."

Mao Zedong

Views on searching the homes of landlords, rich peasants, counter-revolutionaries, bad elements, rightists and capitalist roaders:

Many Red Guards in the city are conducting searches of the homes of landlords, rich peasants, counter-revolutionaries, bad elements, rightists and capitalist roaders to look for bad elements and stolen goods, and they have achieved great success in this area. These revolutionary deeds are commendable. Nevertheless, problems are arising due to a lack of experience, which is then allowing class enemies to take advantage of loopholes and seize opportunities to engage in sabotage. We therefore need to be more vigilant, be well-organized, tighten discipline, and do not give enemies any opportunity. We must do this thoroughly and achieve victory.

Therefore, we propose the following seven provisions:

1. Carry out in-depth investigations and research

Chairman Mao says, "No investigation, no right to speak," and "To investigate a problem is to solve it."

What sort of person belongs to the six black categories? And what sort of person does not belong to the six black categories? To answer the questions, it is necessary to conduct thorough investigations and research. One can integrate the efforts of the Red Guards, the police and residents committees to investigate issues. Do not conduct a search before you have a clear understanding of the situation in order to avoid making mistakes or being used by the bad elements. It is important to strive to conduct thorough searches and not search the wrong homes or miss out homes. You are not to search the homes of people who do not belong to the six black categories. The homes of leading cadres of the state must not be searched.

2. Inform the organization

Before carrying out home searches, it is necessary to inform the local headquarters of the Red Guards, obtain a letter of reference, and contact the local police station or revolutionary residents' committee to get their assistance. You may also seek advice from the work unit of the person whose home is being searched. Any home searched by an organization would be the responsibility of that organization, and any other organization that wishes to intervene must contact that organization.

3. Engage in verbal struggles, be vigilant, and let others expose themselves before we take action

Chairman Mao has taught us that in the course of struggle of the Cultural Revolution, we should "use verbal struggle and not violent struggle." He has also taught us to "gain the initiative and thus force the enemy into a passive position" and "letting others expose themselves before we take action."

We have under the strong dictatorship of the proletariat. Any enemy that wishes to restore the old order or make trouble will find it impossible to achieve. We are not the least bit afraid of them! We shall engage in a verbal struggle with them to prove our incomparable strength. After the verbal struggle, those who should be dictated to shall be dictated to, that which should be expanded shall be expanded and those that should be given a way out shall be given one. But if anyone is dishonest, dares to use force or carries out class revenge, they shall be suppressed immediately and shown no mercy! This is known as letting others expose themselves before we take action. In the course of carrying out searches, be on heightened alert at all times, seize the initiative, strive to wage a verbal struggle to the end, and do not resort to violence.

4. Turn in everything that is captured

Chairman Mao has instructed us to "Turn in everything that is captured."

When searching homes, the main objective is political, and the secondary objective is economic. Confiscated goods are evidences of reactionary behavior, such as firearms and ammunition, weapons, gold, silver and pearls acquired by exploitation and stolen goods. All confiscated goods must remain undamaged, and all be turned in to the state. Cultural relics and historical sites must be protected. Red Guards and organizations must not keep any goods belongs to the six black categories.

5. Handle each case differently, strike at only a few enemies at a time, and isolate the enemy

Chairman Mao has said, "In the struggle against the anti-Communist die-hards, our policy is to make use of contradictions, win over the many, oppose the few, and crush our enemies one by one, and to wage struggles on just grounds, to our advantage, and with restraint."

It is welcomed for the relatives of the six black categories to take the initiative in reporting them, voluntarily ask to inspect their homes, and work alongside the inspectors. We can be lenient to those who do good deeds. The methods and extents of a home search should be in accordance with the target. We must handle each case differently. People must be focused and have a sense of propriety when it comes to confiscated items. We must not disrupt the lives of families. Searches must be conducted carefully and thoroughly. Among the families belonging to the six black categories, many young people aspire to be revolutionaries. This is something they can strive for. As long as they completely turn their backs on their families and resolutely join the revolution, we shall unite with them. We shall win over the majority of them, and fight with only a small number of them in order to isolate the enemy to the greatest possible extent. To achieve this goal, we must conduct investigations and researches, handle each case differently, and wage verbal struggles. During the overall process of home searches, we shall always be vigilant and prevent bad elements from exploiting any loopholes.

6. Defeat enemies and educate the masses

Our searches and confiscations are not simply about striking at the enemy economically. They are most importantly about striking hard at the enemy politically. We need to drag out these parasites, bloodsuckers and murderous butchers, expose them to the light of day and put them in front of large crowds, publicize their numerous sins, organize mass struggles against them, denounce them, conduct large-scale mass education campaigns and spread Mao Zedong Thought. Through struggle, we shall overthrow these bloodsuckers; raise the proletarian consciousness of the masses; improve the prestige of the proletariat; educate and transform those born into families that belong to the exploiting classes, make them aware of their own class branding and help them make a clean break from their families, transform themselves and take the path of revolution; promote unity among the revolutionary masses, unite as one with them, pool the strength and courage of the masses, struggle heroically and see the Great Proletarian Cultural Revolution through to its conclusion. Every Red Guard must work with the masses, conduct propaganda work among the masses, mobilize more of the broad masses and commit themselves to this great movement.

7. Give a way out

As stated by the "Sixteen Points", "Rightists who oppose the Party and socialism should be exposed and overthrown, and their influence should be eliminated, while also giving them a way out to be rehabilitated."

Those who have been proven to be part of the six black categories and struggled against, especially those who have attempted to flee, except active counter-revolutionaries who should be dealt with in accordance with the law, should be given a way out politically. This way out comes with a time limit (September 10th) to leave Beijing (unless there are special circumstances, extension can be granted upon permission by the work unit or unit who carried out the home search) and return to their ancestral home. The reform of such people shall be overseen by the revolutionary masses, who shall give them an opportunity to rehabilitate themselves.

The above provisions are to be implemented by members of the Red Guards Picket Corps and every Red Guards. Police stations and residents' committees should monitor and coordinate their implementation.

Every Red Guard must become a model of compliance with mass discipline. We want everyone to sing loudly the "Three Main Rules of Discipline and Eight Points for Attention" song and become models of compliance with the "Three Main Rules of Discipline and Eight Points for Attention" personally developed by Chairman Mao. Any Red Guard who violates the mass discipline or breaches the "Three Main Rules of Discipline and Eight Points for Attention" shall be the subject of severe criticism from the revolutionary masses. Action shall be taken in serious cases.

We Red Guard soldiers must act in accordance with Mao Zedong Thought, the Party's policies and the "Sixteen Points" at all times, in all circumstances and wherever we go. We shall resolutely oppose anyone who does not act in accordance with Mao Zedong Thought and resolutely support anybody who acts in accordance with Mao Zedong Thought. We shall act in accordance with Mao Zedong Thought regardless of any difficulties we might face.

Study the "Sixteen Points"! Implement the "Sixteen Points"! Publicize the "Sixteen Points"! Defend the "Sixteen Points"!

Resolutely carry out the Great Proletarian Cultural Revolution to the end!

Xicheng District Headquarters of the Capital Red Guards Picket Corps
August 29, 1966

Xicheng District Headquarters of the Capital Red Guards Picket Corps

General Order No. 5

"We must do as Chairman Mao has instructed, and wage a verbal struggle instead of a violent one. We should not beat the others. The same goes for the struggle against capitalist roaders and against landlords, rich peasants, counter-revolutionaries, bad elements and rightists. Violence only affects the flesh; verbal struggle affects the soul. Only through verbal struggle can we fully reveal and profoundly criticize enemies, thoroughly expose their counter-revolutionary intentions, and isolate and overthrow them to the greatest possible extent."

Lin Biao

Opinions on Using Verbal Struggle Instead of Resorting to Violence

In order to defend Mao Zedong Thought, implement the Party's policies, act in accordance with the "Sixteen Points" and thoroughly carry out the Great Proletarian Cultural Revolution, it is necessary to prohibit beating and insulting people, corporal punishment in any shape or form, and obtaining confessions by compulsion in the course of the Great Proletarian Revolution upon this day.

Violence is not allowed in cases where the identity or background of a person is unclear, a person that commits a mistake but is not opposing the Party or socialism, a person that commits a serious mistake but the nature of the error is not clear and those who have already been identified as anti-Party and anti-socialist elements.

We are the most loyal Red Guards of the Party Central Committee and Chairman Mao. We must resolutely act in accordance with Party policies and the "Sixteen Points".

Following Comrade Lin Biao's speech on August 31st, from this moment forth, any Red Guard who violates the supreme instructions, acts in a way that does not accord with Party policies, or beats people at their own wills shall be subject to severe criticism and education.

We must also strictly punish and firmly suppress class enemies who launch counterattacks, engage in class revenge, and seize opportunities to commit violent acts.

The truth is in our hands. The proletarian dictatorship is in our hands. We shall conduct a verbal struggle and thoroughly topple our enemies. We must achieve complete victory in the Great Proletarian Cultural Revolution.

Xicheng District Headquarters of the Capital Red Guards Picket Corps

September 3, 1966

Xicheng District Headquarters of the Capital Red Guards Picket Corps

General Order No. 6

"Present the facts, use reason, shun simplistic and crude practices, prohibit beatings and corporal punishment in any shape or form, and prevent confessions being obtained by compulsion."

"The Twenty-three Points"

"Use verbal struggle instead of violent struggle. This is an important Party policy for the Great Proletarian Cultural Revolution. We must adhere to and implement this policy."

Editorial in *People's Daily*

Supplementary Information on Verbal Struggle

General Order No. 5 was issued by our Headquarters on September 3, 1966.

The General Order stated, "In order to defend Mao Zedong Thought, implement the Party's policies, act in accordance with the 'Sixteen Points' and thoroughly carry out the Great Proletarian Cultural Revolution, it is necessary to prohibit beating and insulting people, corporal punishment in any shape or form, and obtaining confessions by compulsion in the course of the Great Proletarian Revolution from this day forth."

This was not specific enough, so the following supplementary information has been formulated.

1. Verbal Struggle

We must uphold verbal struggle and not use violence. Beating and insulting people, corporal punishment in any shape or form and obtaining confessions by compulsion are not methods of struggle we should adopt.

2. Corporal Punishment in Any Shape or Form

Being made to kneel, lie down, carry heavy loads, parade through the streets, stand for a long time, raise one's hands for a long time, bow or do heavy work for long periods are all considered forms of corporal punishment and are not methods of struggle that we should adopt.

3. Insulting People

Hanging boards around people's necks, making people wear silly hats, singing confession songs, shaving people's heads, etc. are all insults and are not methods of struggle we should adopt.

4. Obtaining Confessions by Compulsion, and Giving Them Credence

Disregarding investigations and researches and disregarding evidence while blindly giving credence to confessions, and obtaining confessions using violence or threats are known as obtaining confessions by compulsion, and giving them credence. This approach is blind, vulnerable to exploitation by bad elements. It is not a method of struggle that we should adopt.

5. Labor

Organizations should participate in work. This will make it easy to transform people. However, it is necessary to treat people based on their circumstances. The elderly, weak, sick and disabled should not be forced to work for long periods of time.

The five points above are intended to compliment General Order No. 5. It is hoped that all Red Guards shall consult and implement them, and the revolutionary masses shall assist in their implementation.

Members of Picket Corps have the right to work in accordance with these provisions and to interfere and put an end to any behavior that does not comply with Party policies.

Acting in accordance with Mao Zedong Thought, the Party's policies and the "Sixteen Points" will never tie our hands or limit the revolution. On the contrary, it will make us more powerful and suitable to wage revolution, and make the Great Proletarian Cultural Revolution more successful and complete. This is what all the class enemies fear the most!

Mao Zedong Thought is unbeatable!

Long live Mao Zedong Thought!

Xicheng District Headquarters of the Capital Red Guards Picket Corps

September 9, 1966

Xicheng District Headquarters of the Capital Red Guards Picket Corps

General Order No. 7

"In the struggle against the anti-Communist die-hards, our policy is to make use of contradictions, win over the many, oppose the few and crush our enemies one by one, and to wage struggles on just grounds, to our advantage and with restraint."

Mao Zedong

"We must differentiate between targets of the four clean-ups campaign based on circumstances and isolate bad elements to the greatest possible extent."

"The Twenty-three Points"

Opinions Regarding the Expulsion of Landlords, Rich Peasants, Counter-Revolutionaries and Bad Elements

General Order No. 4 was issued by our headquarters on August 29th, which contained seven provisions.

The following additional provisions have been formulated based on issues that have been raised in the course of our recent work. Where a conflict exists between this and previous general orders, the provisions of this General Order shall prevail.

Article 1

Having been exposed, landlords, rich peasants, counter-revolutionaries and bad elements who flee from villages or provincial cities to Beijing or those that attempt to conceal their background, history or criminal activities and worm their way into state organs and factories, mines and enterprises, shall be ordered to leave Beijing and return to their ancestral homes. They shall be struggled against by the masses and persecuted by them. The masses know their criminal activities, and shall also supervise their manual labor and reform.

When dealing with such people, it is necessary to liaise with public security organs, who will determine methods for dealing with them. This is to ensure that reactionaries who have committed heinous crimes cannot conceal their identity and get away without punishment.

In order to avoid increasing the burden on people in rural areas, people from these categories who are unable to do manual labor and have no dependents at their ancestral home, or whose ancestral home is Beijing, may be allowed to stay in Beijing and undergo supervised reform. However, if there is significant public anger towards an individual and the masses demand a struggle, the demands of the masses must be met.

If the relatives and children of people from these categories do not themselves belong to the four categories, they shall be allowed to stay in Beijing if they can live independently or if they have dependents in the city.

The deadline for people of these four categories to leave Beijing has been extended from before September 10 to before September 27 (unless there are special circumstances, in which case an extension may be granted).

Article 2

1. Capitalists

Capitalists do not have to leave Beijing; they can remain in their work units to undergo reform.

Patriotic, law-abiding capitalists who support the Communist Party and socialism usually belong to the national bourgeoisie. Our contradictions with them must be handled as contradictions among the people. This is a general principle that we shall not depart from.

2. Rightists

Rightists who have been renounced the label shall no longer be considered as rightists. If the label has been wrongly renounced, they shall be dealt with at the later stage of the movement.

Rightists do not have to leave Beijing, and can remain in their work units where they shall be dealt with through the organizational structure, which will facilitate the struggle against them as well as their supervision and reform.

3. Other People having Historical Problems

Those who have historical problems, have been thoroughly dealt with by a Party organization, with their labels been removed, their behaviors converted, and their civil rights recovered, and who have not been caught in any reactionary acts may stay in Beijing and continue to work at their work unit to undergo further reform. If it is decided that such people were judged incorrectly, they can be dealt with at the later stage of the movement by Party organizations and the masses. There is no need to deal with them now.

4. Reformed Landlords, Rich Peasants, Counter-Revolutionaries and Bad Elements

These categories of people should be treated differently from landlords, rich peasants, counter-revolutionaries and bad elements. They can be allowed to continue working at their work units, to continue living and working at the original place, where they will be supervised and reformed by their local Party organizations and the masses. If they lapse backwards into their old ways, they can be reevaluated by the Party organization and the masses, but there is no need to rush into this.

People from the above four categories who break the law or violate discipline or are active counter-revolutionaries should be immediately reported to the public security organs and relevant departments, so they can be punished in accordance with the law.

Article 3

1. Organizational Procedures

Anyone proven to belong to one of the four categories mentioned in Article 1 must be made to leave Beijing within the given time limit.

The formalities required to organize their departure should be completed with their work unit and local police station and with the help of the home searching unit and residents' committee. It would be better to contact their original place of domicile beforehand. Procedures for changing their household registration should be handled directly by the police station and their work unit. Other units, Red Guard organizations or individuals may indirectly assist, but must not directly interfere. This is to prevent bad elements from causing trouble and obtaining benefits.

2. Necessary Provisions

It is necessary to ensure that such people have the necessary provisions to sustain their living. There is no need to confiscate property that has no political significance. They must be given what they need to sustain their living. Do not resort to violence against them. Their safety on the way of departure must be guaranteed.

These provisions are in effect immediately.

Where any police station, office or relevant unit previously acted in a manner inconsistent with this General Order prior to its promulgation, their case shall be considered by relevant departments.

We firmly uphold acting in accordance with the Party's policies. We shall not forgive our enemies; rather, we shall isolate to the greatest possible extent any bad elements that oppose the Party and socialism, thoroughly overthrow them and ensure that they never rise up.

Xicheng District Headquarters of the Capital Red Guards Picket Corps

September 9, 1966

Xicheng District Headquarters of the Capital Red Guards Picket Corps

General Order No. 8

Supplementary materials and instructions regarding General Order No. 6 and General Order No. 7

As said by Chairman Mao, "The peasants are clear-sighted. Who is bad and who is not, who is the worst and who is not quite so vicious, who deserves severe punishment and who deserves to be let off lightly — the peasants keep clear accounts, and very seldom has the punishment exceeded the crime."

As revolutionary masses and Red Guard soldiers, we are just like this! The Great Proletarian Cultural Revolution is going very well. Throughout the previous stage, the revolutionary masses and the overall orientation of the Red Guard movement has been revolutionary. Their handling of numerous issues, including home searches, the expulsion of landlords, rich peasants, counter-revolutionaries and bad elements, and the struggle against capitalist roaders have all been done correctly, with very few cases being mishandled.

As Chairman Mao said on the dictatorship of the proletariat, "We enforce their dictatorship over the running dogs of imperialism — the landlord class and bureaucrat-bourgeoisie, as well as the representatives of those classes, the Kuomintang reactionaries and their accomplices. We would suppress them; allow them only to behave themselves and not to be unruly in word or deed. If they speak or act in an unruly way, they will be promptly stopped and punished."

We have a stern warning to those who attempt to launch counterattacks to settle scores: in the past, out of bitter hatred of the enemy, our revolutionary masses and Red Guards ransacked your homes, beat you, made you wear tall hats, paraded you through the streets, and sent you to your ancestral home to reform through labor. To us, these things are not a big deal. If you seek to take advantage of the shortcomings in the mass movement, launch counterattacks and carry out class revenge, which would just like lifting a rock only to drop it on your own feet. Every member of the Picket Corps has the right and the duty to assist the revolutionary masses to resolutely suppress all counterattacks of class enemies.

These are supplementary materials and instructions for General Order No. 6 and No. 7:

1. We further declare that, the stubborn capitalists, rightists and the children from families that belong to the four categories who refuse to reform their ways and anger the masses must be dealt with severely in accordance with the requests of the revolutionary masses.
2. Regarding the provision in General Order No. 6, which stated people should not be made to stand and bow for long periods of time, this should be determined based on the requirements of the struggle and shall be handled accordingly by the revolutionary masses.
3. Property gained through exploitation is considered as "property with political significance".
4. For capitalists who remain in the city, their supervision and reform shall be overseen by the people whom they have exploited and oppressed and who know their criminal activities. This is in accordance with the Party's policies, and is an effective method, as it is the most feared by capitalists. We should deal with rightists based on the same principles as capitalists. We should not simply palm off contradictions for others to deal with, and irresponsibly let others clean up the mess.

In the Great Proletarian Cultural Revolution, the most powerful and effective weapon is not violent struggle or corporal punishment, but the invincible Mao Zedong Thought. As we said in General Order No. 6, "Acting in accordance with Mao Zedong Thought, the Party's policies and the 'Sixteen Points' will never tie our hands or limit the revolution. On the contrary, it will make us more powerful and suitable to wage revolution, and make the Great Proletarian Cultural Revolution more successful and complete. This is what all the class enemies fear the most!"

Counterattacks by counter-revolutionary forces are an inevitable result of the development of revolutionary forces. It is an inevitable result after touching their souls, and it is determined by the class nature of revolutionary forces. It is of no great surprise. Their class nature determines that they will always miscalculate the situation, miscalculate the great strength of the people and miscalculate the tremendous power of Mao Zedong Thought. Upheaval is a good thing. Every time there has been a major upheaval in history, it has given strong impetus for social development. It is to be expected that, in the storm of the mass movement, countless intelligent and courageous revolutionary heroes will emerge.

In the raging fire of the Great Proletarian Revolution, a glowing, red new world of Mao Zedong Thought will emerge!

Long live the powerful dictatorship of the proletariat!

Long live the great mass movement!

Long live the invincible Mao Zedong Thought!

Xicheng District Headquarters of the Capital Red Guards Picket Corps
September 11, 1966

Xicheng District Headquarters of the Capital Red Guards Picket Corps

General Order No. 9

"The people, who have already achieved victory in the revolution, should assist those who are struggling for liberation. This is an obligation of our internationalism."

Mao Zedong

Suggestions on Receiving Guests on October 1st

1. The Situation

The Great Proletarian Cultural Revolution is like a surging river flowing east, crashing into the banks of the old world, and shaking the earth.

All the revolutionary people of the world are rejoicing and cheering. They see how deep-rooted Mao Zedong Thought has become in China, and that it emits a brilliant light similar to the red sun; they see Chairman Mao's Red Guards surging forward and showing what they are capable of; and they see that the tide of revolution is unstoppable, and that it is destined to bury the old world.

Conversely, imperialism, modern revisionism and all reactionary forces are scared to death. They have a deep-seated hatred of the great revolutionary movement. They try their best to denigrate and spread fictitious stories about the revolution, attack the Red Guards, and attempt to set off another wave of anti-Chinese sentiment. All we can do is to expose their lies and tell them that they are on their last legs and the end is near to them, as they are just like lifting a rock only to drop it on their own feet.

2. The Task

October 1st is approaching. By then, foreign guests from various walks of life around the world will congregate in Beijing. The fact that they are coming to Beijing represents a victory of us and a failure of imperialism, modern revisionism and all reactionary forces. We Red Guards and revolutionary masses are armed with Mao Zedong Thought, and are patriots as well as internationalists. We have a responsibility and obligation to use the enormous power of Mao Zedong Thought, our revolutionary rebellious spirit as well as revolutionary discipline to inspire comrades of seizing power and crushing the enemy.

3. Provisions

a. Take advantage of visits, open forums and individual discussions with foreign visitors to vigorously promote Mao Zedong Thought, so that they can take the flame of Mao Zedong Thought to every corners of the world and stoke the fires of revolution.
b. Assume the attitude of the master of the house when speaking to foreigners, while respecting their customs. Stand tall, look far, influence them politically and ideologically, and inspire them. Oppose great-nation chauvinism.
c. All members of picket corps and Red Guards must be vigilant to prevent trouble by class enemies and ensure the safety of foreign visitors.
d. Do not get in the way of vehicles carrying foreign guests or surround them. Do not prevent foreign guests from taking photographs, except where you suspect they have ulterior motives, and ensure they are allowed to go about their business freely. Do not interfere with the clothes, adornments or hobbies of foreign visitors.

Red Guards and all revolutionary masses across the city, unite and struggle to fulfill this glorious task!

Long live the Great Proletarian Cultural Revolution!

Long live the great unity of the people of the world!

Down with US Imperialism, modern revisionism and reactionaries!

Long live the invincible Mao Zedong Thought!

Long live Chairman Mao, the beloved leader of people all over the world!

Xicheng District Headquarters of the Capital Red Guards Picket Corps
September 14, 1966

Xicheng District Headquarters of the Capital Red Guards Picket Corps

General Order No. 10

"Students from across the country are now coming to Beijing, and Beijing students are traveling to other parts of the country for the great exchange of revolutionary experiences. We view this as a good thing, and we support you. The CPC Central Committee has decided that college students from all over the country and some representative of high school students should visit Beijing in groups.... We believe that this nationwide exchange of revolutionary experiences will help to promote the further development of the Great Proletarian Cultural Revolution."

(Selected from a speech given by Premier Zhou Enlai at a meeting with revolutionary teachers and students in Beijing)

Welcoming Students from Other Places to Beijing for the Great Exchange of Revolutionary Experiences

The Great Proletarian Cultural Revolution is developing rapidly. Struggles, criticisms and reforms in schools have already developed into struggles, criticisms and reforms in society. The flame of the Great Proletarian Cultural Revolution has already spread from Beijing to the rest of the country, and formed a raging fire. Under the leadership of the CPC Central Committee and Chairman Mao, a new high tide in the great nationwide exchange of revolutionary experiences is emerging.

The nationwide exchange of revolutionary experiences is a great initiative and a good thing. Without this type of exchange, it would not be possible to genuinely mobilize the masses. Without it, the Great Proletarian Cultural Revolution could not develop further. The nationwide exchange of revolutionary experiences indicates that the Great Proletarian Cultural Revolution has entered into a new high phase.

National revolution could never be developed in a balanced way. As Beijing is the center and source of the Great Proletarian Cultural Revolution, it is the location of the CPC Central Committee and Chairman Mao. Thus, it is the responsibility of students from Beijing to travel to other places to fan the flames and study the experiences of others, and it is completely normal and justified for students from other places to come to Beijing to exchange revolutionary experiences and study. There are students from other places who do not fear hardship and do what it takes to come all the way to Beijing. We can learn from their revolutionary attitude and their daring spirit of rebellion. Beijing Red Guards and revolutionary comrades should wholeheartedly support the decisions of the CPC Central Committee, and give a huge revolutionary warm welcome to the revolutionary students from across the country. In order to ensure the success of the great exchange of revolutionary experiences, we requested all Red Guards to do according to the following regulations:

1. All Red Guards should be mobilized immediately to thoroughly study the speeches of Comrade Lin Biao and Comrade Zhou Enlai from their meeting with revolutionary teachers and students in Beijing, and understand the importance of the great nationwide exchange of revolutionary experiences. The majority of students from other places who are coming to Beijing are Red Guards. They are coming for the revolution, and to study. We should give them a warm welcome. For those who are not Red Guards, as long as they are revolutionary, we should offer them a warm welcome as well. It is also necessary to remain vigilant against people who wish to sabotage the exchange of revolutionary experiences.
2. All Red Guards should act immediately to do everything

possible to resolve difficulties for students from other parts of the country who have come to Beijing. We should promote a spirit of fraternity, and make life easier for others by assuming their burdens. The heads of all units should offer housing to students quickly and to the best of their abilities, and contact municipal Party committees to make provisions for the living, eating, transport and medical requirements for students, and try to provide them with what they need during their exchange in Beijing.

3. All Red Guards should be organized immediately to strengthen leadership. Every unit should appoint someone to set up a reception group, and liaise with district and municipal reception groups to get things done successfully.

Xicheng District Headquarters of the Capital Red Guards Picket Corps
September 14, 1966

Xicheng District Headquarters of the Capital Red Guards Picket Corps

Opinions on Launching Comprehensive Rectifications within the Red Guards

(This document is for internal distribution within the Red Guards)

September 26, 1966

Xicheng District Headquarters of the Capital Red Guards Picket Corps

Opinions on Launching a Comprehensive Rectification within the Red Guards

"To accomplish the task of overthrowing the enemy, we must accomplish the task of rectifying within the Party...Once our Party's style of work is put completely right, the people all over the country will learn from our example. Those outside the Party who have the same kind of bad style will, if they are good and honest people, learn from our example and correct their mistakes, and thus the whole nation will be influenced. So long as our Communist ranks are in good order and march in step, so long as our troops are picked troops and our weapons are good weapons, any enemy, no matter how powerful they are, could be overthrown."

Mao Zedong

"If, in the interests of the people, we persist in doing what is right, and correct what is wrong, our teams will surely thrive."

Mao Zedong

We Red Guards were created in the storm of the Great Proletarian Cultural Revolution, and nurtured to maturity by Mao Zedong Thought.

We Red Guards only recently joined the struggle, but have already made a considerable impact. We have the bravery to revolt, to rebel, and to engage in a tenacious struggle against all class enemies. We are afraid of nothing. We have swept away the "Four Olds" and promoted the "Four News". We have spearheaded the struggle, scared the class enemies out of their wits, and rocked the whole society and the old world. In the struggle of the Great Proletarian Cultural Revolution, we have done away with power and prestige, and created immortal feats!

During the storm of class struggle, we have advanced in the shipping lane opened by Chairman Mao. Our general direction has always been correct. Nevertheless, we must be aware of our own shortcomings and errors. We are not afraid of pointing out our own shortcomings, which must be corrected. We must follow Chairman Mao's teachings, educate ourselves in the course of struggle to benefit the people, uphold truth, and correct mistakes. We must take the best interests of the people of China and the whole world as our starting point, take the conditions of our proletarian revolutionary successors as our highest standards, be strict with ourselves, measure ourselves, and transform ourselves.

In the history of our Party, there have been several major rectification campaigns. Chairman Mao once said, "In accordance with Lenin's principles of forging close ties with the masses, acknowledging the pioneering spirit of the masses, carrying out criticisms and self-criticisms, and following years of revolutionary practice, we have come up with a method of rectification..." "The rectification movement is 'a widespread movement of Marxist education.' Rectification means to involve the whole Party to study Marxism through criticism and self-criticism." It is under the wise leadership of Mao Zedong that our Party has previously achieved great successes in the previous rectification movements and made our Party undefeatable.

During the 1942 rectification movement, Chairman Mao personally initiated and led a great and profound struggle along ideological lines. Through the struggle, he consolidated the position of proletarian ideology inside and outside the Party, and greatly improved the thinking of Party cadres, thereby achieving an unprecedented level of unity and writing a magnificent new chapter in our Party's history.

During the rectification movement, a series of essays written by Chairman Mao, such as "Reform Our Study," "Rectify the

Party's Style of Work" and "Oppose Stereotyped Party Writing" had comprehensively and profoundly analysed various erroneous tendencies and their root causes politically, organizationally and ideologically, and pointed out the right direction. These brilliant works have summarized the Party's experiences and lessons on revolutionary struggle in the previous decades. Nowadays, they also have a great significance on revolutionizing the ideology of the Red Guards.

Some negative trends have already emerged among a small number of Red Guards. This is mainly to do with a sense of individualistic heroism ideologically as well as liberalism and factionalism organizationally. These comrades have slackened their efforts when it comes to studying Chairman Mao's works as well as in ideological transformation. As a result, their bourgeois ideology has gained a foothold. If it is allowed to develop and spread unchecked, it will corrupt our comrades, disrupt our teams, destroy the unity of will, unity of action and unity of discipline of the Red Guards, reduce the effectiveness of the Red Guards, and result in tremendous losses for the Great Proletarian Cultural Revolution.

As said by Chairman Mao, "Though the majority of people in our Party and in our teams are clean and honest, we must in all seriousness put things in order both ideologically and organizationally, if we are to develop the revolutionary movement more effectively and bring it to speedier success. To put things in order organizationally requires us to first do so ideologically, and to launch a struggle of proletarian ideology against non-proletarian ideology."

Based on the teachings of Chairman Mao, we believe it is necessary to launch a comprehensive campaign within the Red Guards to rectify ideology, get rid of negative work styles, promote a revolutionary spirit, teach our teams the importance of Mao Zedong Thought, make them more proletarian and revolutionary, and make better use of our combative and pioneering role in the Cultural Revolution.

We believe that those in charge of Red Guards in every school should pay attention to this, integrate it with the circumstances in their school on the basis of investigations and researches, and systematically launch a comprehensive rectification campaign within the Red Guards. The process of a rectification campaign is the process of studying Mao Zedong Thought. Every comrade in the Red Guards should hold high the great red banner of Mao Zedong Thought, repeatedly and carefully study Chairman Mao's works, improve training in Mao Zedong Thought, make full use of the powerful weapons of criticism and self-criticism, check themselves, help comrades, promote solidarity and strengthen our teams to advance the struggle.

This rectification is aimed at breaking private interests and promoting public interests. We must oppose individualistic heroism, be modest and prudent, serve the people wholeheartedly, and always be faithful servants of the people. We must oppose "imperial envoys" and those who take everything into their own hands, promote the practices of investigation and research, and be pupils of the masses. We must oppose those who act arbitrarily and tyrannically, promote proletarian democracy, and be good at listening to different people's opinions. We must oppose those who try to stand out from the crowd and be ostentatious, prevent privilege, continue the revolutionary traditions of the Veteran Red Army, and continue the work style of struggling and working hard. We must oppose liberalism and conciliationism, engage in a fierce ideological struggle, eliminate capitalism, and promote a revolution in our ideology. We must oppose sectarianism, selfishness and the "small circle" mentality, improve the communist spirit, strengthen the unity of the revolutionary teams and fight together. In short, we must resolutely resist and oppose those whose thoughts and deeds are not in accord with Mao Zedong Thought, and we must strongly support, follow and promote all those whose thoughts and deeds are in accord with Mao Zedong Thought!

The Great Proletarian Cultural Revolution has always been a great revolution that has touched the souls of the people, and will inevitably touch the soul of each of us. We Red Guards must have the bravery to face the enemy in our souls, and completely rid ourselves of all non-proletarian things. We must abandon evil individualism, and embrace the brilliance of Mao Zedong Thought!

This rectification movement may involve a thousand or ten thousand items, but the first point is to study Chairman Mao's works. Through this rectification movement, we would reach a new peak in the creative study and application of Chairman Mao's works. We Red Guards must never forget or overlook the importance of studying Chairman Mao's works. That would be the equivalent of overlooking our own lives or the revolutionary cause, and will lead us to the wrong path and mistakes. That would be very dangerous. What experience have we gained? And what conclusions have we arrived? We have learned that Mao Zedong Thought cannot be lost for a moment, and the works of Chairman Mao cannot be left for a moment.

During this campaign, we recommend everyone to study the following works by Chairman Mao, namely "Reform Our Study," "Rectify the Party's Style of Work," "Oppose Stereotyped Party Writing," "Combat Liberalism," "Serve the People," "In Memory of Norman Bethune," "On the Correction of Mistaken Ideas in the Party," "Our Study and the Current Situation," "Preface and Postscript of Rural Surveys," "Speech at the Assembly of Representative of the Shaanxi-Gansu-Ningxia Border Region" and "The Role of the Chinese Communist Party in the National War." Comrades can focus on studying them based on their own backgrounds.

In addition, we have selected relevant instructions of Chairman Mao and Lin Biao aimed at a small number of Red Guards with undesirable tendencies. These are attached and should be studied for reference.

This campaign is a comprehensive, top-down movement. Leading Red Guards should participate enthusiastically, serve as examples to others, and take the lead in studying Chairman Mao's works as well as ridding their minds of non-proletarian thoughts.

This campaign is a revolution involving the transformation of the subjective world in the storm of class struggle and in the process of transforming the objective world. It is an ideological training in the struggle and on the battlefield. It is about training and consolidating a new army for better carrying out the Great Proletarian Cultural Revolution.

It is entirely foreseeable that the Red Guards will flourish after this comprehensive campaign. We Red Guards shall be more worthy of our position as the young red soldiers of the Party and Chairman Mao, the loyal sons and daughters of the revolutionary people of China and the whole world, trailblazers of the Great Proletarian Cultural Revolution, and reliable reserves of the People's Liberation Army. Red Guards who grasp Mao Zedong Thought will have great material strength, and it will signal that our teams are in good order and march in step, our troops are picked troops, and our weapons are good weapons. We will then form a mighty torrent to utterly destroy the old world, and create a brilliant new world!

We will remove all pests and enemies!

Xicheng District Headquarters of the Capital Red Guards Picket Corps
September 26, 1966

Appendix 2

Compilation of State Affairs

Volume 1107

Published by *People's Daily* on April 3, 1979

Suppression of the Xicheng District Picket Corps was a Conspiracy Against Zhou Enlai by Lin Biao and the Gang of Four

Throughout the Cultural Revolution, Lin Biao, Chen Boda, the Gang of Four, Kang Sheng, Xie Fuzhi and other careerists colluded to create storm after storm and frenzied opposition to our beloved Premier Zhou Enlai. At the start of the Cultural Revolution, they used the opportunity presented by the suppression of the Xicheng District Picket Corps to go after the friends and family of corps members and instigate a sinister conspiracy against Premier Zhou. As a member of the headquarters of the Xicheng District Picket Corps who suffered persecution and one who knows about the injustices suffered by corps members, I have the responsibility to tell others about what had happened. I do so not only in order to publicly vindicate the Xicheng District Picket Corps, but also to lay bare the conspiracy against Zhou Enlai concocted by Lin Biao and the Gang of Four.

(1)

The full title of the Xicheng District Picket Corps was the Xicheng District Detachment of the Capital Red Guards Picket Corps. It was established on August 25, 1966. At that time, Lin Biao and a group of careerists at the Central Cultural Revolution Group hijacked the revolution for their own personal interests, and stirred up troubles in an attempt to seize power. Under their bewitching and instigating efforts, ultra-leftist ideas were spread among the population, the "five great leaders" of the Red Guard ran amok, beatings, lootings and destruction of property was widespread, Party and government organs were attacked, cadres and the masses were filled with fear and panic, and society descended into chaos. In the midst of this "revolution" and waves of rebellion, our beloved Premier Zhou Enlai played an indispensable role in impressing upon the Red Guards the need to act in accordance with the "Sixteen Points" and implement Party policies. This was Premier Zhou's struggle to resist the perverse acts of traitors to the nation, despite the prevailing historical conditions. As hot-blooded young people and spurred on by the slogan "it is right to rebel" that was so popular at the time, we too were caught up in the fanaticism of the Red Guards. However, filled with traditional revolutionary thoughts nurtured and taught to us by the Party and the people over past years and with a firm grasp of right and wrong, we instinctively resented these rampant "revolutionary acts" and were unhappy about the chaotic and turbulent social situation. Inspired by Premier Zhou's repeated persuasive speeches, out of a desire to act spontaneously, with a purpose of implementing the "Sixteen Points" and maintaining social order, the Xicheng District Detachment of the Capital Red Guards Picket Corps was jointly established by Red Guards from 50 middle schools in the Xicheng District of Beijing.

(2)

Within the Xicheng District Picket Corps' short lifespan of less than one month (from late August to late September), it issued ten general orders. These general orders, which were complied with the "Sixteen Points," the Party's policies, Mao's teachings and the guiding principles of Premier Zhou's speeches and were targeted at the social conditions at the time, laid out specific and detailed provisions on protecting the Party Central Committee, government agencies, revolutionary cadres and state secrets, maintaining social order, opposing the use of violence and corporal punishment during denunciations and home searches, as well as maintaining policies on national bourgeoisie, foreign affairs, and receiving foreign dignitaries. Amid the wave of rebellion at the time, the Party, government authorities and security system, whose hands were tied, welcomed our general orders. A number of government departments in Beijing and Party committees in some provinces reprinted our general orders and posted them in public places to spread our messages. Many cadres and members of the public inconvenienced by rebellious acts supported the general orders out of a desire for calm, with many also opposing the rebels on those grounds. After issuing several general orders, various agencies, organizations, cadres and the masses had called on the Xicheng District Picket Corps to solve the problems they faced, which led to the Picket Corps taking action to maintain order.

Premier Zhou heard about the Picket Corps' positive role in maintaining social order, and was quick to offer his praise, stating, "The Red Guards have many innovations, one of which is the picket corps." He later personally asked representatives of the Xicheng District Picket Corps to attend a reception of Red Guards at Tiananmen Square hosted by Chairman Mao. He also met several members of the Xicheng District Picket Corps at the State Council, where he spoke to us in detail about the important task of maintaining the order at Beijing Railway Station, and instructed the former Secretary-General of the State Council, Comrade Zhou Rongxin, to arrange housing, transportation, and printing facilities to facilitate our activities. Afterwards, Premier Zhou requested our assistance for a number of tasks through Zhou Rongxin, Xu Ming (former Deputy Secretary-General of the State Council) and other people, including the protection of the Panchen Lama at a denunciation meeting organized by students of the Institute of Nationalities and protecting the family of Cheng Yanqiu from being raided.

Many central leaders expressed their praise and support toward the general orders and actions of the Xicheng District Picket Corps. On August 31, 1966, when comrade Ye Jianying met several of our members on Tiananmen Gate Tower, he explicitly stated that our general orders were well written. He enquired in detail about the difficulties we faced in terms of our publicity efforts, and stated that he was willing to offer his help in that area. When the Xicheng District Picket Corps went up against the "East Is Red" Red Guards from Geological Institute at the Ministry of Geology in an attempt to guard confidential archives, several of our members were invited to the State Council by Xu Ming to discuss the ways of resolving the crisis, and we met comrades Li Fuchun and Li Xiannian there. On hearing about our actions, they agreed that we had acted correctly for the sake of protecting state archives. Comrade Tao Zhu met several members of the Xicheng District Picket Corps who were on duty and encouraged them. When Chairman Mao received the Red Guards at Tiananmen Square, Zhou Enlai as well as many other central leaders and marshals all wore Picket Corps armbands to show their support to us.

With the support of Premier Zhou and other central leaders, we were greatly encouraged and were with a high morale. We were involved in many activities with a purpose of maintaining social order. During the receptions Mao gave to Red Guards, we were assigned the glorious task of working alongside the People's Liberation Army to protect Chairman Mao. In accordance with Premier Zhou's instructions, members of the Xicheng District Picket Corps worked tirelessly with the staff at the railway sector to maintain order at Beijing Railway Station and provide services to passengers. In response to the instructions of Party and government organs, the Xicheng District Picket Corps sent many of its members to the Ministry of Metallurgical industry, the Ministry of Petroleum and other ministries to help protect state secrets and cadres, and stop rebels from ransacking them. In conjunction with the foreign affairs department, the Xicheng District Picket Corps participated in the Sino-Japanese Youth Carnival, providing security at the Beijing Hotel and other locations to ensure the safety of foreign guests. We also dispatched our members on several occasions to stop beatings and the use of corporal punishment against famous people, such as Liu Shikun, during denunciations and home searches. We were also involved in protecting precious national relics (such as the relic of the tooth of the Buddha), meeting members of the public, dispute resolution, shoveling manure with workers and a host of other activities.

In the society at that time, on one side, there were Xicheng District Picket Corps and other similar mass organizations supported and sponsored by Premier Zhou and many other central leaders who wanted calm, alliance and observance of Party policies. On the other side, there were Lin Biao and careerists from the Central Cultural Revolution Group as well as rebel organizations, such as the university Red Guards Third Division manipulated by them, who wanted to overthrow everything and cause chaos. Thus, conflicts were inevitable. Within less than a month, the Xicheng District Picket Corps was involved in two fierce struggles. One was at the Ministry of Geology, against the "East Is Red" Red Guards from Geological Institute led by Wang Dabin and Zhu Chengzhao. The other was at the Air Transport Association close to the Ministry of National Defense, against the "Red Flag" from Beijing Aviation Institute. These struggles were later enormously exaggerated and came to be referred as the "Ministry of Geology Incident" and the "Air Transport Association Incident", which involved the "suppression of revolutionary rebels" by the Xicheng District Picket Corps.

Many people also wrote to us to express their strong support. The famous Ironman Wang Jinxi from the Daqing oilfields once visited our headquarters to express his unequivocal support. He later wrote to us to request a Xicheng District Picket Corps armband, and told us that he wanted to set up a Daqing Picket Corps. Shortly after the Xicheng District Picket Corps was established, other districts and counties in Beijing, as well as provinces and cities around the country, had set up their own picket corps.

Being young and sincere, and having weathered some struggles at the beginning, we never expected that our enthusiasm and devotion would get us into misfortunes. Looking back now, given the worsening political situation, that trouble was as inevitable as we would have conflicts with rebel factions. In the end, during the peak of criticism against the bourgeois line three months later, the Xicheng District Picket Corps was brutally suppressed.

(3)

On December 16, 1966, at a meeting of more than 10,000 people at the Workers' Stadium in Beijing, Jiang Qing suddenly and despicably launched an attack on the Xicheng District Picket Corps, calling for its merciless and resolute crackdown. It was claimed that the Xicheng District Picket Corps was protecting "monarchists" among the "capitalist roaders" and suppressing "executioners" among the rebels, thereby was extinguishing the fire of revolutionary rebels. It was also claimed that the Xicheng District Picket Corps was carrying out beatings, murders and various other evil deeds. Jiang Qing publicly named Wang Renzhong, Zhou Rongxin, Yong Wentao, Kong Yuan and Xu Ming as those who worked behind the scenes and ordered the Xicheng District Picket Corps to commit such acts.

As soon as Jiang Qing gave her orders, suppression of the Xicheng District Picket Corps and persecution of those believed to have supported it had begun. *Red Flag* magazine whipped up public opinion against us, while the Minister of Public Security and lackey of Lin Biao and the Gang of Four, Xie Fuzhi, were to ensure if Jiang's orders were carried out. Many members of the Xicheng District Picket Corps (such as Dong Biwu's son Dong Lianghe, Su Yu's son Su Hansheng and me) were imprisoned, abused in all sorts of ways, and interrogated regardless of night or day. Some senior comrades mentioned by Jiang Qing at the meeting were subsequently denounced. I was also mentioned by Jiang Qing, and it was claimed that my parents were also at fault. This led to my father, Kong Yuan, being thrown into prison and my mother, Xu Ming, committed suicide on the day I was arrested.

While in prison, we protested bitterly and argued that it was not a crime to be devoted to the Party. They claimed that we were royalists, but we pointed out that we had always acted in accordance with the "Sixteen Points," the Party's policies and Chairman Mao's teachings. However, fair conclusions have now been made on our so-called crimes: Lin Biao and the Gang of Four have been forever nailed to the historical pillar of shame; the crimes of Kang Sheng and Xie Fuzhi have been exposed to the public; the counter-revolutionary clowns known as the "five great leaders" of the Red Guards had stood in front of judges in people's courts; and members of the Xicheng District Picket Corps, along with thousands of revolutionary masses labeled as "royalists," have been shown to have acted in the interests of the country. But we must never forget that even in the days of Lin Biao and the Gang of Four, when the Xicheng District Picket Corps suffered persecution, our beloved Premier still insisted that the Picket Corps had rendered a great service.

The second count of "carrying out beatings, murders and various other evils," which many people believed and led them to turn against the Picket Corps, was even more groundless. The crafty tactics of Lin Biao and the Gang of Four involved pinning on the Xicheng District Picket Corps the excesses of Red Guards from different schools who were under the influence of their ultra-leftist ideology. As we all know, however, as evidenced by the general orders and our many activities of maintaining the social order, we resolutely opposed beatings, lootings and the destruction of property or any behavior that violated Party policies.

Even during our interrogation, faced with the irrefutable evidence provided by us, the interrogators had to admit that we had not committed any crime. Nevertheless, Lin Biao and the Gang of Four ensured that we were sentenced to long periods of detention. It could be thought that they made such a big deal about the Xicheng District Picket Corps, because we were young and powerful, and could have resisted or caused trouble to them, thus we had become a major obstacle for them to seize power. But this was not the case. Members of the Picket Corps were only energetic, innocent and naïve teenagers. The real power lay in the masses. The Xicheng District Picket Corps was suppressed, in the words of Xie Fuzhi, "with a purpose of setting an example." They thought that it would suppress the discontent and opposition of the masses to their rule. Moreover, the unjust case against the Xicheng District Picket Corps coined by Lin Biao and the Gang of Four also had a more sinister and despicable motive: to target at Premier Zhou Enlai. As a representative of the interests and hearts of the Party and the people, Zhou Enlai, along with a number of the older generation of proletarian revolutionaries and many Party, government and military cadres, were the real obstacles for this group of careerists to seize power. They were fully aware that many central leaders had openly praised and offered support to the Xicheng District Picket Corps, so they decided to crack down on us in order to go after our supporters in an attempt to topple them.

As far as I know, the suppression of the Xicheng District Picket Corps was the first of multiple conspiracies concocted by Lin Biao and the Gang of Four aimed at persecuting Zhou Enlai and other central leaders during the Cultural Revolution. The exact details of this conspiracy still remain unknown by most people, but the tactics used in such cases at the time were widely acknowledged. The interrogators followed the instructions of their masters, and used fascist methods, such as extorting confessions by means of torture and coercion, in order to get to our supporters, particularly central leaders and senior cadres. In addition to Zhou Enlai, the targets of their investigations included leading cadres such as Ye Jianying, Li Fuchun, Li Xiannian, Chen Yi, Xu Xiangqian, Tao Zhu, Yu Qiuli, Liao Chengzhi and Wang Renzhong, as well as senior cadres such as He Changgong, Lü Dong, Zhou Rongxin, Yong Wentao, Kong Yuan and Xu Ming. Because so many members of the Xicheng District Picket Corps were children of leading and senior cadres, many people were implicated in the case. Xie Fuzhi once claimed that "All the sons of marshals and generals are members of the Xicheng District Picket Corps and the Joint Action Committee," and he thus persecuted a number of old comrades for the acts carried out by their children. They even went so far as to force Xu Xiangqian's son, Xu Xiaoyan and a group of other children of cadres to confess (who were Picket Corps members) about our military training, so as to cook up that the Picket Corps were carrying out armed training classes with the conspiracy of an armed insurrection.

(4)

Still young in age, we had never been subjected to the iron fist of the proletarian dictatorship before. We were unable to see the counter-revolutionary nature of Lin Biao and the Gang of Four, in the face of our interrogators and their attempts to force confessions from us. Despite these facts, we remained firm in our belief in the causes of the

Party and the people and in our deep-seated respect for Premier Zhou Enlai and the older generation of revolutionaries, and we stayed vigilant to attempts by interrogators to implicate our supporters. We did not let them cheat us, and we never yielded. We argued the facts and lived up to the support and advice from Premier Zhou and the central leadership, who encouraged us to do deeds welcomed by cadres and the masses and for the benefit of the Party and state. In order to defend Premier Zhou and the older generation of revolutionaries, we insisted that any mistakes made by the Xicheng District Picket Corps were our own faults rather than the adults'. Despite building a fake case against us, we were eventually released on the instructions of Chairman Mao. With that, the conspiracy to incriminate our supporters failed.

Jiang Qing once claimed that people would be surprised to learn whom the supporters of the Xicheng District Picket Corps and Joint Action Committee were. She also warned that she would round up the supporters of the Picket Corps and sentence them to death. This was a thinly veiled threat to Zhou Enlai and revealed the deep-seated hatred she harbored towards him. It depicted her sinister attempt of using the crackdown on the Picket Corps to strike at the Premier. On April 22, 1967, members of the Xicheng District Picket Corps and the Joint Action Committee were released. That day, Zhou Enlai received us in the Great Hall of the People and made a speech that confirmed the real reason for the suppression of the Picket Corps. He said, "The Xicheng District Picket Corps has rendered a great service. Dong Lianghe and Kong Dan, I have known you both since you were very young and watched you grow up. I am also responsible for the mistakes you made. I did not help you well." We were moved to tears by his words. We did not realize at the time, however, the depth of meaning when he talked about responsibility for mistakes. This was a reference to the difficulties he faced as a result of the case against us that had been concocted by Lin Biao and the Gang of Four. It also revealed that the real target of the crackdown was Premier Zhou himself.

The conspiracy to suppress the Xicheng District Picket Corps in order to oppose Premier Zhou and persecute the older generation of revolutionaries, revolutionary cadres and young revolutionaries needs to be completely exposed. At the same time, in order to redress some of the wrongs suffered by deceased victims and restore the political reputations of members of the Picket Corps who suffered persecution, I strongly appeal to the relevant parties for the vindication of unjust charges of those involved, so that we may embark on our new endeavors with a greater motivation.

Kong Dan
Postgraduate student at the Graduate School of Economics
of the Chinese Academy of Social Sciences

Appendix 3

Letter from Kong Dan to Comrade Chen Yun in 1984,

Subsequent Instructions from Central Leaders, and Related Documents from 1980

Document of CPC Central Committee in 1980

[Issued by the CPC (1980) No. 77]

It has been pointed out on Page 57 of "Two Investigation Reports Approved and Transmitted by the CPC Central Committee to the Central Commission for Discipline Inspection Regarding Kang Sheng and Xie Fuzhi", and under the item that cites Xie Fuzhi's crimes, who "cooperated with Jiang Qing, Kang Sheng, Chen Boda and others in cooking up charges, extorting confessions by torture, and creating a large amount of unjust, false and erroneous cases":

"(4) Xie Fuzhi, together with Lin Biao, Jiang Qing, Kang Sheng, Chen Boda and others, labelled the mass organizations in Xicheng District, namely Xicheng District Picket Corps and the Red Guards Joint Action Committee as reactionary organizations and arrested more than 200 people, most of whom were children of cadres. Xie Fuzhi concocted the 'Suggestions for Dealing with Detained Reactionary Students in the Course of Crack Downs on Counter Currents' and conspired to punish some young people as 'counter-revolutionaries' and for 'ideological reactionists.'"

Kong Dan's letter of accusation is quoted in Appendix 12 ("Xie Fuzhi Ordered the Use of Torture to Extort Confessions Which Lead to Unjust, False and Erroneous Cases") of Document 77.

Politburo Meeting Document (1984) No. 2

Comrade Kong Dan and Comrade Dong Zhixiong's Letter to Comrade Chen Yun

Proceed in accordance with the suggestions of Comrade Chen Yun. First send to comrades Deng Xiaoping, Zhao Ziyang and Li Xiannian for them to read over. Then invite Comrade Qiao Shi to publish all comments and materials as Politburo documents and send them to each comrade.

Hu Yaobang, 28th February

Comrade Hu Yaobang, Deng Xiaoping, Zhao Ziyang and Li Xiannian (with Comrade Ye Jianying not included for the moment),

I suggest that this letter and materials on Chen Chusan be printed and distributed among the Politburo and Secretariat, as well as the Party Steering Committee and Central Organization Department. Kong Dan's opinions are correct, so relevant departments should study them. These Red Guards do not belong to "the three kinds of people", and the good people among them should still be considered as targets for the third echelon. Purging the Party of "the three kinds of people" involves a political struggle, but we must prevent some one to muddy the waters. We must be especially vigilant against people like Chen Chusan and prevent them from sneaking into the third echelon, but we should also give such people a way out.

Chen Yun, 27th February, 1984

Li Xiannian's comments:
I totally agree.
1st March
(Already Read by Comrade Deng Xiaoping, Zhao Ziyang and Qiao Shi)

Comrade Chen Yun,

We were the members of senior old Red Guards during the early stages of the Cultural Revolution, and we would like to share with you some thoughts on how we think the Party should deal with the senior Red Guards.

The senior Red Guards are some of the children who born into families of cadres, workers or peasants, and who were in middle school or university during the summer of 1966. Impacted by the "leftist" line, they spontaneously organized themselves to participate in the Cultural Revolution, and they gradually withdrew from the movement after the Party Working Conference in October 1966 which highlighted the "bourgeois reactionary line". During the middle and the latter stages of the Cultural Revolution, they had continuously suffered from oppression.

During the rectification movement nowadays, there has been a prevalent opinion among Party members, saying that the senior Red Guards were a rebel faction. As a result, it has been said in some places and work units that the senior Red Guards should be included in "the three kinds of people", who were responsible for the mistakes during the destroy the "four olds" campaign. For some senior Red Guards, because they had held responsibility or were involved in famous organizations during the Cultural Revolution, such as the Xicheng District Picket Corps and the Joint Action Committee, their employment and promotion prospects have been affected.

We feel that this is in violation of the guiding principles in relevant documents and instructions of leading cadres of the CPC Central Committee, and that this is in need of clarification and rectification. Otherwise, it will be detrimental to the whole Party and hinder the purge of "the three kinds of people" and the works on developing the "third echelon."

The senior Red Guards was a political force. During the Cultural Revolution, the majority of them behaved admirably at important times, and their behavior could stood the test of time. They had deep affections for the Party as well as the older generation of proletarian revolutionaries, and were quick to express their dissatisfaction and resist "leftist" mistakes during the Cultural Revolution. They also cherished an undying hatred towards the perverse acts of Lin Biao and the Gang of Four.

Of course, members of the senior Red Guards were not perfect and had made mistakes. First of all, they were generally the first students to criticize school leaders and their "revisionist educational line." The direction was totally wrong. Second, some among them (mainly underage middle school students) took things too far during the destroy the "four olds" campaign, including using violence against teachers, searching the homes and confiscating the property of landlords, rich peasants, counter-revolutionaries, bad elements and rightists, and in the case of a few, killing people. Nevertheless, these mistakes by members of the senior Red Guards are essentially different from the mistakes by rebel organizations against all levels of Party committees and the older generation of proletarian revolutionaries, and they are very different from those of "the three kinds of people."

Throughout the Cultural Revolution, there was a desperate struggle between Party cadres at all levels and the older generation of proletarian revolutionaries on one side, and Lin Biao and the Gang of Four on the other. During this struggle, the old Red Guards supported the former and resented the latter. The Xicheng and Dongcheng Picket Corps made up of Beijing middle school students, and the First Division of university students all provided strong support to Premier Zhou Enlai as well as the senior Party, government and military cadres, and were used to control the situation, protect veteran cadres and maintain social order (including defending state organs, protecting archives and preventing excesses). The Joint Action Committee was in particular established to oppose the Central Cultural Revolution Group. Those organizations were all suppressed by the Cultural Revolution Group around the December of 1966, and were labelled as conservative and reactionary organizations. Some of the members had experienced different forms of attacks and persecution. Lin Biao and the Gang of Four even went after their friends and family members who were veteran cadres and proletarian revolutionaries. Since then, the organizations of senior Red Guards ceased to exist, but many of its members experienced a long period of oppression during the key moments of the Cultural Revolution, such as the movements against the "Black Wind of December," "Seizure of Power of January" and "Counter-current of February"; campaigns to "criticize Lin Biao and rectify the Party's style of work," "criticize Lin Biao and Confucius", "criticize Deng Xiaoping"; and the Tiananmen incident. Ideologically and politically, the old Red Guards were opposed to Lin Biao and the Gang of Four. Those who closely followed Lin Biao and the Gang of Four consciously acted as powerful tools of the Cultural Revolution Group (whether as ultra-leftist rebels or part of the "policy faction"), and they all targeted Party cadres at all levels and the older generation of proletarian revolutionaries. They actively participated in power struggles in various localities and departments, including breaking up government organs, robbing files, fighting other factions, manufacturing protests, seizing so-called "traitors," "spies" and "capitalist roaders," engaging in "programs" with veteran cadres, implementing a so-called "dictatorship of the masses," besieging Zhongnanhai, organizing denunciations of central leaders, and stealing and disclosing Party and state secrets (of course, the members of these rebel organizations should be dealt with in accordance with Party policies and based on their specific actions at the time). By comparing the activities, organizations and backbones of the senior Red Guards with those of these rebels, one can see that they are fundamentally different in nature. Labelling the senior Red Guards as "rebels" would muddy the waters and divert the attention away from "the three kinds of people."

During the early stages of the Cultural Revolution, some senior Red Guards were guilty of beating people labelled "class enemies" (including landlords, rich peasants, counter-revolutionaries, bad elements, gangsters, etc.), looting their homes and destroying the "four olds" (including some temples and works of art). This all happened under the destroy the "four olds" campaign, which lasted for only a short period of time (just a month or two), and we believe that those could be considered general errors. Of course, some circumstances were serious, such as those who beat people to death. If they were not dealt with at the time, they should be investigated and dealt with now. But these events cannot be discussed in the same breath as the beatings, looting and destruction by "the three kinds of people." As we know, the so-called "the three kinds of people," regardless of their kind, they all served the conspiracy of Lin Biao and the Gang of Four to seize power, which first and foremost is a serious political issue. The senior Red Guards, however, despite responsible for some beatings, lootings and destruction out of immature foolishness at the start of the Cultural Revolution, did not support Lin Biao and the Gang of Four's attempt to seize power. If such issues are labelled as those committed by "the three kinds of people," it will blur the political nature of "the three kinds of people."

The senior Red Guards and "the three kinds of people" belong to the same generation and are now mostly in their 30s or 40s. As Comrade Chen Yun has pointed out, it should be made clear who was second, third and fourth in command behind Nie Yuanzi and Kuai Dafu. The veteran cadres do not know. Only those who were Red Guards, and later became part of the conservative faction and "carefree clique" know who once targeted veteran cadres. As such, we feel that during this instance of Party consolidation, although members of the senior Red Guards should re-examine their past, learn from their mistakes and improve their awareness, they should not be investigated any further for mistakes or general errors made during the early stages of the Cultural Revolution, nor should the charges against them by the Central Cultural Revolution Group be used as a basis for investigating them. On the contrary, they should be fully recognized as having been part of the mainstream movement during the Cultural Revolution and mobilized, together with the vast majority of young people, as a positive factor in the struggle against "the three kinds of people."

These are some of our personal thoughts. We look forward to hearing from you.

Yours sincerely,

Kong Dan, National Economic Commission and CPC Member
Dong Zhixiong, Ministry of Metallurgical Industry and CPC Member
February 23rd, 1984

About Kong Dan

Kong Dan was born in the prefecture of Yanbian in Jilin Province of China in 1947, and graduated from the prestigious Beijing No. 4 High School in 1966. He was born into a so-called "Red family" — his father, Kong Yuan, was the head of the Investigation Department of the CPC Central Committee, while his mother, Xu Ming, was Deputy Secretary-General of the State Council. Kong's talents gradually began to emerge during his days at Beijing No. 4 High School. He was given a citywide award for being an excellent student upon graduation, and was recommended for admission to the senior grades at Beijing No. 4 High School without taking the entrance examination. In his second year at senior high school, Kong was appointed deputy secretary of the Communist Youth League Committee at school. He was also among the first group of high school Communist Party members and model students in Beijing after the Socialist Education Movement.[1] At the start of the Cultural Revolution, he was appointed as head of the Cultural Revolution Committee of Beijing No. 4 High School, and he established a unique leadership system Youth League Committees in Beijing among different grades in high school based on his personal understanding of the mass movement, with the hope of bringing the student movement under the control of the Communist Youth League.

Subsequently, along with Chen Xiaolu and Dong Lianghe, Kong helped set up the Xicheng District Picket Corps of the Capital Red Guards and was placed in charge of it. In those days, the picket corps issued a series of orders with an attempt to establish order amid the unrest. Later on, Kong was ordered to disband the picket corps, after

1 Also known as the Four Cleanups Movement, the movement was launched by Mao Zedong in 1963 in an attempt to eliminate "reactionary" elements within the Communist Party of China.

being accused by the Cultural Revolution Committee of suppressing the masses and obstructing the Party's overall goals, for which Kong was sent to jail. Meanwhile, Kong's parents were labeled as "sinister supporters of the Xicheng District Picket Corps" by Jiang Qing, which directly led to Kong's father being imprisoned as well and his mother's suicide.

Following his release from prison, Kong had been treated as a deviationist for a long time. In 1968, he was detained and investigated by school authorities for opposing the Cultural Revolution Committee, which resulted in his being sent to work for a production team in northern Shannxi Province for four years. Upon his return to Beijing, Kong worked as a librarian in an economic research institute, and was admitted by Wu Jinglian, an economist, as his first postgraduate student in 1978. After graduation, Kong worked as secretary for the director of the National Economic Commission, Zhang Jinfu, before being transferred to China Everbright Group, and later, to CITIC Group.

During his time in managing the two central government enterprises, Kong saved them from three major crises. He even managed to turn these crises into business opportunities and helped develop both groups. Under his leadership, CITIC Group became a Fortune 500 company and one of the most profitable central enterprises in China due to its sustainable and stable development model.

Following his retirement, Kong still spends his time thinking about the nation's future as well as exploring a Chinese-style development path for large state-owned enterprises.

From Red Guard to Business Mogul:
An Oral Biography of Kong Dan

Dictated by: Kong Dan
Compiled by: Mi Hedu
Translated by: Central Compilation and Translation Bureau
Proofread by: Wang Bo
Edited by: Zhang Yucheng
Cover design by: Tu Hui
Published by: The Commercial Press (H.K) Ltd.,
8/F, Eastern Central Plaza, 3 Yiu Hing Road,
Shau Kei Wan, Hong Kong
Distributed by: The SUP Publishing Logistics (H.K.) Ltd.,
3/F, C & C Building, 36 Ting Lai Road,
Tai Po, New Territories, Hong Kong
Printed by: Elegance Printing & Book Binding Co. Ltd.,
Block A 4/F, Hoi Bun Industrial Building,
6 Wing Yip Street, Kwun Tong, H.K.

First Edition, First printing, December 2015
ISBN: 978 96207 5669 6
Printed in Hong Kong